Praise for Sp

"This is a refreshing and heartei
with a rich and skilful integration
and case studie

Katrina Shields, author of the Australi:

"Nuclear disarmament, as this thoughtful book suggests, is more than a matter of dismantling the weapons. We must also dismantle our minds and hearts to change our current ideas of true security."

Bruce Kent, Vice President of the Campaign for Nuclear Disarmament

"We've tried to heal what ails us and our world with smartness, money, technology, economic growth, policy, and politics--all necessary and all insufficient. Having tried everything else, it is now time to add spirit exercised with discipline, going to the heart of the matter where wholeness, healing, and Holy converge. Highly recommended."

Professor David W. Orr of Oberlin College, author of *Down to the Wire*

"The perilous path we tread is littered with burnt out, sold out, freaked out activists. If we wish to engage effectively and for the long run in this world full of wounds, for our efforts for Earth and Justice to be truly sustainable, it behoves us to take great care of our psychological and spiritual wellbeing. This book provides us with an important tool for the journey."

John Seed, Australian deep ecologist and founder of the Rainforest Information Centre

"There is so so much that we activists can learn from religious faiths: about how to mobilise people, earn their commitment, and speak to their sacred values. From the spiritual traditions we can learn how to sustain ourselves in the long struggle. So, to my fellow activists, even the most sceptical, I insist read this excellent book and learn some vital lessons from the most successful and longest lasting social movements in history."

George Marshall, founder of the Climate Outreach Information Network

SPIRITUAL ACTIVISM

LEADERSHIP AS SERVICE

ALASTAIR McINTOSH & MATT CARMICHAEL

Published by Green Books
An imprint of UIT Cambridge Ltd
www.greenbooks.co.uk

PO Box 145, Cambridge CB4 1GQ, England
+44 (0) 1223 302 041

First published in 2016, in England

Matt Carmichael and Alastair McIntosh have asserted their moral rights
under the Copyright, Designs and Patents Act 1988.

Front cover illustration by Vic Brown, GalGael Trust
Interior design by Jayne Jones
Cover design by Glyn Bridgewater

ISBN: 978 0 85784 300 5 (hardback)
ISBN: 978 0 85784 414 9 (paperback)
ISBN: 978 0 85784 302 9 (ePub)
ISBN: 978 0 85784 301 2 (pdf)
Also available for Kindle.

Disclaimer: the authors and publisher accept
no liability for actions inspired by this book.

In writing relevant parts of this book Alastair McIntosh acknowledges support
from an Arts and Humanities Research Council grant, Caring for the Future
through Ancestral Time, held by Professor Michael Northcott at the School of
Divinity, University of Edinburgh.

10 9 8 7 6 5 4 3 2

CONTENTS

THE AUTHORS

Alastair McIntosh has been described by BBC TV as "one of the world's leading environmental campaigners." A pioneer of modern land reform in Scotland, he helped bring the Isle of Eigg into community ownership. On the Isle of Harris he negotiated withdrawal of the world's biggest cement company from a devastating "superquarry" plan. Alastair guest lectures at military staff colleges, most notably the UK Defence Academy. Over nearly two decades he has addressed 6,000 senior officers from eighty countries on nonviolence. His books include *Soil and Soul: People versus Corporate Power* (Aurum), *Hell and High Water: Climate Change, Hope and the Human Condition* (Birlinn) and *Rekindling Community* (Green Books). He is a fellow of the School of Divinity at the University of Edinburgh and a visiting professor at the College of Social Sciences, University of Glasgow. A founding director of the GalGael Trust, which tackles urban poverty, he lives with his wife, Vérène Nicolas, in the Govan area of Glasgow, Scotland. He has taught spiritual activism in Europe, North America, Australia, Indonesia, Moscow and Beirut.

Matt Carmichael has been campaigning on global justice issues in his home city of Leeds, England, since the mid 1990s; and in the past decade on climate change and fuel poverty. He led workshops on spiritual activism at two Camps for Climate Action, and as chair, guided the Leeds activist hub, Tidal, from its church-based origins to becoming a fortifying force in Leeds activism, open to all perspectives. He was a founding member and secretary of Schumacher North and created the Delta Course, an introduction to spirituality for people disillusioned with, or uninterested in, religion, but open to life. He has a degree in theology and is also an inner-city secondary school teacher, a homemaker, a writer, and as can be seen scattered throughout this book, sometimes a cartoonist.

To Kath, agent of change and of my becoming (Matt)

To Tom Forsyth of Scoraig (Alastair)

Alastair gratefully acknowledges Francis Camfield's Trust
and the Joseph Rowntree Charitable Trust for support
in the early stages of what became this book; also,
all at the Centre for Human Ecology
who upheld its original
teaching context,
generously.

Beyond

"Out beyond ideas of wrongdoing and rightdoing there is a field.
I will meet you there." **Rumi**

Peace, you say?
You're not from round here are you?
Peace.
That well hasn't been used for years. Probably filled in,
Buried in shrubbery by now.
Mother used to talk about it, or was it her mother?
They'd gather there, draw water. Sit together. Talk.
All sorts of scandals.
It's on the edge of the village somewhere.
You have to go through the Angers, on foot.
Out past the tree of the knowledge of good and evil.
Might need something to cut through all the crap.
Are you really that thirsty?

Matt Carmichael

INTRODUCTION

You hold in your hands a book that has evolved over a quarter century of university teaching and nearly a century of life experience between Alastair and Matt. We first met at a gathering of activists called *The Summat* that was held in Leeds in 2009. Alastair spoke to a packed audience on "spiritual activism" - the applied spiritual underpinning for social and environmental change in the world - and afterwards, agreed to Matt using his teaching materials. These had originally been developed and accredited for use as part of a master's degree taught by the Centre for Human Ecology variously in the University of Edinburgh, the Open University and the University of Strathclyde, where he was visiting professor in human ecology.

The two of us are a generation apart. Alastair has hit his sixties (second time round) and Matt is a generation younger. The teaching of the former had a profound impact on the latter, but the material needed to be updated to pass on the flame between generations. Matt experimented with using it in a series of evening workshops that he ran in Leeds under Schumacher North, an offshoot of the Schumacher Society. So it was that a partnership developed between us, resulting in this synthesis of time-tested fabric embroidered through with bright new threads.

The causes to which any one of us might apply ourselves in life should be more than just personal passions. They should also be wake-up calls to those around us. Equally, wake-up calls to our own deeper selves and thus, spiritual journeys; a form of activist pilgrimage through life. What makes "spiritual" activism so exciting is that it approaches demanding issues in ways that invite an ever-deepening perception of reality and of our positioning - individually and collectively - within it.

We invite you to join us on that walk of discovery. It rescues new life even in the jaws of seeming hopelessness. Time is precious. Let us embark.

Matt & Alastair
Leeds & Govan, 2015

CHAPTER ONE

Activism and Spirituality

What is an activist?

Like all words charged with power, most people will feel a certain ambivalence towards the term "activist". Many shy away from applying it to themselves. An activist is one who acts to bring change in the way our relationships are structured, that is, change in community, often taking one to a point of discomfort. Dom Hélder Câmara, a Brazilian archbishop who practised liberation theology, said; "When I give food to the poor, they call me a saint. When I ask why the poor have no food, they call me a communist." We too, if we are to be activists, must expect to be judged, labelled, and sometimes misjudged.

Some people are born activists, some choose to become so, and some have activism thrust upon them. Matt's friend - we'll call him James - became a highly effective activist when he was falsely accused of criminal offences at work. In the process of defending his name, he found himself tackling corruption and incompetence at the management level of an organization that was supposed to be serving some of the most damaged people in society. As such, activism entails an openness to life and how it might change us. One thing leads to another; we become both transformers and the transformed.

Some years ago, Alastair ran a workshop on Spiritual Activism at Iona Abbey with the veteran Quaker peace worker, Helen Steven. There was a mismatch between theme and participants. Many were in groups that had come for a spiritual holiday and activism did not speak to their needs. Initially we had an uncomfortable time together. As one woman put it; "Your Jesus is not like mine. Mine is always gentle, kind, and a healer."

"So is mine!" said Alastair, "which is why he turned over the money-changers' tables in the temple, told the rich young man to give it all away and challenged hypocritical family values."

The world of activism contains all the "usual suspects". There's the anti-frackers, the feminists, the tree-huggers, ban-the-bombers, the occupiers, climate campers, living wagers, Idle No More, community organizers, whistleblowers, trades unionists and myriad others who protest, demonstrate and reclaim the streets - and occasionally the front pages - in the name of a more just and sustainable society. However, the activist tag is not reserved only for those who are up against the "big things". Each of us must dig from where we stand. To be an activist is, at its most elementary, to be active, to be alive, to seek to use our lives to give life. Our calling is to be movers and shakers, the social salt and pepper that troubles the "Roman peace" of those who seek a quiet life untroubled by injustice.

To be an activist, therefore, is not necessarily to be admired or even understood. It takes courage to stand up, stand out and hold a mirror up to oneself and others. As the poet Adrienne Rich said; "I stand convicted by all my convictions - you, too." But the blessing that comes from the wrestling is that it opens the blocked-up watercourses and reveals, as another feminist writer, Audre Lorde, puts it; "the passions of love, in its deepest meanings." We are on a journey that reconnects to the lifeforce.

Activism and community

As people who act to bring change in the way our relationships are structured, activists act upon community, our togetherness. Why is community so central?

- because community is where life comes to pass
- because human being is relational and not individual
- because our ultimate fulfillment lies in our deep connections
- because many of our outer material problems can only be solved by working on the inner basis of human relationships.

Alastair called his best-known book *Soil and Soul* and to this, his friend Satish Kumar of Schumacher College and *Resurgence* magazine, eloquently added a third pillar to characterize the fullness of community;

"soil, soul and society."

- "Soil" as our relationship with the Earth - the biosphere of cosmos, land and nature.
- "Soul" as our relationship within ourselves through psychology, spirituality and what might be called "the sacred".
- "Society" as our relationship with one another.

To bring all three of these together helps to build a holistic worldview, one that liberation theology calls "integral human development". To fail to integrate them helps to explain some of history's failures. We may perceive, for instance, how easily the French and Russian revolutionaries slid into their oppressive ways without a spiritual underpinning that carried a deeper sense of purpose, meaning, values and tenderness. Victor Hugo, who lived through the aftermath of the French Revolution, observed that; "revolution changes everything except the human heart". In turn, we may ask what kind of human hearts were needed to avoid bloody vengeance when South Africans overturned apartheid and in what culture such hearts were cultivated.

This triune basis of the human ecology that is human community in its fullness can be glimpsed in teaching and stories from all over the world. For example, after long preparation, the Buddha goes and sits under a Banyan tree (soil), receives enlightenment (soul) and then sets out to build the Noble Sangha of community among the people (society). The black American civil rights activist, Martin Luther King, often expressed his dream of humankind(ness) as the Beloved Community. At a rally in 1956 to celebrate the desegregation of bus seats in Montgomery, Alabama, he told the crowd:[1]

> The end is reconciliation; the end is redemption; the end is the creation of the Beloved Community. It is this type of spirit and this type of love that can transform opponents into friends. It is this type of understanding goodwill that will transform the deep gloom of the old age into the exuberant gladness of the new age. It is this love which will bring about miracles in the hearts of men.

George MacLeod, who founded the Iona Community in Scotland, used to say; "Only a demanding common task builds community." We would suggest that activism is the process of building community in all three of its dimensions - social, environmental and spiritual. This does not mean building sameness, or conformity. True community, being constantly resourced from the creative wellspring of life, will always be in human hands a "community of contested discourses". It will be work in progress and yet, as where nature's biodiversity flourishes freely, a functioning ecosystem of interdependence.

The alternative, which is offered by much of mainstream society, is to seek our fulfilment not in *being* but in *having*. Such is the realm of consumerism where each of us competes with everyone else to hoard our trinkets. The rules of the competition allow us to harm one another in myriad ways, and this is called "freedom". Cosmetics manufacturers make us feel ugly, banks trap us in debt and all of us buy prawns or mobile phones inextricably bound up in a web of interdependencies that has cost someone far away their land, livelihood or life. Thus alienated, we use our purchasing power to shore up our damaged egos in a further zero-sum competition for social status. Our basic human need for community is continually undermined, and the market provides a never-ending stream of surrogates, always promising that tomorrow, one day, just around the corner, all our problems will be solved by "progress".

The Cycle of Belonging

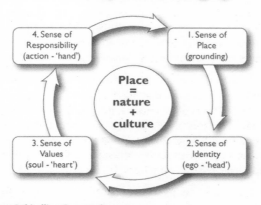

Diagram from *Rekindling Community*
Alastair McIntosh, Schumacher Briefing No. 15, Green Books, 2008

In contrast, community subverts consumerism by plugging us back into the deep networks of life, which meet our real need for belonging. We therefore describe healthy growth as the stimulation of a *cycle of belonging* - belonging to the fullness of community. Discovering our *sense of place*, a grounding in the physical reality of bodily existence on Earth, is usually the starting point in this cycle. A grounded sense of place contributes to a *sense of identity*. Identity encodes a *sense of values* or qualities of being that abide in the heart. These activate our *sense of responsibility* - the capacity to respond to others by being activists.

Whereas community degeneration comes about by damaging the cycle of belonging at any point, community regeneration comes from its rein-forcement. We therefore have the choice in life of either destroying or reinforcing, of rejecting or participating in a cycle by which the fabric of the Earth that sustains us is itself sustained. That, through the cultivation of interrelationship with one another, in right relationship with one another.

Activism and leadership

Ever since Hitler's demise, activists of many kinds have been acutely aware of the problems of leadership and power. We take as our subtitle "Leadership As Service" because we recognize the importance of these issues in considering how to build community. For example, the Camps for Climate Action have been organized using models developed in the 1960s, which enable consensus decision-making in large groups without the need to select leaders - though not without some difficulties.

The global Occupy movement of 2011 took this consensus-seeking to another level, and (with the exception of the City of London occupation at St Paul's cathedral) did not make any policy demands. Rather, Occupiers asked the public what kind of society they wanted, the clear message being that in a system where "the 1%" have taken control of democratic structures, the answers would be very different from what "the 99%" apparently voted for.

Working through what that might mean in political practice, and finding agreement, remains work in progress. Radical movements tend to be strong on critiques but less so on solutions. One model of bottom-up, community-based democracy in action is provided by the Zapatistas of Chiapas in Mexico. For two decades, the indigenous people have been able to defend parts of their lands against the ambitions of the Mexican government, which seeks to exploit it for natural resources. A makeshift army, the EZLN, took control of Chiapas in 1994, on the day when the North Atlantic Free Trade Agreement came into effect. It continues to defend the region and has occasionally engaged in battles with the Mexican national army. However, in the event of a full-scale civil war, the Zapatistas know that they would be overwhelmed almost immediately, so they rely on peaceful tactics to prevent this scenario from arising. The popular press frequently identified Subcomandante Marcos as a "leader" in ignorance or defiance of the Zapatistas' organising philosophy. Marcos had no decision-making power, only a communicating role on behalf of the people.

Care must be taken with a model like this. What works in a largely indigenous society might not translate well to an urbanized western population. Also, merely getting rid of the language of leadership does not get rid of leadership itself. Even in Chiapas, every local community entrusts responsibility to elected people to discuss and represent the community's views at the next level up and feed back faithfully, and this continues all the way up the structure of accountability to Marcos and his team. Any army, the EZLN included, relies on a chain of command (as exemplified in Marcos' title: sub*comand*ante). The model is strikingly similar to the bottom-up system of soviets advocated by Lenin, which he so deftly used to manipulate the political situation rather than represent the people.

After the fall of Hitler, many social psychologists in Europe and America, particularly those of the so-called Frankfurt School, studied power and leadership to try to understand better how fascism had gripped Europe and destroyed millions of lives. The 1960s saw many "alternative" movements spring up. These hoped to operate in structureless, leaderless ways. Thinkers like Marilyn Fergusson in *The Aquarian Conspiracy* argued that an "Age of Aquarius" was upon us in which "new wave" movements would "co-respire" towards a transformed society. Similarly, Alvin Toffler's *Future Shock* portrayed "the collapse of hierarchy" and Theodore Roszak explored alternative values in *The Making of a Counterculture*.

The 1970s saw a new wave of realism as it became apparent that many of these alternative movements had failed, often leaving hurt and exploited people in their wake. During the 1980s, many non-governmental organization (NGO) management texts addressed these issues. In one of these, four members of the failed publishing collective, *The Leveller*, issued a particularly influential little volume, tellingly entitled: *What a Way to Run a Railroad: An Analysis of Radical Failure*. Landry, Morley, Southwood and Wright asked why it was that so many right-on organizations of the era had crashed. They concluded that in the drive to be anti-authoritarian, the baby of *legitimate authority* had been thrown out with the bathwater. Their stinging tone is captured in the following lines:[2]

> Skills were seen as 'capitalist' and therefore reactionary by their very nature [but] creditors are rarely impressed by rhetoric... The Left avoids the idea of management by calling people 'coordinators' - as if the skill of management was merely that of stopping people bumping into each other.

Sadly, there was a lot of bitter truth in their critique. Some issues to which we would draw attention and which have prompted us to dig deeper in writing this book are the following.

- **"The Tyranny of Structurelessness"** - In animal social groups, including human ones, there is always a structure.[3] In other words, there is always power. Well-meaning people can be naïve about the possibility of self-serving individuals existing, and exploiting open doors to power. Whatever the organizing structure of a group, it needs to be constantly held in the light of recognition and accountability. The maxim: "Power denied is power abused" warns us that losing awareness of where power lies and how it is being used leaves us vulnerable to tyrants or self-serving factions who wish to exploit it.

- **"Rebels Without a Clue"** - As a one-time General Secretary of *War on Want* confided to Alastair when they were experimenting with counter-hierarchical job rotation; "The trouble is that while I can do the receptionist's job, the receptionist can't do mine."

- **"God Gets what Man Rejects"** - Inclusive organizations can attract a disproportionate number of people that more mainstream groups

have rejected. Such people can introduce creativity and innovation and become a part of demonstrating what it means to be caring and inclusive, but they can also damage the organization, rendering it oddball and dysfunctional. Group wisdom or policies need to be developed to define what burden of society's casualties can be carried, what support and constraints should be in place, and when to draw a line to prevent the organization's main point from being subverted. At the GalGael Trust in Govan, Glasgow, there is a poster on the wall that says; "I will wash your feet, but you may not wipe your feet on me." In other words, mutual respect is of the essence.

- **"Pay Peanuts, Get Monkeys"** - It's a reality that most people measure their self-worth in terms of what they get paid. Low pay can mean high staff turnover and that undermines the economic rationale of low pay. Equally, many organizations undergo a crisis when they start paying for work that had previously been voluntary; payment can upset the whole volunteer ethos. As implicit or explicit leaders in activism, we need to be conscious that not all our colleagues may share our strength of motivation. Some will be discomfited by it. Self-exploitation can be harmful both to ourselves and the motivation of others. What are the solutions to these tangles? Only awareness, sensitivity and openly talking the issues through.

None of the questions implicit in making these points are to suggest that we should give up the pursuit of bottom-up and "organic" forms of organization. They are merely to help us face square on the need to take stock of failures, and press on with our lives' work - all of us - of becoming more "sorted". The task of building an alternative society runs very much deeper than many caught up in the wave of postwar nineteen-sixties idealistic hope had anticipated. Rather than *deny* power, it requires us to understand, work with and, as we shall see, seek to *redeem* power.

Activism with a spiritual basis

In the next chapter we will explore some meanings of "spirituality". For now, we'd like to enter our subject by asking why spirituality is becoming an increasingly hot topic among activists. We'd like to explore four inter-related ways in which activism becomes a spiritual question.

Firstly, activism is all about putting our highest values into practice in the world. Spirituality involves an awareness of where those values come from at a deep psychological level: our motives, passions and drives. This is not to deny that values are shaped by the external forces of history, economics, culture and religion, but to ask additional questions. Why do I feel so strongly about this? Why don't other people? Why are my values clashing with what I find happening in mainstream society? What am I getting out of putting myself in the line of fire? Am I really doing it to benefit society? If my motives are complicated, can I still be confident that I'm doing the right thing? From what psychological soil are they being nourished?

Such soul-searching questions inform, refine and ultimately strengthen our activism. As spirituality involves the inner life, it can provide tools for addressing these challenges with a more penetrating integrity.

Secondly, spirituality is a way of knowing. It provides a basis for understanding what may be the further reaches of reality. Activism tests our convictions, demanding that we query our own basis for believing that we sense a better way in which the world can be. Spirituality brings such otherworldly ways of knowing, being and doing as music, poetry, art and prayer. These can hold us in ways that are bigger than just the cause for which we might be fighting. This can help us to see beyond the usual parameters of success or failure and friend or foe. It brings us to an awareness of the process by which we work and not just the tasks set as objectives. All of this renders us more open to compassion.

Thirdly, there is the primacy of truth. Activists can so easily fall into the same trap as the powers they come into conflict with; that of ignoring inconvenient truths. Such blind spots and self-referential bubbles undermine our work. Because truth is so vital to spirituality, the activist motivated from this depth never has a final, dogmatic solution; the complexity of the real world and the limits of our own understanding do not allow it. A spiritual activist is one who puts truth before all else, hence the title of Gandhi's autobiography: *Experiments with Truth*. Truth spoken to power has its own power. Gandhi called it *satyagraha* - a Sanskrit word that means "truth force", "soul force", "God force" or, perhaps most interestingly, "reality force". He believed that at its heart lay *ahimsa* - a Sanskrit word that, from about 1920, he translated as nonviolence. Truth is a power easily lost or abused if those who wield it are not themselves deeply committed to integrity.

Fourthly, we may find ourselves desperately needing spirituality when we're up against it, when we are exhausted or our back is to the wall, and we're getting shot at. As an old woman on the Isle of Lewis told Alastair of her youth, when so many of the young men in the village were serving on the Atlantic convoys; "You don't find many atheists on a life raft." There will be times when we might feel that we are carrying the cause or the movement. Other times, we may find that it is carrying us, and that can be a very humbling but powerful experience. John Seed, the Australian rainforest activist, often says; "I thought that I was saving nature, but then I found that nature was saving me."

Is all of this mumbo jumbo or, as our American friends say, "woo-woo"? A generation raised with little or no experience of religion is vulnerable to the pejorative terms and simplistic caricatures of spirituality that pervade popular discourse. There are all kinds of good reasons why society has rejected traditional conservative religion, but it would seem that this is not the end of the story. God may have been proclaimed dead, but the "Holy Ghost" keeps coming back!

It would seem that religion served deep human needs for meaning and affirmation which shopping, porn and football cannot adequately replace. For today's activists, several issues are converging to spur a renewed and refreshed spiritual narrative. Since at least the 1960s, activists have been joining the dots of multiple global crises. These range from nuclear proliferation to ecological devastation. They include grotesque social inequalities and massive power imbalances. Until the collapse of the Iron Curtain, the dots for many radical thinkers were joined by finding – through the lens of Marx – the roots of the problem in the creation and maintenance of the capitalist system. Religion was deeply implicated in this – "the opiate of the masses" – even though Marx can be read as a spiritual thinker. However, the failure of state communism to offer a viable alternative pressed many activists to take a deeper look. At the same time, environmentalism was rocketing up the agenda as pollution injured life on Earth. The energy intensity, mostly based on fossil fuels, by which we built up an unprecedented combination of population and material consumption is forcing planetary climate change. In some scenarios the consequences of global warming threaten a human-induced Armageddon. The search for meaning and deeper answers about life is no longer just a moral crusade; it is a fight for life and dignity, indeed, for existence.

For many activists, the roots of these problems lay deeper than class struggles, of key importance though these are. Further questions had to be asked of a 500-year-old philosophy – the project of modernism – which viewed the land and oceans as dead, and reduced humanity to the status of machines that may or may not contain ghostly wisps of free will.

Meanwhile, as aeroplanes and media shrunk the globe, we became familiar, even if in tokenistic ways, with land-based indigenous (tribal, aboriginal or native) cultures from Australia, New Zealand, North America and India whose mythologies seemed to speak to the spiritual vacuum. As a generalization, these connected human identity with the natural world. They didn't cut down forests, in part because they lacked the technology so to do, but also because the spirits of their ancestors lived there. The mountains were their gods, and rivers, goddesses. Suddenly mythology – romanticised though it often was – didn't seem so daft. It enshrined wisdom that protected people from real harm; wisdom we'd somehow lost.

So it is that a new opening has come about for thinkers who underpin their activism with faith, or a generalized spiritual perspective. Such fields as liberation theology and engaged Buddhism that have been going on for decades are drawing fresh interest. In Spain, for example, an organization called Ecodharma runs courses in spiritual activism, and many non-religious young activists practice yoga, Buddhist meditation or Reiki. An alternative story is emerging which transcends materialism without diluting the commitment to social and economic justice. This is despite the many evident problems inherent in "doing spirituality" with activists who are repelled by traditional religion, are suspicious of mystical claims, or may have experienced the spiritual abuse of compulsory religion. The bottom line is that many activists are re-evaluating their own traditions or discovering spirituality for the first time.

From this place, many of us find that far from being yet another concept or an optional extra in life - perhaps even a lifestyle choice - spirituality becomes the *underpinning* of what we are about. It becomes the magic horse on which we ride, or the tiger's mouth in which we sit in the heat of conflict, teeth sharpened by awareness of our predicament as dancers between sharply contrasting worldviews.

We love the story of the Buddhist monk who, after staying for the night but having no money, left for his kind hosts the next morning a piece of parchment with the words; "The best place for meditation is in the mouth of the tiger."[4] Then there's the tale of the Chinese sage who was chased (by that very same tiger!) over a precipice. As he fell, he grabbed hold of a blossoming bush and hung there, midway between the precipitous drop and the wild beast's teeth, and thought to himself; "What beautiful blossoms!"

Such is the capacity to remain alive and thrive. As Alice Walker says - each of us is a revolutionary petunia - "blooming... for deserving eyes... for its Self" - even in, perhaps especially in, the jaws of adversity.[5] There is in this both wit and wisdom, and not a little holy foolishness.

We live our lives, all of us, on a long front of possibilities with many different positions. Whatever might be our activist callings, what matters is that we live our lives authentically; that we live from out of our hearts. From there, as the old Ned Millar lyric has it, the practicalities are just to; "Do what you do do well."

In February 1969, the great modern spiritual activist Dorothy Day wrote these lines in *The Catholic Worker*, the newspaper that she edited. Really, these are all we need to live within our limitations, yet reach towards the furthest stars and so, to bloom.

> The thing is to recognize that not all are called, not all have the vocation to demonstrate in this way, to fast, to endure the pain and long-drawn-out nerve-racking suffering of prison life. We do what we can, and the whole field of all the Works of Mercy is open to us. There is a saying, "Do what you are doing." If you are a student, study, prepare, in order to give to others, and to keep alive in yourself the vision of a new social order. All work, whether building, increasing food production, running credit unions, working in factories which produce for true human needs, working the smallest of industries, the handicrafts - all these things can come under the heading of the Works of Mercy, which are the opposite of the works of war.

Some people argue that to devote one's efforts primarily to the Works of Mercy in this way is a displacement activity from the "real world" of politics, including party politics and policy development. For example, Alastair was pressed on this point at an academic conference. He replied that politics can happen on many different levels, but the challenge left him ill at ease and slightly struggling to convince.

Later on, he found that an email had arrived. It was from an astonished senior civil servant. There she had been, sitting in a committee of the European Parliament, and his work had just been pivotally quoted by a much respected British diplomat on climate change.

Spiritual activism works mainly at the pre-political level. It digs the pilot channels into which subsequent political processes can flow. The personal is political, the political is personal, and not all that glimmers on the surface knows the springs that rise from deep below.

CASE STUDY

Mahatma Gandhi: The Power of Simple Service

***Gandhi Graffiti San Francisco* by Victorgrigas**
Wikimedia Commons

In his autobiography, *Experiments with Truth*, Gandhi tells how, as a young man, he went to the offices of the Congress party in the hope of gaining experience. Every activist has to start from somewhere, and even Gandhi realized that he had to find himself an apprenticeship, as it were.

Bhupenbabu and Ghosalbabu were the secretaries. He went to Bhupenbabu and offered his services. No joy. Bhupenbabu had no work that was not already being covered, but suggested that the keen-eyed young man might try Ghosalbabu.

Not discouraged, Ghandi went to Ghosalbabu. He looked Gandhi up and down, smiled and said; "I can give you only clerical work. Will you do it?"

"Certainly. I am here to do anything that is not beyond my capacity."

"That is the right spirit, young man," and turning to the other volunteers who surrounded him, Ghosalbabu announced; "Do you hear what this young man says?"

Only later did Ghosalbabu enquire about the new volunteer's credentials. It was the attitude of being willing to do whatever was most needed that unlocked the door.

Gandhi goes on to describe how, within a few days, he had met most of the leaders of the party. He noticed their lack of work discipline; they had little regard for economy of energy and wasted much time. More than one did the work of one and many important tasks were left unattended. He managed to summon the charity within himself to hope that, were he walking in their shoes, he might have found it impossible to have done much better and this attitude, he recorded; "saved me from undervaluing any work."[6]

Gandhi would have loved the maxim of George MacLeod, who founded the Iona Community; "God is never served by inefficiency." Elsewhere, this great leader of the Indian independence movement wrote that he considered cleaning the toilets to be the highest function. Why? Because the most lowly is the most vital.

Another thing about Gandhi is that he understood the importance of the activist living in the moment; their relationship to time. One day much later in his career, he was travelling by train to address an important party meeting when a journalist asked; "What do you intend to say to Congress?"

He answered; "How do I know when I have not yet arrived?"

CHAPTER TWO

Spirituality Justified

A contested concept

"It means just what I choose it to mean," said Humpty Dumpty to Alice, and there is a danger that when we talk about spirituality we enter a Never Never Land of fantasy that, as the existence of religious cults suggests, can be both delusory and harmful.

In this chapter, we explore the meanings and validity of the hotly contested word spirituality. We see it as central to activism because it is, first of all, a way of knowing. That leads on to a way of doing, and from there, to a way of being in what becomes a positive feedback loop. We could argue about the ordering of those three attributes. It is not a logical sequence of priorities because they all reinforce one another. You have to know it to be it and thus to do it; but equally, you have to do it to know it and be it, and so on, in various permutations. That's why we are sympathetic only up to a point with retreat- and workshop-junkies who say; "I have to get my inner stuff together before I can engage with the world." It's a half-truth but, equally, it is only by engaging with the world that the stuff in question can be processed in the first place. If you don't do a bit of everything all at once, you're likely to get stuck - hence the "junkie" designation.

By engaging with activism at the deepest levels of what it means to be human, we open doors of perception through which we can better see our human nature ecologically; that is, in its total context within the universe, the Earth, the land, culture, society, history, community, family and so on. Academic rigour is of great assistance in this, provided it is kept in context and not allowed to induce *rigor mortis* by attempting to over-control and simplify complex life systems.

Spiritual but not religious?

For a little bit of rest and recreation after an intensive bout of activism during the First Gulf War in 1991, Alastair went on a 10-day Vipassana Buddhist meditation retreat that involved getting up every day at four in the morning and sitting for fourteen hours a day. Ouch! But it did leave an impression, and not only on the posterior.

"I don't get it," he said to one of the teaching staff, an old woman from Sri Lanka. "You Buddhists keep saying that you don't have a God, but everything I hear you say about the Buddha Nature seems to be about God."

"Well, what do you mean by God?" she asked.

"Buddha Nature," he replied. "The creative power of love pumping out life to make reality."

"But your Western missionaries came to us and taught that God is like a bearded old white man in the sky."

"I don't believe in that God either," he said, and both laughed, but this does touch on a very important point; religion and spirituality are not necessarily the same thing.

Matt's spiritual journey remains outside religious boundaries. On one level, this is simply a matter of beliefs. Religions (not unreasonably) use beliefs to define the boundaries of their communities, and Matt's honest opinions do not sit well with any religion he has yet explored. But there's another level too. It was, in fact, at one of Alastair's workshops on spiritual activism that he experienced a profound sense of calling to keep following a path outside religion.

As the group sat in a circle at the end of an intense weekend, Matt listened to the contributions of others and hadn't considered anything he might want to say himself. Without warning, he found himself in tears, trying to articulate a deep feeling of spiritual homelessness. Spiritual activists tend to be a caring bunch, and afterwards they came up to say; "If you need someone to talk to..." and "Thanks for sharing your pain..." But somehow their kind words felt all wrong. Matt's experience had left him with a profound feeling of being affirmed, a kind of elation that, despite all his doubts and fears, he was on the right path after all - at least for today.

A religion is a coherent worldview emanating from a shared sense of sacredness in an experientially knowable ground or focus of being. This offers a framework for life, meaning and governance to the community of adherents that it constellates. The word "religion" derives from the Latin, *re*, meaning "back" or "again", and *ligare* meaning "to tie". One way to understand religion is as that of the spiritual, which has been "tied back down" and integrated into social structures. This etymology aptly implies the free-ranging nature of spirituality. At its best, religion is a human-made trellis upon which the wild vine of raw spiritual life, the spirit-driven life of the soul, can be invited to grow. It raises us towards the sun.

At worst, on the other hand, religion forces and prunes growth in particular directions. When it is blind to the value of or feels threatened by a limb, it lops it off. Instead of supporting the development of spirituality, bad religion can inhibit or kill it. This is why most of the great religious teachers have been reformers: Jesus was reforming Judaism; Buddha, Hinduism; Guru Nanak of the Sikh tradition, Islam and Hinduism; Confucius, the ancient Taoist traditions (though some would say, deforming). So it goes on, for all religions need periodic reformation; thus the Protestant principle of *semper reformanda*, which means, when unpacked; "The reformed church is the church that is always reforming itself."

Different religions that are based on life as love made manifest can be likened to the many pathways up a mountain. Each has its rough and smooth, its steep climbs and its easy steps. From the bottom, confronted by its immensity, the other paths may not be visible. What little we might glimpse of them might even seem to be wrong ways. However, from the mountaintop - from the God's-eye-view - even the most meandering eventually converges. This is why the mystical worldview is called the "perennial philosophy". The unitive vision perennially recurs across cultures, space and time. The Truth that sets us free is made of many lesser truths.

Many people today find they cannot participate in organized religion because of a multitude of real or perceived problems including, variously, its obsequious relationships with power, obscure and pernicious dogmas, its obsession with sex and rigid gender roles, sexual abuse, sectarian prejudice and its association with holy wars. There has been a growing trend for people therefore to define themselves as "spiritual but not religious" and with it, a rise in new religious movements. These purport to cut through the deadening baggage and get to the source of life, offering more freed-up spiritual paths. Questions arise such as how liberated these really are. The "New Age" started in the postwar years of the mid-20th century and was, initially, a new take on moribund mainstream spirituality.[7] By the 1970s, what had been a breath of fresh air was becoming tainted by those who tag on to exploit any spiritual revival. New Age became a term of abuse, especially by fundamentalist Christians who felt threatened by competition, and could see the mote in others' eyes while missing that within their own. As we have said, all religions – including those that claim not to be religions – have a periodic need for reformation through theologies of liberation. These are questions that will emerge frequently throughout this book.

What is spirituality?

Having made a distinction between religion and spirituality, how is the sense of spirituality used? Three definitions would be:

- The presence of God, Goddess, Allah, Christ, Brahman, etc. in our lives.
- The inner aspect of reality.
- That which gives life and, specifically, life as love made manifest.

The first understands the spiritual as the expression of our relationship to a supreme being that may, to varying degrees, be personified. It is the idea that there's *more* to life than just our own little egos going about on legs of meat. The spiritual journey explores, seeks and, hopefully, receives revelation surrounding that "more".

In this discussion we are taking it for granted that many different words from many different traditions can be used to designate "God". This is how mystics usually understand divine realities, but the conventionally religious can be very possessive of their terminology and consider, for example, that Allah does not pertain to God, or that Christ is the only valid path to God.

Our second definition of spirituality draws on the theology of the late

Walter Wink, a key figure in spiritual activism. Wink saw the spiritual in structural terms. His work suggests that all things in this world have an outward material face, but also an inner spiritual dynamic that animates them, that brings them to life or implicit meaning. A human being is, yes, flesh and bones and genetic code. But there is also an inner spirituality that finds incarnation through the body. Equally institutions, nations, corporations and even buildings and natural objects can all be considered to have their own spirituality because they embody values and meanings. It is this with which the activist wrestles.

The third definition views the human experience of the divine as being centrally about life and love becoming manifest in the world. Gustavo Gutiérrez is the Peruvian father of liberation theology - theology, we might say, that liberates theology itself so that it can measure up to the task of liberating humankind. Perhaps like Mahayana Buddhism with its *Tibetan Book of Great Liberation*, Gutiérrez sees that true religion is the practice of setting life free. Thus his formula:[8]

To liberate = to give life

Spirituality under intellectual fire

Broadly speaking, one studies a theology, observes a religion, but lives spirituality. We can speak meaningfully of all three being in relationship with one another, even if that friendship might often be strained. However, the same is less easily said of spirituality in relation to the materialistic frameworks that dominate much of our mainstream thinking and intellectual institutions. Spirituality sits uneasily with modernist and most postmodernist ideologies. These see it as a delusion, to be exposed and deconstructed by the cold light of reason. This is because modernism has interpreted rationality to be positivist, meaning that only positive phenomena - capable of being felt and measured through the senses or scientific instruments - are considered real. We could summarize some of the main points of disagreement as follows:

1 Epistemology
Epistemology is the study of the nature and structure of knowledge. It concerns what we think we know and don't know, and

how or why we think we know or don't know about things. In many disciplines the epistemological basis of knowledge seems obvious. For example, the physical sciences are substantially based on *empiricism*, a word that means by experience or experiment. However, it is often used synonymously with *positivism*, which is pretty much taken to mean materialism in the word's philosophical sense – that is, the belief that only matter (and physical energy) exist and everything else, from mind to magic, is an illusion. In empiricism, knowledge flows from unifying the evidence of the senses with reason. Everything that is "inner" is either dismissed out of hand or explained in a reductionist manner, radically narrowing the range of things it is possible to know. Thus, the British logical positivist philosopher AJ Ayer, in his landmark book, *Language, Truth and Logic*, dismissed all metaphysics (which includes religion and ethics) as "literally senseless"! For thinkers in the tradition of Ayer, if you can't count it, it doesn't count.

In contrast, a spiritual worldview permits not just sensory and rational impressions of reality, but also those that come from intuition and feeling. This radically *widens* the scope of what can be known and allows for a sense of *meaning* to inform our understanding and experience of reality. The danger is that this could admit delusion. It can pull us out of line with a grounded reality, and that can become a cause of suffering. Equally, however, the *nihilism* or emptiness of a materialistic worldview causes suffering. It's not just religions that can cause wars; it can also be the abject atheism of a Joseph Stalin or Pol Pot.

2 Wholes

In a poem whose title is translated as "Lousy at Maths", the Sufi poet Hafiz tells of a group of thieves who steal an enormous diamond. They celebrate by getting drunk – and promptly fall out, deciding in the end to divide the gem amongst them and destroying its value in the process. It illustrates how we experience realities *as wholes*, but how materialism breaks them down into parts such as atoms, cells, genes or bits of data. This is *reductionism*. At its best, it represents focus; at its worst, tunnel vision.

Einstein pointed out that it might be possible to describe a Beethoven symphony as a variation in wave pressure hitting the eardrum, but there would be no point. In doing so you lose the meaning, the experience of the music. It's only as a whole, and not as a scientific description of parts, that music makes sense. Just as with Hafiz's diamond, those who are obsessed with counting but miss the immeasurable whole turn out to be lousy at understanding the true worth of things. As Oscar Wilde said, they "know the price of everything and the value of nothing".

Seeing things as wholes involves acknowledging the extraordinary degree to which everything is *interconnected*. Whole things are not only more than the sum of their parts because of the complex ways in which the parts which make them up are interlinked, but also because of the way in which the whole is woven into larger wholes. In science, ecology has been prominent in acknowledging this sense of "emergent properties", by which the whole is greater than the sum of its parts. Other disciplines are following suit, for science is not locked in its older paradigms, and increasingly this is allowing the consideration of spirituality to be brought into scientific discourse, especially in the human sciences.

3 Essence

Whole things have their own qualities, which are an aspect of what makes them more than the sum of their parts. Just as what makes your house a home cannot be located in any particular object, brick or memory, what makes you *you* is a feature of the *whole you*. When we try to discern what makes you you, we find ourselves talking in intuitive terms about your *essence*.

This "essence", though, is anathema to materialist thinking. After all, where is it? How can it be measured? What experiment could be conducted to isolate it? The very notion of isolating it, so vital to positivism, makes no sense if it is an emergent property arising from the whole, any more than it would make sense to try to isolate the poetry from a poem, leaving only a jumble of prose.

Modernism, however, rejects essentialism and postmodernists have mostly arrived at the same conclusion. Indeed, many postmodernists dismiss everything, even "nature", as being the social constructions of human minds. Realities can be remade and unmade as we please. Quite how some of them would do out in a boat in a force eight is a good question! "Deconstruction" has a valuable place where applied to taking to pieces, for example, oppressive power structures such as patriarchy. However, when it strips out poetry, soul and grace, it results again in nihilism. The essence is lost, as if the alcohol had been squeezed out from the whisky. Speaking for ourselves, we'd be a little wary of post-modern party time.

A philosophical defence of spirituality

An agnostic (*a* - "not", and *gnostos* - "known") claims not to know whether there is a God or any sort of spiritual underpinning to reality. However, a full card-carrying atheist permits no such receptivity. Atheism bluntly asserts that there is no theistic principle; there is no God, Buddha Nature or anything else. It is an assertion of philosophical materialism. This, however, lands atheists with a problem. They claim that their argument follows from reason - atheism has been called "the Church of Reason" - but reason hinges on the principle of causality, which is the logic of logic. It entails the belief that nothing can come into being without a cause.

Cold logic on its own would expect there to be nothing, but look up at the starry universe, and our eyes behold an astonishing fact. *There is some-thing* where one would expect *nothing*. What's more, science holds that this whole shebang - space, time and the kitchen sink - began some 13.8 billion years ago.

Either this coming into being had a cause, or it didn't. If it had a cause, that cause must itself stand outside of space and time. That is to say, it must be grounded in eternity. Such - with or without the baggage - is the usual definition of God.

It might be objected that if eternity "just is", the universe too should be accepted on the same basis and not need to be explained. This, though, would be to confuse categories. The universe and eternity are not symmetrical. The universe exists within the fabric of its own space and time. In contrast, eternity has "no vestige of a beginning, no prospect of an end."[9] The *Bhagavad Gita*, the gospel of Hinduism, is explicit on what this implies. Here Krishna as the incarnation of the divine principle, the embodiment of eternity, says; "All beings have their rest in me, but I have not my rest in them... I am the source of all beings, I support them all, but I rest not in them."[10] Equally explicit is the *Tao Te Ching*. It says of the underlying cosmic principle, the Tao; "The myriad creatures all rise together/ And I watch their return.../ This is what is meant by returning to one's destiny."[11]

Atheism of the most hard-line variety is left with one further recourse if it is to duck the latent theistic pitfalls of eternity. This is to argue that the Big Bang (or whatever marked the universe coming into being) required no cause. Such is the argument from *acausality* - "without cause".[12] The problem with acausality is that it contradicts causality. It crashes the very structure of logic. Something that comes into being without a cause is the definition of magic. This leaves such an atheist caught between a rock and a hard place. To put it tongue-in-cheek, as perhaps befits such endlessly abstract arguments: either, reality is rooted in eternity, which raises vexing theological questions, or, bring on the faeries!

Rediscovering pre-modernism

The intellectual movement we call modernism has its roots in the Renaissance, which began around the fourteenth century. Classical thought, most notably through Aristotle, Plato and the Roman writers, was rediscovered and applied. This led to the 18th-century Enlightenment, with the advent of modern science and the technological age we now inhabit. It has brought tremendous power, but at the same time undermined our capacity to know what to do with such power. Why? Because it struggles to accommodate spiritual principles that provide the foundation for ethics, meaning and values. When we are "lousy at maths", we are simply unable to value the whole planet, the diversity of humanity, the vast ecosystems which support life and the uniqueness of individuals. Instead, we break everything up for parts with an economic value, and turn the world into a giant scrapyard. It is no coincidence that Hafiz's diamond reductionists were thieves.

Let us use an example to see the extent to which modernism has boxed knowledge in to narrow compartments based on questionable values.

The home page of the British Library's website proclaims itself to be the place to "Explore the world's knowledge". In the United Kingdom, PhD theses are submitted for public record to this library as standard. That process requires a form to be completed that is supported by an A4 sheet headed "Subject Categories". Through these, the thesis is catalogued.

The sheet lists the main groupings of what the Library recognises as human knowledge. There are some 200 categories gathered under 20 major headings. For example, there are major headings for *Biological and medical sciences*, for *Chemistry* and for *Physics*. That seems fair enough, but there are also major headings (out of the mere 20 available) allocated respectively to *Aeronautics, Military sciences, Missile technology, Navigation, communications, detection and countermeasures, Ordnance, Propulsion and fuels,* and *Space technology*.

In other words, more than one third of the headings of what is deemed significant knowledge relate to aerospace/military matters. In contrast, just one major heading covers the whole of *Humanities, psychology and social sciences*. Within this, just one subcategory, coded 05H, is afforded to the entire corpus of knowledge lumped together as: *Philosophy; theology; religion*.

At least there is humour in the listing. Under *Space technology* there are seven categories, including code 22F for *Extraterrestrial exploration*. Let us be clear about the priorities that this reveals; the British Library appears to afford the same weight to *Philosophy; theology; religion* as it does to extraterrestrial affairs!

This is just one example of how the modern utilitarian worldview crushes alternative representations of reality. Attention to technological detail has subsumed the conceptual latitude that might have been afforded to human depth.

We do not want to devalue modernity's emphasis on rationality and evidence-based knowledge. Neither do we wish to devalue postmodern thought where it deconstructs oppressive fabrications of race, gender, religion and social class. But we do wish to challenge the oft-shared presumptions of modernism and post-modernism of having bettered the soulfulness of those ancient and indigenous worldviews that can be found - albeit often laden with their own baggage - in premodern thought.

We hope this is adequate to show that far from being intellectually dishonest, weak or inferior, spirituality can be a way of waking up intellectually to the depth of the problems we face today. The cracks in the modernist project now sundering ecosystems and societies everywhere are partly related to its own intellectual weaknesses, especially the tendency to fragment wholes. Spirituality values wholes as sacred. Sacredness is not a capitulation to superstition. Sacred is the appropriate adjective for whole things that cannot be taken apart and put back together again, and therefore cannot be valued in material terms: healthy forests, snow leopards, clean rivers, starry nights, daughters and brothers and lovers and friends. If nothing is sacred, nothing is safe from the mechanizers of life and calculators of profit; and until we find ways to resacralize our world appropriately, there can be no end to the carnage.

This gives fresh wings to the once-pervasive human understanding that things have soul, that there's more to life than just the posturing of an intellect under the ego's control. The intellect is important. Not least, it helps to protect us from false or distorted spiritual claims. Of deeper consequence, though, is the need to open up the doors of perception; an opening of both mind and heart in ways that take our activism for environmental, spiritual and social change - soil, soul and society - beyond the ordinary limits of vision and endurance.

CASE STUDY

Julia Butterfly Hill: Breakdown to Breakthrough

It is common for a shamanic calling to be prefigured by a life-threatening illness, a brush with death, or other traumatic incident. In his classic work on shamanism, the Romanian historian of religion, Mircea Eliade, calls them "initiatory sicknesses".[13]

Julia Hill had been like any normal teenager who graduated from high school at sixteen and started working in a restaurant. One night, as a designated driver taking a friend home from a party, she had a crash. "The steering wheel in my head, both figuratively and literally, steered me in a

Julia Butterfly Hill by Carl-John Veraja, Wikimedia Commons

new direction in my life."[14] Before that, she had been obsessed with career and material success. Afterwards, her passion shifted to life and the planetary future. Her chosen "forest name" was "Butterfly", based on a totemic childhood experience.

Before she climbed the 55 metres (180 feet) to a wooden platform in a giant redwood tree called "Luna", no-one had sustained a tree-sit for longer than 90 days. Cold weather, isolation and physical danger always brought them down. Julia, however, stayed in Luna for 738 days, spanning two of the worst winters on record. She makes clear in her account that spiritual experiences of inner transformation were key to her endurance. During one particularly violent storm she realized that Luna herself survived not by bracing herself against the wind, but by bending with it:[15]

I suddenly understood. So as I was getting chucked all over by the wind, tossed left and right, I just let it go. I let my muscles go. I let my jaw unlock. I let the wind blow and the craziness flow. I bent and flailed with it, just like the trees which flail in the wind. I howled. I laughed. I whooped and cried and screamed and raged... Everything around me was being ripped apart. My sanity felt like it was slipping through my fingers like a runaway rope. And I gave in.

"Fine. Take it. Take my life. Take my sanity. Take it all."

Once the storm ended, I realized that by letting go of all attachments, including my attachment to self, people no longer had any power over me. They could take my life if they felt the need, but I was no longer going to live my life out of fear, the way too many people do, jolted by our disconnected society. I was going to live my life guided from the higher source, the Creation source.

I couldn't have realized any of this without having been broken emotionally and spiritually and mentally and physically. I had to be pummelled by humankind. I had to be pummelled by Mother Nature. I had to be broken until I saw no hope, until I went crazy, until I finally let go. Only then could I be rebuilt; only then could I be filled back up with who I am meant to be.

Now that she has entered her forties and mid-life, it will be revealing to watch how Julia's life story continues to unfold. All of us who might have cut our activist teeth in the shimmer of springtide must face the question of what happens when the oil in the lamp of youth runs low. Do we run dry - burn out or sell out - or will we find ways to drill down to fresh wells? Julia has spoken frankly of how she has become limited by her old role; "But it's hard to figure out what next because there's this entire reality that's been created around this role that I play... I just know that there's aspects of it that need to shed."[16]

Trees are not alone in needing to shed their leaves. Like hard-worked fields depleted of their nutrients, activists too need times to rest their lives awhile in fallow.

CHAPTER THREE

Higher Consciousness

Side-effect or reality?

For some people, the question of whether spirituality is "for real" does not require evidence; it seems self-evident. For others, a case that can be more strongly argued is required. They might say; "This talk of spirituality is all very well, but is there any evidence?" There are various ways of addressing this question. The one that we wish to follow here hinges on the nature of consciousness.

To many behavioural scientists the ego self and its field of consciousness is a side-effect of brain evolution. As Hans Eysenck of the Institute of Psychiatry has said; "consciousness is an epiphenomenon of brain activity."[17] Here the brain might be likened to an island in the sea, and the ego, a lighthouse on the top that sweeps out its brain-generated beam of consciousness. A spiritual worldview, though, sees it differently. Here consciousness is a quality of an intangible and indestructible quality called the soul. Not only that, but individual soul, through its connection to the divine Spirit, is connected to the cosmos. Consciousness is a quality not of the brain, but of reality as a whole. The pioneering Canadian psychiatrist, RM Bucke, called this "cosmic consciousness". He defined it as "a consciousness of the cosmos, that is, of the life and order of the universe," adding from his own experience and an extensive literature review that it brings with it "indescribable feelings of elevation, elation and joyousness, and a quickening of the moral sense."[18] Here the brain is not the source of consciousness, but more like a tuner or reducing valve that limits the universal down to the singular. As such, the ego's limited field of consciousness is our individualized and manageable share in an infinitely vaster transpersonal (or interconnected) whole.

To imagine that the brain generates consciousness is, we would argue, as misinformed as thinking that the radio in your kitchen generates the programmes that are broadcast over the airwaves. Bucke saw that this has ethical implications. As the "geologian" Thomas Berry put it, if you start off with the view that the universe is a dead "collection of objects", you end up interpreting consciousness as only a side-effect. This was the soulless viewpoint that allowed Descartes and his circle to nail dogs to boards by their paws for vivisection, insisting that their cries were only the mechanistic creakings of an unoiled machine. In contrast, if we entertain the possibility that the universe is in some very deep sense alive, that it comprises a "communion of subjects", then we come to very different conclusions about our own relationship to the rest of reality.

Mainstream science is still working with Eysenck's mechanical view, but some disciplines are more open to the possibilities than others. When two articles highlighted the lack of any satisfactory definition of life in biology, *New Scientist* magazine published Matt's letter suggesting that the whole universe is alive, "After all, even the vacuum of space is fizzing with subatomic activity as particles bubble in and out of existence."[19]

States of consciousness

The veteran American consciousness researcher, Charles T Tart, argues that levels of consciousness in others or in nature can only be appreciated from within states of consciousness that are capable of appreciating them. Further, he suggests that the "Two Cultures" divide between scientists and the humanities in academia is best resolved by coming to see that knowledge itself is specific to the state of consciousness out of which it arises.

In other words, knowledge and its epistemological validity varies with the level of consciousness. Both reductionist psychology and holistic transpersonal (or spiritual) psychology need to be understood as discrete state-of-consciousness-specific sciences. Tart gives the example of a volunteer in a study into the effects of LSD, who tells his investigator; "You and I, we are all one, there are no separate selves." The investigator reports that his subject showed a "confused sense of identity and distorted thinking process". Each is reporting what is obvious from within his own state of consciousness. Each thinks the other mad![20]

To take another example, it makes perfect sense to a poet to equate one's lover with a rose. Metaphor is the *lingua franca* of poetry. But as a Zen aphorism cautions; "Do not show your poem to a non-poet!" The men in white coats would soon turn up if you went to the park and made love to a rosebush. Normal state-of-consciousness paradigms of reality would kick in with an ouch!

Transpersonal psychologists hold that psychosis, when it is not caused by brain dysfunction, is often best understood as an extreme confusion of categories between different states of consciousness. This is why the brain needs to set boundaries. The problem of limited spiritual vision arises when those limitations get so constricted that we find ourselves locked up in cognitive straitjackets. Go to either extreme, and the men in the white coats win! The healthy development of consciousness is a question of balance, and that, as the Buddhists teach, is a question of learning to live in right or mindful relationships.

Mystical experience and brain function

In 1882, the psychologist William James published a paper in *Mind* about the inhalation of nitrous oxide. He urged others to repeat his experiment in which "the center and periphery of things seem to come together. The ego and its objects... are one... God and devil, good and evil, life and death, I and thou..." His experiment had induced an altered state of consciousness - in this case a mystical experience - by affecting the function of his brain. He surmised:[21]

> Rational consciousness... is but one special type of consciousness, whilst all about it, parted from it by the flimsiest of screens, there lie potential forms of consciousness entirely different. We may go through life without suspecting their existence; but apply the requisite stimulus, and at a touch they are there in all their completeness... No account of the universe in its totality can be final which leaves these other forms of consciousness disregarded.

While some would say he lost his mind, others would say he opened it, cutting out the reducing valve to have an experience that was "psychedelic" - from Greek words meaning mind-clarifying or mind-manifesting.

In short, James had got stoned on laughing gas. Eighteen years later, his classic study for the Gifford Lectures drew on a great many accounts of spontaneous religious experience, many of which had been collected by the Quaker-born psychologist, Edwin Diller Starbuck. [22]

What entitles us to speak of spiritual experiences - or "peak" experiences as the humanistic psychologist Abraham Maslow called them[23] - as if they comprise a discrete level of reality? Walter Stace identified nine characteristics that are commonly present in mystical consciousness.[24]

1. A sense of undifferentiated unity - sometimes called "the hallmark of mystical experience".
2. Objectivity and reality - the experience seems more real than real.
3. Space and time - feel as if their limitations have been transcended.
4. Sacredness - a sense of which pervades the experience.
5. Deeply-felt positive moods - joy, blessedness and especially love.
6. Paradoxicality - normal categories of logic seem to drop away.
7. Ineffability - the experience cannot adequately be expressed in words.
8. Transiency - the intensity of the experience usually passes fairly quickly (which is one feature that differentiates it from psychosis).
9. Positive changes - in attitude and/or behaviour towards life, often permanent.

The philosophical *Argument from Mystical Experience* holds that because, in mystical states of consciousness, a person feels themselves to be at one with the Ultimate - the universal "I am" of the divine - then that person is justified in believing in the existence of the same. As James put it; "Mystical states, when well developed, usually are, and have the right to be, absolutely authoritative" to the person who experiences them.[25]

Thus the *Mandukya Upanishad* says of God as understood in Hinduism; "In the union with Him is the supreme proof of His reality. He is peace and love."[26] Christians would say the same of Christ, Taoists of the Tao, and so it goes on across different traditions, but while the defensively religious will usually insist on difference, the mystics commonly hold that the same underlying reality is being glimpsed through differing cultural lenses.

The strength of this "seeing is believing" argument is that it is empirical. Mystics who have encountered the divine usually hold that their basis for believing in the same is at least as strong as their basis for believing in ordinary reality. This lays no requirement on others to accept the authority of the mystic. It does, however, invite consideration that there may be levels of consciousness other than the "normal" one waiting to be investigated. If you have never been to Trinidad, you can still accept that it exists because of corroborated reports of others who have been there. Such corroboration is know to researchers as "consensual validation".

Furthermore, the "normal" state of consciousness may only be normal to those who hold a given worldview. In his remarkable tome, *The Master And His Emissary*, Iain McGilchrist, an Oxford don, consultant psychiatrist and neuroimaging researcher, brings together recent advances in brain research. He explains that the left and right hemispheres of the brain each facilitate a very different way of perceiving the world.

The left hemisphere deals with details, is highly focussed in its attention and seeks clarity and certainty. "Clarity", as McGilchrist says; "describes not a degree of perception, but a type of knowledge." The left hemisphere has no perception of the flow of time – and therefore no sense of narrative – and is very literal in its interpretation of meanings. The right deals with wholes in their whole context. It is intuitive, concerned with emotions and relationships and alive to the unexpected. The left constructs and then pays exclusive attention to its own reality, whereas the right synthesizes the model created by the left hemisphere with everything else. In Tart's terms, each hemisphere supports necessary and essential states of consciousness, but the left's narrow state of consciousness is unaware of what the right perceives, whereas the right's wide-angle state of consciousness is fully aware of what the left perceives.

However, it is what McGilchrist does next that is really startling. First, because of the left's narrowness, he notes that there is a serious problem in the relationship between the hemispheres; "Despite an astonishing degree of ignorance on the part of the left hemisphere about what its partner… the right, is up to, it abrogates decision-making to itself in the absence of any rational evidence as to what is going on" and "lays down the law about what only the right hemisphere can know." So, whereas the right hemisphere, with its big picture, is the natural "master" of his book's title; and the left hemisphere, its natural "emissary" attending to the administrative detail, it is the emissary with its more limited vision that wants to be in charge. Precisely *because* it understands so little of what the master perceives, it thinks it knows everything, but lacks the generalist's overview.

McGilchrist goes on to suggest that all of human history is the result of people perceiving reality through these different lenses of consciousness, because; "What we attend to, and how we attend to it, changes it and changes us." Interpreting Western culture through this set of insights, he finds that the left hemisphere has staged a kind of slow, internal coup, usurping the right hemisphere's rightful role as master of perception. Thus:[27]

> Denial, a tendency to conformism, a willingness to disregard the evidence, a habit of ducking responsibility, a blindness to mere experience in the face of overwhelming evidence of theory: these might sound ominously familiar to observers of contemporary Western life... [If] the story of the Western world is one of increasing left-hemisphere domination... we would expect a sort of insouciant optimism, the sleepwalker whistling a happy tune as he ambles towards the abyss.

The neurology of mystical experiences cannot be simplistically associated with one hemisphere or the other. However, the right hemisphere is open to what is new, alive, astonishing and Other, so when evidence of the transcendent nature of reality presents itself, the "master" hemisphere, given enough space by the "emissary", does not reject it, but learns.

What does entry into transcendent states of consciousness feel like? People report peak and mystical experiences as being like waking up out of a dream. When asleep, a dream self occupies a dream world in which one interacts with other dream people. It all feels perfectly real until the alarm clock goes off. Only then does one realize that the dream was a mental fantasy entertained by one's now-awakened mind. As a person slips into mystical consciousness it may feel as if their ordinary sense of self and the everyday world fall into proportion from the vantage point of a greater perspective, just as the dream self did for the awakened sleeper. From this seemingly higher vantage point, other people may no longer appear to be separate entities struggling against all the others in the world, but part of a greater whole that is bound up together in the whole of Creation. Such is the sacred sense of unity that is the hallmark of mystical consciousness.

Some practical examples might help to illustrate. Professor Robert Greenway, a pioneer of ecopsychology, would specifically set up the conditions to invoke what he calls the "wilderness effect" with his students by spending prolonged periods in nature. From his studies of 1,380 people who had been taken on these camping trips, 90 per cent described "an increased sense of aliveness, well-being, and energy" and 38 per cent described life changes that "held true" five years after their return from what he led them through. The following describes the experience of twelve people who were near the end of a two-week trip up the Eel River in northern California.[28]

> We had gone as deep into the center of the wilderness as we could, and as deep into our hearts and minds. We had adopted games and structures we knew would open us beyond our familiar constraints. Now, in the fullness of our opening, our ability to feel and understand reached unexpected depths... We came upon a huge pool that seemed bottomless – shadings of blue-green darkening almost to black in the depths... We knew without speaking that we had found "the place". We fell silent at the sight, knowing that this would be the turning point, "the most sacred", the place of deepest wilderness, for this day, for this trip, for this time in our lives, and perhaps in our entire lives... We swam, crawled onto the hot rocks... most of us slept for a time. Later some spoke of amazingly vivid dreams... Distance disappeared and there was an openness into ourselves that was an openness to each other that embraced the pool, the river, and further out into the wilderness, the "other world", the whole Earth, the universe.

An example of a mystical experience with more explicitly religious overtones is from George Fox, the seventeenth-century founder of the Quaker movement. Notice, again, the sense of illumination.[29]

> I now came up in the spirit past the flaming sword into the paradise of God. Everything was new. And the whole creation gave off another smell to what I knew before, beyond what I could ever

express in words. I knew nothing but purity and innocence and rightness as I was renewed in the image of God by Jesus Christ, so that, as I say, I entered the state that Adam was in before he fell. The creation was opened up to me... Great things I was led to by the Lord and wonderful depths were revealed to me, beyond what I could ever put in words.

And just to remember to bend the gendering of God, here is a lovely description from the scholar Carol Christ, author of *Rebirth of the Goddess*, whose experience has helped to shape her theology.[30]

As my mother died, I felt the room fill with an immense power of love. This did not feel like my mother's love for me or mine for her; rather it seemed to me to be a great power of love that included us both and everything else. Since that moment I have felt this power of love in everything while going about my daily life. Sometimes I feel it more intensely, and sometimes I need to remind myself of it; nonetheless, from the moment of my mother's death, I have never doubted that a great matrix of love supports and sustains the world... I define Goddess in terms of this experience.

Are higher states "abnormal"?

The chief counterargument to mystical states is that they are "abnormal". Especially if chemically induced, they cannot reveal truth as authoritatively as does "normal" perception. Bertrand Russell put it like this; "We can make no distinction between the man who eats little and sees heaven and the man who drinks much and sees snakes. Each is in an abnormal physical condition, and therefore has abnormal perceptions."

We might respond that there is an important qualitative difference between the hallucinating alcoholic and the mystic. Charles T Tart holds that we must distinguish between higher and lower states of consciousness. A lower state is one where normal perceptual and cognitive functioning are impaired, such as being "blind drunk". In a higher state, however, normal faculties remain available but outgrown.[31]

Ram Dass, the American spiritual teacher, tells of walking into a mental institution back in his hippy days wearing a long robe and beads to visit his brother, who was locked up in a suit and tie.

The brother says: "I don't understand, why am I in a hospital and you are out there free? You look like a nut."

Ram Dass says: "You think you're Christ?"

"Yeah."

"Well, I'm Christ too."

"No, you don't understand," protests the brother.

"That's why they're locking you up," says Ram Dass. "Because you think that you're the only one!"[32]

That's the difference between the psychotic and the mystic, between a lower and a higher state of consciousness.

Among today's vast and growing body of studies of these phenomena, is the work of the Alister Hardy Religious Experience Research Centre. Founded by an eminent biologist, this has conducted cross-cultural studies asking; "Have you ever been aware of or influenced by a presence or power, whether you call it God or not, which is different from your everyday self?"

In Britain, the USA and Australia, typically 34 per cent of the population answer "yes" to this question.[33] Of those reporting a religious experience, trigger factors include listening to music (at the top of the list); prayer; natural beauty; listening to a sermon; watching little children; reading the Bible; other reading; childbirth; sexual activity; doing creative work, and physical exercise. Interestingly, no one in these studies reported such an experience as a result of using drugs.[34]

There is much debate about how natural and valid drug-induced experiences may be. Problems of legality have minimized research. The social history of this is analysed by Ram Dass and Ralph Metzner (who were colleagues with Timothy Leary at Harvard University) in their recent valedictory retrospective, *Birth of a Psychedelic Culture*. The classic study remains the "Good Friday Experiment" of Pahnke and Richards, who found that subjects taking a dose of psilocybin rather than a placebo had pronounced experiences of mystical consciousness.[35] It is one thing, however, to take a helicopter ride up above the clouds and to see that the mountaintop exists. It is quite another to climb the mountain through the course of life and to come to fully own the experience.

Automatization of the mind

A recent debate in this area concerns the discovery that surgical or electromagnetic stimulation of the brain can induce feelings associated with out-of-body experiences and some of Stace's nine characteristics of mystical consciousness. Claims that the brain might have a "God spot" have led to speculation that such states may be explained away as side-effects of neurological activity.[36] However, if the brain's visual cortex is stimulated, flashes of light will be hallucinated. This does not mean that light is an artefact of brain malfunction. On the contrary, the brain is furnished to detect light precisely because light is "for real". Similarly, the brain may have the wherewithal to process transcendent experience because reality is transcendent. Questions about the existence or otherwise of "God" thereby connect to questions about the existential status of anything, and in particular, to the psychology of perception (how we sense) and cognition (how we think about it).

One clue as to what might be going on in peak and/or mystical states is that they are very commonly described in terms of "freshness", "seeing the world with new eyes" and even, being "born again". The clinical psychiatrist, Arthur Deikman, carried out a celebrated series of experiments into this using meditation.[37] These were based on earlier studies that suggest that the brain does its housekeeping by *automatizing* - rendering automatic - many perceptual and cognitive processes. Because individual consciousness can't attend to everything, once a skill like riding a bicycle is learned, the need to invest it with attention can be allowed to drop below the threshold of consciousness, thereby freeing consciousness to look at the birds, the bees and the view.

Deikman got his subjects to meditate on a beautiful blue vase. Afterwards, they reported shifts in awareness: the vase was not just blue, but very blue; its shape intensified. He suggested that the process of intense concentration re-invested reality with meaning because it *de-automatized* what had been automatized. After all, why should there be any limit on how blue and shapely a shapely blue vase is perceived to be? Mystical experience, he therefore concluded, might be a radical form of de-automatisation. Of course, the poets had beaten him to it, for as William Blake had written in *The Marriage of Heaven and Hell*; "If the doors of perception were cleansed, everything would appear to man as it is, Infinite: for man has closed himself up, till he sees all things through narrow chinks of his cavern."

It is certainly true that the essence of much spiritual practice is the cultivation of "presence" to life around us. Mystical teachers will counsel trying to bestow everything we do with *awareness* - be it walking, eating, breathing or making love - and it is said that the longest journey is that from the head down to the heart.

Mark Twain wrote that "familiarity breeds contempt", succinctly implying, perhaps, the automatization or "taking for granted" that can lead to monstrous desensitization. Developing the presence of spiritual awareness may, conversely, be seen as a resensitization to reality that breeds the opposite of contempt - namely, reverence in the "sacrament of the present moment".

Here we may return to our distinction between spirituality and religion. Perhaps a key danger in religion is that the attempt to build a structure for spirituality can so easily ossify it. Dogmatism can automatize the very qualities that spirituality tries to de-automatize. We have therefore reached a point where weighing up the validity of mystical experience also sheds light on activism; both value that which might otherwise have been marginalized.

A spiritual paradigm therefore demands that we rethink our epistemology - both by challenging what constitutes knowledge and developing insight into how that knowledge is structured. Activism so informed can engage at very deep levels in the psyche. These are levels of which most people are, quite literally, unaware. While our opponents in struggling for the things that matter may have the resources to buy political influence and newspaper column inches, we, though materially poor, may have psychospiritual riches. These are not without their own power. To understand this better we need to deepen our understanding of the psyche.

CASE STUDY

Gerard Winstanley: The Spirit that Made the Globe

In 1649, immediately following the Civil War in England, Gerard Winstanley and a few dozen local labourers sowed parsnips, carrots and beans on wasteland at St George's Hill in Walton-on-Thames, Surrey. Rocketing food prices had left many of them starving, but their bid for survival came not so much out of desperation as inspiration.

During their short-lived attempt to establish a just social order, "Digger" communities sprang up in at least three locations in the south of England. Following the example of the Anabaptists, they declared independence, refusing

***Winstanley* by Clifford Harper**
© Clifford Harper

to submit to the unjust rule of Church and magistracy. They equated monarchical tyranny with the reign of Babylon over the chosen people of Israel in the Hebrew Bible, and, when brought before Lord Fairfax to explain themselves, Winstanley and his collaborator Everard refused to remove their hats since "he was but their fellow creature".

Winstanley was a failed cloth trader who had been reduced to herding cows. Far from resenting his lowly status, though, a journey into intense personal spirituality, transcending his initial flirtation with the Anabaptists, turned his understanding of the social order on its head. Commentators tend to miss the point that his radical social ideas were entirely reliant on "the misty regions" of his theological speculations, as is evident from one of the most famous passages in his writings:

The great Creator Reason made the Earth to be a Common Treasury, to preserve Beasts, Birds, Fishes, and Man, the lord that was to govern this Creation; for Man had Domination given to him, over the Beasts, Birds and Fishes; but not one word was spoken in the beginning that one branch of mankind should rule over another. And the Reason is this: Every single man, Male and Female, is a perfect Creature of himself; and the same Spirit that made the Globe dwels in man to govern the Globe... He needs not that any man should teach him, for the same Anoynting that rules in the Son of man teacheth him all things.

Here we have a qualified environmentalism, a fully-fledged egalitarianism and a clear statement of gender equality, focusing its political demands on land ownership. Not only Winstanley's dignified confidence, but his *reasoning* is based on his theology, which chimes with the perennial philosophy of the mystics of all ages. He claims that "the same Anoynting" given by God to Jesus Christ is available to all humanity, thereby obviating the need for religious authority. By asserting universal salvation in this way, he challenged the Puritan teaching of double-predestination; that some were pre-ordained by God to go to Heaven, and the rest, in a handcart to Hell. In so doing, he subverted the special claims of earthly powers to their own anointing, and with it their presumption of God's blessing for their reign.

Winstanley's longing was for the "Law of Righteousness" to reign in the hearts of all people, by which he meant an end to self-interest and a recognition of the equal status of all people before God. He envisioned a time when landowners might become righteous, but in the meantime he laid claim to the marginal lands where the poor and disenfranchized could experiment with a new social order. Freed from wage labour they would control their own production directly from the land; this was a direct reversal of the impact of the enclosures.

Alas, it was not to be. This spiritual activism proved too threatening to local landowners and the Rump Parliament chose to overlook the organized arson and thuggery that ended the Digger experiment after only a year. However, Digger tracts were translated into French and influenced the thinking of revolutionaries in Bordeaux. Because of their remarkably prescient analysis, they have continued to inspire activists ever since their rediscovery in the late 19th century.

In 1999, a small community of modern-day Diggers occupied a site at St. George's Hill, now an enclave of the superrich. They hoped to erect a beautifully carved stone memorial to the Diggers, but were evicted from the site and the memorial removed.

Far from being just another of the many 17th-century religious sects, the Diggers stand out because of what we now recognize as their incisive thinking, nonviolent methods, reasonable demands, and lasting legacy. "By their fruits shall you know them."

CHAPTER FOUR

The Structure
of the Psyche

Psychology colonized

Three words are crucial that are often used interchangeably. "Soul" is of proto-Germanic origin linked to a word meaning the sea, and sometimes said to suggest "coming from or belonging to the sea" because the Otherworld was likened to an ocean, lake or land beyond the seas. In transpersonal psychology - psychology that accepts a spiritual basis to being - the soul is often spoken of as the Self, sometimes capitalised to distinguish the great or deep self from the small or lesser self or ego.

"Spirit", shares the same Latin root as words like inspire and respire, meaning to breathe; and specifically, to breathe life into something. In the Judeo-Christian tradition, the Spirit is usually seen as the aspect of a person's being where the divine meets with and breathes through the soul, this divine presence itself being spoken of as the Holy Spirit or, in older terminology, the Holy Ghost.

"Psyche" comes from the Greek, and also means breath or soul. In art and literature it is often symbolized as a moth or butterfly. Carl Jung popularized the use of psyche in a holistic sense to refer to the inner totality of what it means to be a person - mind, soul and Spirit. This includes the self-awareness of which we are conscious, the realm of the unconscious that is personal to us, and the deep structures of the unconscious that, Jung believed, are collective or transpersonal to us all.

It follows that the discipline of "psychology" ought to mean "the study of the soul" and be implicitly transpersonal. To use it as a byword for behavioural, cognitive or perceptual science is to colonize and degrade the term.

At heart, behaviourism is an approach that builds psychology up from the model of Pavlov's dog. If you stimulate an animal, it produces a response, and human behaviour can be understood as a network of stimulus-response interactions. Cognitive approaches join up the dots by viewing the brain like a programmed computer, the scripts of which process information.

Both of these approaches - that are self-evidently valid, up to a point - have been applied in ways that are reductionist to the point of being simplistic, indeed, deterministic. Michael Eysenck, the son of the intelligence psychologist Hans Eysenck, and a leading cognitive exponent, illustrates this:[38]

> Determinists argue that a proper science of human behaviour is only possible if psychologists adopt a deterministic account, according to which everything that happens has a definite cause. Free will by definition does not have a definite cause. If free will is taken into account, it becomes impossible to predict human

behaviour with any precision. According to determinists, it is often possible with other sciences to make very accurate predictions from a deterministic position (eg forecasting planetary motion). If determinism is regarded as not applicable to psychology, then it is either a very different science to physics, chemistry, and so on, or it is not really a science at all.

Notice the logic. To be a "proper science", psychology must be deterministic, which is to say, based on causality. This rules out free will because it is not bound by causality. Therefore, we do not have free will. Eysenck does, however, have the honesty to admit that; "these arguments were greatly weakened by the progress of science during the twentieth century." In physics, Heisenberg's Uncertainty Principle basically says; "you never quite know!"

Our quibble is not with rational science, which proceeds on the basis of carefully tested hypotheses that are capable of being disproved. Our objection is when this approach is allowed to judge the legitimacy of realms of experience which lie beyond its carefully defined limitations. For example, science can explain how the telescope or microscope reveals macro or micro space, but not the experience of the "wow" factor that happens in the inner spaces of the mind when we look through them. Yet it is this wow factor that motivates the love of science. As Abraham Maslow argued from his experience studying biology, without love there would be no new knowledge. Unfortunately, psychology, as a young discipline during the 20th century, was so anxious to be accepted as a "proper science" that, for two-thirds of that century, it wrote off much of its own field. Thankfully such "physics envy" is now softening.

The rise of transpersonal psychology

In the second half of the 20th century, reductionist approaches came to be seen by many outside mainstream academic psychology as constrictive. Jung's work gained a fresh lease of life. It was boosted, not least, by growing numbers of people who had experienced altered states of consciousness - meditative, psychedelic and otherwise - as well as the influence of such writers as Hermann Hesse, Alan Watts, Timothy Leary and the Beat Generation poets. Having first been mooted by William James as early as

1905, the term *trans-personal* (originally hyphenated) later found currency to describe an approach based on an acceptance that personhood is, at some level, profoundly interconnected, which is to say that we are spiritual beings. In parallel, the term *psychospiritual* allowed bridging between those who prefer to see things only in terms of standard humanistic psychology, and those who see such psychology as a spiritual doorway.

It was initially in northern California that transpersonal psychology developed academic credentials. Being holistic and more of a whole worldview than a fragment, the field defies succinct definition. One attempt, recently proposed by prominent scholars, is as follows:[39]

> Transpersonal psychology is a transformative psychology of the whole person in intimate relationship with an interconnected and evolving world; it pays special attention to self-expansive states as well as to spiritual, mystical, and other exceptional human experiences that gain meaning in such a context.

In addition to Jung's pioneering work, the transpersonal pedigree owes much to the justice-based biblical values that were held by earlier generations of North American radicals, especially slavery abolitionists and women's rights campaigners such as Lucretia Mott and the Grimké sisters. These were people not afraid to put their spiritual beliefs to social effect. Expansive ideas from Eastern religion melded in through 19th-century American Transcendentalist writings such as those of Ralph Waldo Emerson, Walt Whitman and Henry David Thoreau – the latter, in 1849, also authoring the seminal essay; *On the Duty of Civil Disobedience*. Moving in to the 20th century, radical social and political thought that revolved around the question of *what a human being is* developed further through black civil rights activism, the Catholic Worker movement, opposition to the Vietnam War, the hippie and "back to the land" experiments, radical feminism, modern environmentalism and indigenous people's emancipation.

Along such avenues as these the burning desire for social transformation, the love of nature, and personal and group consciousness expansion, often ran hand in hand. So it was that spiritual activism was born, or more accurately, reborn. By the end of the 20th century *ecofeminism* had made its appearance on campuses and around protest campfires with its cogent arguments that patriarchy has oppressed both women and nature alike.

Around the same time, deep ecology, often providing the philosophical basis of radical environmentalism, championed the notion that the human self is ultimately at one with the "ecological self" - the human person being part of nature personified. Self-realization therefore implies a growth in consciousness to renew ecological right relationship. There is no separate "human" from "environment". There is no dead, mechanical universe.

Moving to the cusp of the 21st century, North American campaigns to protect old growth forest and European ones to stop motorway building continued the tradition of "alternative" or "progressive" thought. These drew teachings from traditional ecological knowledge (TEK) and indigenous Earth-centred spiritualities such as manifested in movements ranging from India's Chipko "tree-huggers" (who used the vulnerability of their bodies to protect threatened forests) to the more recent Sarawak Dam protests. Most of these "direct actions" were a collision between premodern animistic (or ensouled) worldviews, and the materialistic mechanistic modernism of advanced capitalism. These battles - often based around the land, the spirit of place, the need for belonging and a sense of peoplehood - continue today. Their urgency to sustain a sense of life ensouled summons up prophetic responses from around the world. For example, in 1977 the Six Nations Iroquois Confederacy produced an *Address to the Western World* that solemnly issued what it called "a basic call to consciousness".[40] Or more recently, as Eriel Deranger of the Athabasca Chipewyan First Nations puts it in her statement (used as a website banner by the indigenous treaty rights and sovereignty movement *Idle No More*):[41]

> Our people and our Mother Earth can no longer afford to be economic hostages in the race to industrialise our homelands. It is time for our people to rise up and take back our role as caretakers and stewards of the land.

Psychohistory, feudalism and rationalism

To understand more deeply why this linking of the psyche, activism and the environment has become such a mark of resistance across today's world, we need to understand the psychological history of what we lost. We need to feel where these losses leave our humanity. Our focus here will be Eurocentric, but similar patterns can be recognized probably across all colonized parts of the world.

During the Europe of the Dark Ages, neo-Roman structures of power became indigenized in the rise of feudalism. Feudalism is the principle that a king or queen (usually someone we might otherwise describe as a war criminal) establishes power and defends the peace in a kingdom, using a federal structure of noblemen endowed with land to draw wealth and military muscle from the land and its tenants.

The plus side of feudal power is that robber-barons or their descendants often want to clean up their act - particularly where organised religion puts the fear of hellfire into them or where real spiritual light breaks through, as it did with the Russian count and novelist, Leo Tolstoy. As such, feudalism often provided patronage for the arts and religion. However, the quid pro quo is that the arts, religion and intellectual institutes pay fealty by holding up a mirror that ennobles feudalism and sustains social approval accordingly.

The Renaissance in Europe, which had its earliest stirrings in the 13th century, held up precisely such a mirror, re-integrating the imperialism of Greco-Roman feudal thought back into the European mainstream. Central to this was Greek rationalism, drawing particularly on the work of such philosophers of military city-states as Plato and Aristotle. This movement gave us the *Summa Theologica* of Thomas Aquinas (1255-1274), which remains the uncontested cornerstone of Roman Catholic theology to this day. It was the heyday of counting angels on pinheads. The "Scholastics" or "Schoolmen" as they were nicknamed, believed that Aristotelian logic could make sense of all God's creation, and rationality became the stairway to Heaven.

Under the doctrine of the divine right of kings, to challenge sovereign power was to take on God Himself, and so to be a heretic was dangerous precisely because it risked deranging the patterns of reason by which the Powers that Be had canonized their own legitimacy. However, as the culture of reason developed, it started to contest the very theology that had given it birth. In the 16th century, Europe went through the Reformation, a re-forming of the Church around the ideas of *protestors*, or "Protestants". The problem with being a Protestant is that by setting up your own church you experienced the ontological insecurity of having to question whether your ideas were correct. Getting it wrong risked being burnt at the stake and eternal hellfire to follow. The advancement of systematic (orderly and *rational*) theology became even more important and with it, a fear of the inner movement of the Spirit and spiritual ideas, because these cannot be controlled. Rationality therefore became ever more unyielding, and as a professor of divinity at Edinburgh University is reputed to have told his first-year students at the start of term; "There is only one way to spell *mysticism* in this faculty, and it begins: m-i-s-t..."

Rationalism received a further boost with the 18th-century self-styled Enlightenment. Building on the Reformation's audacity to question religious dogma, thinkers like Voltaire saw that God could be reasoned out of the picture altogether. Man, not God, became the measure of all things. So it was that modernity's faith in a materialistic and deterministic form of science became paramount in Europe, usually to the advantage of the rising mercantile and professional bourgeois classes who increasingly assumed the reins of culture and the Protestant faith. Power was shifting. Those who controlled the means of production as driven by the industrial revolution's technology were replacing those whose power was based on sovereignty over the land. As power shifted, so too did war, from having been a "sport of princes" with a certain chivalry, to a contest of machinery that culminated in the industrial warfare of the 20th century.

Mainstream religion kept going, but with shrinking congregations and spiritually eviscerated from within. By the start of the 21st century it had withered in the public eye to a whimpering reactionary voice on sexual affairs, its hierarchies (with notable exceptions) more concerned about gay ordination than liberating the Spirit and championing the great concerns of the era. That said, it is when old growth has died back that new seeds can find the space and light in which to germinate; such are the seeds of spirituality. First, though, let us step back a little, to the 19th century and its psychopathologies of reason, the better to understand how a new sense of spirituality has started to emerge.

Sigmund Freud

The problem with the "supremacy of reason" is that it reduces what it means to be human and denies the beauty and potential of *experience* by locking people in to a narrowly analytical state of consciousness. By the time a young doctor called Sigmund Freud arrived on the scene in 19th-century Vienna, many of the bourgeoisie were marooned on an island of grey matter an inch beneath the left hemispheres of their skulls, unable to find peace with their bodies, souls or world. In trying to understand their suffering, Freud argued that civilization had not come without a price tag.

We all seek pleasure, especially sexual pleasure, but Freud held that the "pleasure principle" of what he called the *id* (the "it", the instinctual self) was a destructive force like the magma in an active volcano ready to erupt. In a civilised society it had to be kept in check, or repressed, by the "reality principle" of the ego, the conscious "I". While perhaps painful for the individual, this provided a double-fillip of benefits. On the one hand, repressing psychological energy (libido) contributed to the stability of law, order, rationality and "polite" society. It rescued us from what 19th-century colonialists liked to think of as the savagery of the peoples they had so mercifully subjugated. On the other, that highly charged energy had to go somewhere. In a healthy situation it got re-channelled into cathartic pursuits like the creative arts, business and scientific endeavour.

From where does the conscious ego derive its norms of acceptable behaviour, its conventional morality? Freud thought they were dictated to it by the "superego", the internalized voice of such conditioning influences as parents, teachers, priests, the government and other authorities including, not least, their personification as "God". Religious experience such as the hearing of an inner voice can be likened, he said, to "a hallucinatory psychosis," and God, at least for the male of the species, accountable as an unresolved Oedipal complex in which the son battles it out with his father,[42] as if God is merely a communal father figure projected out onto a supernatural movie screen. Religion, he asserted in his essay, *The Future of an Illusion*, is chiefly a symptom of "human weakness and helplessness". Of its doctrines, "all of them are illusions and insusceptible of proof".[43]

Freud reminds his readers at the start of this essay that; "the principal task of civilization is to defend us against nature." That is to say, to defend the psyche from being overwhelmed by the *id's* primal urges which would lead to savagery if given free expression. Religious teachings are "neurotic relics", but their historical worth has been as evolutionary stepping-stones in "our appointed task of reconciling men to civilization".

Reason was the prize for becoming civilized. Freud concludes; "The time has probably come, as it does in an analytic treatment, for replacing the effects of repression [i.e. religion] by the results of the rational operation of the intellect."[44] Quite whether this further crowning of the rational faculties confuses cure with cause is a good question. Most of today's post-Freudians would take a more nuanced understanding of "reason". Addicted to the rationalist paradigm as he may have been, Freud nonetheless forced its adherents to face up to the non-rational passions of the worlds within. He opened a door on the unconscious and thereby paved the way for one of his students, Carl Jung, who was able to reconnect psychology and spirituality, setting reason back in to its rightful context.

Carl Gustav Jung

The son of a Protestant Swiss clergyman, Jung rejected mainstream religious dogma as a child when he had a "fantasy experience" of God shattering the local cathedral by dropping an almighty turd! He read his spirituality from the book of nature and later from mythology, the experiences of his patients, and travelling among tribal peoples. His was a profound deep ecology long before Arne Næss popularized the term, recognizing that human nature and natural nature are a co-evolved unity. For example:[45]

> Plants interested me too, but not in a scientific sense. I was attracted to them for a reason I could not understand, and with a strong feeling that they ought not to be pulled up and dried... Plainly the urban world knew nothing about the country world, the real world of mountains, woods, and rivers, of animals and "God's thoughts" – plants and crystals... I realised that for all its wealth of learning the urban world was mentally rather limited.

Jung rejected Freud's sexual reductionism. Repressed sexuality was certainly one cause of neurosis or psychological pain and dysfunction, but the libido, as Jung used the word, was not just sexual energy. He saw it as a much more widely construed psychic energy that gives vitality to the whole person. Neurosis was maladaptation to reality – for reasons of which the most central was not being true to ourselves and our world.

Thus; "People who know nothing about nature are of course neurotic, for they are not adapted to reality."[46]

It is this re-orientation towards a more complete reality that marks the pivotal importance of Jung. If Freud, coming from a materialistic, rationalist and reductionist paradigm, had found a door, then Jung's ideas were the key that flung it open in to an alternate spiritual reality. Here was nothing short of a reversal of the direction in which the mainstream Western psyche had evolved for the past half millennium. This is both why he deserves to be taken seriously and the very reason why he has not been taken seriously by cognitive-behaviourist psychology, which is still rolling with the momentum of the supremacy of reason. Jung did not overthrow reason, or *thinking* as he called it. Rather, he set it back into a context where it was balanced out with three other ways of knowing that comprise his four psychological functions - *feeling*, *sensing* and *intuiting*.

Jung's psychology is therefore a question of balance, of restoring equilibrium within the psyche. For all his flaws, he was a healer concerned with the restoration of meaning in a world that had reasoned away mythology and mystery. This may not have gained traction with the kind of psychologists whose laboratory careers advanced by giving electric shocks to rats, but their star is falling; Jung's is rising.

Key Jungian concepts

As the new millennium dawned, Jungian terminology gained popular and political currency. Concepts like the collective unconscious and the psyche found growing usage. While we cannot pretend to offer any more than a cursory overview, it might be helpful to introduce some of Jung's main concepts as are relevant to spiritual activism.[47]

- **the psyche:** Jung saw the psyche as comprising "the totality of all psychic processes, conscious as well as unconscious". It incorporates both the realm of consciousness and the unconscious. While the psyche starts for each one of us with individual consciousness it extends into social structures, the natural world and ultimately, has its bedrock in the divine as the central dynamo of reality. This is shown visually below.

Simplified Structure of the Human Psyche
(based on C. G. Jung)

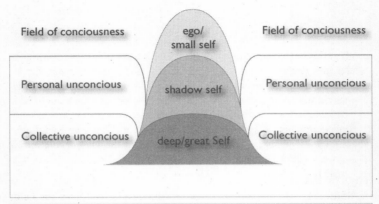

The Transpersonal Basis of Community
After Jolande Jacobi, 1942

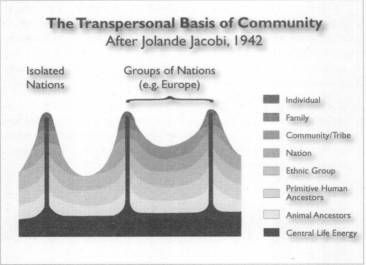

Diagrams from *Rekindling Community*
Alastair McIntosh, Schumacher Briefing No. 15, Green Books, 2008

- **the unconscious:** Whereas Freud had seen the unconscious as a repository for personal repressed experience and instinctual drives, Jung saw it on a vaster scale. For him, the personal unconscious of each one of us rests within the collective unconscious in which we all partake by virtue of our shared humanity. Ultimately, this embraces all reality - everything which we are not consciously aware of. He wrote:[48]

    In addition to our immediate consciousness, which is of a thoroughly personal nature and which we believe to be the only empirical psyche (even if we tack on the personal unconscious as an appendix), there exists a second psychic system of a collective, universal, and impersonal nature which is identical in all individuals. This collective unconscious does not develop individually but... consists of pre-existent forms, the archetypes, which can only become conscious secondarily and which give definite form to certain psychic contents.

- **libido:** Freud popularized the term, which is derived from the Latin for *desire* or *lust*. However, Jung uses it far more broadly to refer to psychic energy in general, a force which gives life and dynamism to individuals and groups. Some commentators equate Jung's conception of the libido with the oriental *chi* and the Hindu *prana*. Jung speaks of *libidinal fields*, drawing an analogy with magnetism or gravity, suggesting that libidinal energy forms its own force fields, patterns and shapes that carry meaning within the psyche.

- **complexes:** In the personal unconscious, influential events power their way through libidinal fields like ships through the water, creating eddies of charged psychic energy called *complexes*. These are emotional force fields coloured by the meaning they embody. Jung therefore refers to them as being "feeling toned". If someone is said to "have a complex" we mean that there is an emotionally charged zone within their psyche - a "touchy" area. This might manifest as a phobia, an obsession, a passion, predisposition or fascination. A complex in itself is neither healthy nor unhealthy. It is simply part of the muscle tone and knots of psychic texture. Only when a complex brings an individual into conflict with wider reality does it constitute a *neurosis*.

- **the ego and the Self:** Central to the Jungian concept of what it means to be a human being is an interplay between the ego and the deep inner Self, or soul. Ego is the conscious "I". Self is Jung's word for the core of our being, around which all other parts of the psyche are constellated. The Self is "that of God" or Buddha Nature within. To use Hindu terminology, it is˙ the *atman* or individual soul that is, ultimately, at one with *Brahman* or universal soul. Matt illustrates this using the image of the Earth. Our individual egos are rooted in our individual bodies, but our souls go deeper. Through the collective unconscious we share the soul of our home-town, and at deeper levels, of the region or nation, or continent. Ultimately, our souls deepen into the soul of the whole Earth.

- **the persona:** The ego is the small or outer self that fronts up who we are in the realm of consciousness, but usually it will wear the masks or personae of differing identities for different contexts. For example, one might wear differing personae whether in the role of an activist, when practising a trade or profession, or at home as parent or lover. While opinions vary on the matter, we do not think that spiritual development should be about trying to delete the ego and living only from the Self. Rather, the name of the game is for the one to relax into its seating in right relationship with the other. This entails coming to know, accept, and at the risk of a wry smile, to find ourselves.

- **Individuation:** *Individuation* in Jung is not individualistic. It is the awakening of the Self through becoming a true individual; the process of becoming a centred self rather than self-centred. Also known as self-realization (because it "realizes" or makes real the deep Self), a failure to individuate through the stages of life leaves us wallowing in fads, fashions and behaviours that are not to our own selves true. Much neurosis, especially where it expresses a loss of meaning, represents a failure to individuate and the corresponding inner call to wake up.

- **the shadow and shadowstrike:** Just as the ego is the part of our psyche that is grounded in consciousness, so Jung posits an alterego that relates to the unconscious - the *shadow*. This represents the parts of ourselves that we usually deny - our darknesses - the potential murderer, the cheat, the rapist, the liar and swindler. They don't exist?

Then ask why there are so many examples in history of otherwise decent people doing terrible things when the conditions were right. The problem, said Jung, is not that we all have shadows. The problem is that we deny them, and the shadow denied is the shadow that trips us up. Road rage is one example of what we call "shadowstrike", where unprocessed aspects of ourselves can flare and project on to others in flashpoint incidents. Driving can be a good spiritual instructor! The good news is that the shadow is a gold mine. It is the cutting edge of where spiritual development happens, harbouring our inner curriculum and all our undeveloped potential. If you want to know what your shadow looks like, says Jung, think of a person you despise.

- **the contrasexual partner:** Jung held that within the psyche of every man is a feminine counterpoint - the *anima* - and within every woman is a masculine *animus*. This is part of the reason why gender issues can be so highly charged in activist organizations and movements. We are dealing not only with injustice in the outer world, but also the inner development of addressing imbalances in what it means to become a whole person.

- **archetypes:** Just as the personal unconscious is shaped by complexes, so the collective unconscious is constellated by shared libidinal fields that Jung called *archetypes*. These operate at a depth of being that is beyond rational thought - a level sometimes called the *Mythos* - the realm of myths, metanarratives, patterns and symbols - a realm that communicates not by reason but through poetry, dream, and vision. We glimpse the expression of archetypes in such universally recurring themes as kings and queens, wise old women and men, heroes and tricksters, cowboys and Indians, gods and monsters, and David and Goliath. Our egos can become "inflated" by an archetypal motif and its perhaps shockingly powerful energy. Other times the motif might be projected by others. Ideally we can surf such narratives, but the individuating human being should be wary of how far they let themselves be sucked into believing their own legend and getting swamped as the wave breaks. Humility is of the essence in spiritual development, not least for protection. Humility can, however, include allowing oneself to be called to the service of taking on and then laying down an archetypal role. The biographies of the saints often illustrate this. Rarely are they bombastic because they understand the dangers of archetypal ego inflation.

Abraham Maslow and Manfred Max-Neef

Whereas Freud was anxious to construct an unchanging dogma out of his schema, Jung hoped that his work would never ossify into an "ism". Indeed this was central to their falling out. Fortunately, both have been well served by subsequent psychoanalysts (Freudians) and analytical psychologists (Jungians) who have taken their thinking forward. Here we will explore some key figures most relevant to spiritual activism.

Abraham Maslow was an American humanistic psychologist who can be thought of as post-Jungian. The titles of his best-known books nicely sum up his concerns. *Toward a Psychology of Being* suggests that living from the vantage point of a centred Self is at the core of being human. This entails orienting our lives towards higher values that he called Being values or metavalues, such as joy, beauty, justice, truth, simplicity, wholeness and love.

What is it that makes these values "higher" and thus "meta"? Maslow says they can only be defined in terms of one another. For example, you can only define beauty in terms of other such metavalues as love, integrity and harmony. Together they form parts of a higher whole of what it means to be a human being.

Metavalues point us, to use another Maslow book title, towards *The Farther Reaches of Human Nature*. This involves what he called *self-actualization* - Jung's "individuation" - which other writers call "self-realization" or "becoming a person".[49] Self-actualisation comprises the apex of a pyramid that has become famous in management studies and educational theory as Maslow's *hierarchy of human needs*. He suggested that human needs develop in five stages, and that usually a higher stage does not evolve until lower ones have been satisfied. Physical needs are at the bottom, with relationship needs in the middle. The highest level, the need for *self-actualization,* takes us into the realm of creativity and altruism - the values traditionally associated with spiritual development.

Maslow's model has been criticized as being very much a Western model and not applicable cross-culturally. Applied rigidly, it would suggest that the poor or sick are incapable of a spiritually developed life, which is manifestly untrue. Nevertheless, it has helped to make higher needs respectable in mainstream academia and management. Many high-achieving individuals are not satisfied only with the mundane rewards of the job – they also seek self-actualization. In the NGO sector, self-actualising need fulfilment can be the driving factor in staff motivation and a key point to keep in mind when working with volunteers... especially where it is not possible to contribute towards all of their subsidiary needs.

A Chilean thinker, Manfred Max-Neef, has addressed the cultural criticism of Maslow's model by developing a matrix of fundamental human needs.[50] This can be re-drawn as a wheel, to which, following a discussion that Alastair had with Max-Neef where he said that spirituality is implicit, we have added transcendence.

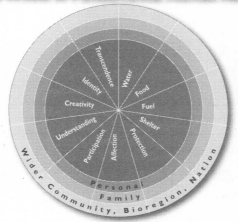

The Wheel of Fundamental Human Needs

Manfred Max-Neef's Fundamental Human Needs
(As expressed in a circle by *Training for Transformation,* with transcendence added)
From *Rekindling Community,* Green Books, 2008

Max-Neef suggests that some needs might be addressed through singular satisfiers. For example, feeding a baby from a bottle is a singular satisfier of the need for food. Others can be violative satisfiers, like prisons can serve the need for protection but violate the need for understanding. Ideally we should try and seek synergistic satisfiers. Here, for example, a community garden might satisfy the need for food but also the needs for protection, affection, understanding and creativity.

The Max-Neef wheel can be used in group exercises by shading in the portions to see how rounded a life a given individual or group might have, and where the gaps are. We like to ask; "If this was a bicycle wheel, how smooth or bumpy a ride would you have?"[51]

Roberto Assagioli

Assagioli developed a school of psychotherapy that he called *psychosynthesis* - a concern with the healing integration of the psyche around the Self. Contrasting his approach with Freud's, he explained that psychosynthesis; "insists that the needs for meaning, for higher values, for a spiritual life, are as real as biological or social needs. We deny that there are any isolated human problems."[52] Assagioli also provides a delightful example of a kind of inadvertent spiritual activism. In 1938 he was arrested and imprisoned by Mussolini's Catholic-fascist government for the crimes of promoting humanism and being Jewish. He was kept in solitary confinement for a month, and after the war he began his work on psychosynthesis. Throughout his life, Assagioli credited this period with the inspiration for psychosynthesis. He said he spent the time meditating and turned his punishment into an opportunity to investigate his inner self.

What makes his work most distinctive is his refinement of the Jungian personal unconscious into a lower, middle and higher realm, as illustrated in his widely known egg diagram. The higher personal unconscious he also calls the *superconscious*, implying very deliberately that not all that emanates from the unconscious is of a "basement" nature, but that the unconscious is also the source of transcendent experience. Such a view is implicit but not explicit in Jung's model.

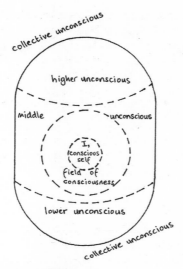

Roberto Assagioli's "Egg" Model of the Psyche
Redrawn from *Psychosynthesis*, Turnstone Books, 1975, p. 17

Wilhelm Reich

Wilhelm Reich was a post-Freudian who died in mysterious circumstances in an FBI jail in the 1960's. His work is marred by cranky ideas such as boxes to accumulate "orgone" sexual energy. Relevant to activism is a notion built on his work called the "Creative Orgasmic Cycle", the idea that activity in an organization or movement is cyclic, and we function best if we understand that its stages parallel those of making love.

A group comes together in the first place because of a shared *desire* focussed round a common purpose. This leads to the second stage - group development by way of *nurturing* - that is to say, by getting to know one another physically and emotionally. The third stage is *energizing*. Here ideas start being put into action. Energy builds up, people get excited and new ideas crystallize. Fourth, a *peak* or *climax* is reached as intermediate or end-point goals are achieved in a burst of yippee oomph. Lastly, the group takes a little time *relaxing*, tidying up after the party and taking stock.

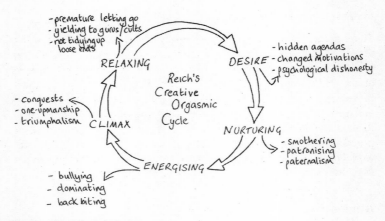

The Creative Orgasmic Cycle
Redrawn from *Co-operative and Community Group Dynamics*, Barefoot Books, 1980

This model holds potential for activists considering the problem of leadership. It suggests a sort of rotating hierarchy in which no-one exerts influence for too long, and which recognizes the different leadership skills that different individuals have to offer. In the nurturing stage, the natural leaders are those who are good at welcoming, forming connections and helping others to do the same. As the group moves into the energizing "can do" stage, ideally those with experience take a dynamic but appropriate lead. After the climax, leadership moves towards those who are good at bringing things to closure, celebration and affirmation... until it's time to start all over again.

Randall, Southgate and Tomlinson, who apply Reich's work to group dynamics with this model, say a typical response is; "This orgasmic cycle sounds like fun, but why are *our* meetings so *appalling*?"[53] Their analysis of dysfunction at various stages in the cycle - the "spin-off" shadow side of each stage shown above - is helpful.

Another feature of this model is its recognition that, while impotence is no fun, neither does a healthy organization run on Viagra. That only leads to burnout. In the organizational ecology of activism, shared activities need to run according to their seasons.

These models remind us that all group dynamics are the collective patterns that emerge from the individuals that comprise the group and their social settings. To parody the expression - "I'm OK; you're OK" - there's also a wry truth in the shadowy counterpoint; "I'm fucked up; you're fucked up." Asking why it is that people's repressed thoughts and feelings emerge so strongly in group situations and around impassioned causes, Randall and Southgate suggest that these experiences trigger unresolved processes from our family and childhood pasts. As such, the activist must work constantly on their personal psychodynamic if they are to be creative and not unwittingly destructive within groups.

Alice Miller

Reich also worked on *The Mass Psychology of Fascism*, linking the rise of Nazism to blocked psycho-sexual processes. However, if we head down that route here, we will find ourselves wallowing in men, men and even more besuited men of the mid-20th century. It was women like Melanie Klein and Karen Horney who did so much to propagate, mitigate and develop Freud's thought, and others like Jolande Jacobi and Frieda Fordham who interpreted and popularized Jung. From an activist's perspective, the Polish-born Swiss, Alice Miller's 1987 work stands out. *For Your Own Good: The Roots of Violence in Child-rearing* follows a similar trajectory to Reich in analyzing the psychopathology of Adolf Hitler and the child murderer, Jürgen Bartsch. However, where Reich saw sex, Miller saw a deficit of unconditional love in early childhood. She argues that if a child is not loved for itself, it loses touch with its true Self and the resultant trauma can project outwards in later life with chilling consequences.

Others have explored this psychodynamic, for example, the director of mental health for the Massachusetts prison system, James Gilligan, who concluded that early abuse can kill connection with the soul and leave a person feeling, and sometimes acting, like the "walking dead".[54]

While these studies are deeply disturbing, they are also profoundly hope-giving. They suggest that a fundamental human problem is a loss of the capacity for empathy, the ability to feel *with* another person. It is a fruit of love and grows when nourished with love. In asking how the deepest structural problems of our times can be addressed, working with the psychology and spirituality of love would appear to be a core part of the answer.

Lessons from social psychology

One implication of understanding family and social factors in child development is that it teaches us to be wary of blaming individuals alone for things that are wrong in the world. More widely, we need to understand individuals in the contexts of the wider fields within which they have developed and find expression.

As children, we take it for granted that a parent takes responsibility for us. The process of growing up, though, is one of gradually learning to stand our own ground – of individuating our ego identities from those in authority. Healthy parenting and schooling allows this to happen at a rate that is sensitive to the child's readiness. However, what happens when the prevailing social climate might be unhealthy and, even with adults, may cause them to regress into childlike dependency and obedience?

Social psychology is the study of how people act in groups. It includes the study of:[55]

- *compliance* – the process of getting another to do what you want them to do – for example, sorting rubbish into what can be recycled.
- *conformity* – which procures compliance by creating social pressure – for example, causing young people to feel odd if they do not wear the same brands of clothes as their peers.
- *obedience* – as the eliciting of naked compliance and conformity driven by fear and/or an overwhelming deference to authority.

Here we can only sample insights that the activist might find helpful. The following are all in Pennington's *Essential Social Psychology*.[56]

In one study, the "Peg-turning Test", researchers gave students a really boring job to do – turning pegs in a peg board for a full hour. They were divided at random into two groups. One was paid $20 for their work and the other, just $1. The question was: how would each report their job satisfaction afterwards?

Perhaps counter-intuitively, the highest satisfaction was reported by the low-paid group. Why? Because those on high pay could justify their time purely in terms of the money. They could say; "It was dead boring but the pay was good." The low-paid had to find other reasons to explain their compliance. These came out with qualitative justifications: "Well, it was really quite a relaxing way to spend an hour."

The implications for voluntary organizations are striking. Change and growth can mean that some people have to start being paid. The salaried may re-frame their values as the new "professionals", while those who soldier on unpaid may feel "perceived demotion" and that the organization has "lost its soul".

Another experiment demonstrates the "foot-in-the-door" technique, where procuring minimal compliance can lead to greater acquiescence. The researchers asked homeowners if they would display a very large sign in their garden which read; *DRIVE CAREFULLY*. The group that was asked straight up demonstrated only 17 per cent compliance. However, in another group that had first been asked to display a much smaller sign bearing the same words, the compliance rate rose to 75 per cent. This is why sympathizers to an activist cause are often asked first to sign a petition before being asked to consider a donation!

Various experiments demonstrate that many people will lie or distort the evidence of their own experience to avoid being seen as out of step with their fellows. In 1951, Solomon Asch published a famous experiment in which people had to judge which of three lines was nearest in length to a comparison line. Subjects were brought into a room where, unbeknown to them, everybody else had been primed to lie. Just over a third of participants gave the answer the rest of the group gave, even though it was unmistakeably wrong. Interviewed afterwards, they justified their responses by saying they didn't wanted to spoil the experiment, or didn't wish to cause disharmony. The good news is that readiness to conform appears to have declined dramatically since the conformist 1950s. Other studies suggest that conformity is higher in non-student populations, and in collectivist societies where fitting in with everybody else is expected.

Asch's work on conformity had a dramatic spin-off that became the most celebrated and ethically controversial social psychology experiment ever,

Stanley Milgram's electric shock test. [57] Milgram found that 65 per cent of people were willing to administer what they believed to be a potentially fatal electric shock to a subject *provided* they were sufficiently convinced by the authority of the experimenter in telling them to increase the voltage.

Lastly, much work has been conducted into the power of social roles, including how prejudice plays out. Philip Zimbardo's Stanford Prison experiment randomly divided volunteers into "prisoners" or "guards" in a make-believe jail constructed in a basement at Stanford University. The volunteers knew how arbitrarily this had been decided, yet Zimbardo recorded that; "in less than a week middle class Caucasians of above average intelligence and emotionally stable Americans became pathological and anti-social." The guards became brutal in their domination and the prisoners pathetic in their learned helplessness. The experiment was terminated prematurely because the power of social roles had proved so much more disturbing than anticipated. [58]

Such experiments as these go a long way in suggesting how it is that ordinary people can become extraordinarily brutal under conducive social circumstances. The history of war crimes testifies that atrocities are more the rule than the exception. If we can deepen our understanding and grounding, however, it is astonishing what can change. Colonel David H Hackworth was a highly decorated Vietnam veteran in the US Army. On retirement in 1971, he said that battle; "is like working in a slaughterhouse. At first the blood, the gore, gets to you. But after a while you don't see it, you don't smell it, you don't feel it". [59] One would think that such a man was beyond the pale, but after moving to Australia, Hackworth lived to be awarded a United Nations peace medal for his antinuclear work. [60]

A similar effect was observed across England in the summer riots of 2011, when otherwise upstanding citizens – a teaching assistant, a chef, an accounts clerk – suddenly turned into arsonists and looters. Five people died and hundreds of small businesses were ruined. One could also argue that the response of the police and courts displayed the same conformity, as they abandoned legal principles in an attempt to appease the political and public desire for retribution. Manchester police used Twitter to celebrate a five-month sentence handed down to a woman who had not taken part in the riots, for receiving a pair of stolen shorts; they later apologized and the sentence was reduced on appeal. The detaining of under-18s without criminal records was criticized by UNICEF for possibly breaching the UN Convention on the Rights of the Child. One teenager, detained on arson charges and later released because there was no evidence, returned home to find his own flat had been burned down.

On the one hand, these are the dynamics of how, as Lord Acton suggested; "Power tends to corrupt and absolute power corrupts absolutely." They suggest that our ability to identify right and wrong and hold out for the good under countervailing conditions is despairingly limited if not hitched to the sources of life. Furthermore, such negation of empathy is not restricted to battlefields and riots; the same can happen in movements for positive social change.

On the other hand, these dynamics offer promise for activists wishing to puncture the bubble of conformity and compliance, which can so easily hypnotise a community. When Milgram ran his shock studies in a seedy downtown zone that lacked the university's prestige, or with experimenters not wearing white coats, the compliance rate fell. If there were two experimenters, one of whom broke ranks and dissented, the compliance rate fell all the way to zero. These experiments testify to the power of activists, even when few in number, bearing witness to the emperor's lack of clothes. As we saw with de-automatization, there is power in restoring attention to what is being overlooked or undervalued.

Activism, identity and psychotherapy

In most of the above discussion, representation of the psyche has been through models made of working parts. This is, of course, a mechanistic and therefore limited way of describing psycho-social reality. Jung speaks of the archetypes and other psychic elements not as rigid expressions, but rather, as being more like containers that can hold broad-brush forms and potentialities. When we speak of the persona, ego, shadow or Self, it is misleading to think of these in concrete terms or as parts that are separate from one another. Rather, they are fluid principles that, as mediators of the life force, have more in common with the currents of a river or movements in the weather than the building blocks of psychic Lego.

The interplay between the psyche and the world impacts on our identity, and thus, on the ego. For some activists this may demand ego-strengthening so that challenging situations can be resolutely stepped into and confronted. For others, it may mean learning to stand back from the ego and to work in less assertive ways so that, for example, others are not overshadowed, or to allow for a cooling off or self-protection. Whatever is appropriate, our identity is likely to be bound up in what we do or don't do. Making the gradual shift from being egocentric towards becoming a more centred self is therefore an essential process to sustain and endure the vicissitudes of activist life.

Mostly the inner life is a flux of the joyously functional and the pathetically dysfunctional. Serious activists must therefore be prepared to work on their own inner lives and those of their groups so that they can grow more fully into their calling. For some, the best way to do this is with the help of trained psychotherapists. However, most of these lack experience of the activist calling. Neither do all have spiritual depth.

Transpersonal psychology is a modern expression of a timeless spirituality. It therefore has antecedents in prophetic and shamanic traditions that contribute depth and perspective. To these bodies of knowledge we shall now turn.

CASE STUDY

Basava: The Moving Ever Shall Stay

Eight-hundred and fifty years ago, a highly educated Indian mystic called Basava was appointed as finance minister by King Bjjala of the Kalachuri dynasty. He succeeded in increasing the kingdom's prosperity while promoting equality and human dignity. As one of his sayings went; "The cow does not give milk to whoever sits on its back, but it gives milk to whoever squats at its feet." *The Times of India* in 1918 claimed that he implemented a; "comprehensive programme of social reform with the elevation and independence of womanhood as its guiding point." In 1924, Gandhi said of him; "It has not

Lord Basavanna, **courtesy of Lingayat**
www.lingayatreligion.com

been possible for me to practise all the precepts of Basava... One does not find even shades of casteism in him." - the caste system being the rigid social class system of institutional Hinduism.

Basava was also radical in his religious beliefs, suggesting a personal mysticism that took him beyond the bounds of tradition. As so many mystics have done, he undermined religious authority and taught that pilgrimage and temple worship were not necessary, because everyone was equal in God's eyes.

Basava based his private life and his public work on two principles: *kayaka* - the sacredness of work - and *dasoha* - the sacredness of giving and sharing. In this way, good work was encouraged as beneficial in its own right, rather than a bad thing to be compensated with a wage. The proceeds of profitable work were then shared and never concentrated in too few hands.

For Basava, "work is worship" and, and as such, to separate the product or the profit from the process was harmful. One of the things which makes work *kayaka* is that it is done for the benefit of all, and not just for the worker, employer or shareholder. The social aspect of being human is emphasized in *kayaka* so that the work actually heals social divides, rather than creating, widening or maintaining them as in the worst excesses of capitalism.

Basava spread his philosophy through popular poems known as *Vachanas*, which explained his radical social ideas in terms of Vedic principles[61]:

> The rich will make temples for Shiva.
> What shall I, a poor man, do?
> My legs are pillars, the body the shrine,
> the head a cupola of gold.
> Listen, O lord of the meeting rivers,
> things standing shall fall,
> but the moving ever shall stay.

Basava became revered as a saint, but not before he had made powerful enemies of those who benefited from the injustices of patriarchy and the caste system, such as the aristocratic Brahmin priests. He invited Dalits (untouchables) to dine at his home and was eventually exiled for refusing to retract his support for a Brahmin-Dalit marriage. It is said that he spent the journey to the neighbouring state preaching about the dignity of labour and the equality of all people.

CHAPTER FIVE

Movements and their Movers

Leadership and conscientisation

Most activists will be familiar with being part of a movement. We speak of the Civil Rights movement, the green movement, the feminist movement and the movement for social justice. It expresses being part of something that is interconnected - a greater good. It is dynamic - *dynamis* being the Greek root for power - and so the psychodynamics of a movement concerns power and specifically, power that has its source at archetypal levels in the psyche. This is why hitching our campaigns to stories, and helping great stories to emerge out of our campaigns, is such an effective means of communicating and motivating.

Secular society is mistaken if it thinks that we can understand movements only by studying the individuals or ideologies that go into them. We fall short if we think we can deal with terrorism simply by taking out a Bin Laden or a Saddam, or for that matter, a Bush or a Blair. Neither can we deal with it by challenging its belief systems using rational arguments on their own. Reason is imperative, but alone it is like trying to understand a forest ecosystem using only photographs.

Vision, values and motivation cannot be conjured up by the ego's willpower on its own, or you end up with a hollow, burned-out activism. Instead, we need to understand that these qualities start in the creative realms of the unconscious. Our task is to birth them into consciousness. This is why so much activist work is about consciousness raising and, fast on its heels, the activation of conscience to motivate action. Both "consciousness" and "conscience" have their root in the same Latin verb, *conscire,* "to know with", or "to know thoroughly". To become conscious is to know well, and equally, to know deeply with others. This is why it is important to understand that a movement is a community – a context in which knowledge is developed, tested and applied with others and not just on our own as lone rangers.

It was from this same Latin etymology that the Brazilian educator who wrote *Pedagogy of the Oppressed,* Paulo Freire, popularized the term *conscientisation.* The word sounds more elegant in its original Portuguese, but is now widely used in its English form, especially in community development and popular (people's) education. We would define conscientisation as the raising of both consciousness and conscience through action and reflection so that people think critically about their lives, enabling transformation towards a fuller humanization.

As Freire wrote (in the days before gender-inclusive language); "To surmount the situation of oppression, men must first critically recognise its causes, so that through transforming action they can create a new situation – one which makes possible the pursuit of a fuller humanity." That includes the humanity of the erstwhile oppressor. "The pedagogy [or conscientisation] of the oppressed is an instrument for their critical discovery that both they and their oppressors are manifestations of dehumanization."[62]

An activist who is engaged in the great work of rehumanization is engaged in conscientisation. This refutes "power over" others and works to develop the empowerment of "power with" and "power from within". The leadership required for this work is servant leadership; a leadership of doing, seeing and being. It means, quite simply, enquiring constantly where we can be of most service, and usually this requires a willingness to move in and out of roles of greater and lesser prominence. Such is what the young Mahatma Gandhi understood when he turned up at the Congress party and humbly offered to do whatever task was most pressing.

If a movement might be likened to an ocean lying at the interface with the collective unconscious, the organization is a ship upon its outer surface and we, its crew. Our demanding common task is to keep everything ship-shape, to set a course, keep a weather eye out for currents, shallows and rocks. Usually, especially in larger groups of people, this requires allocating roles at differing levels of skill and authority, yet while this perhaps entails appointing a captain, everybody knows that the one who really matters, most of the time, is the cook!

Jesus taught a sermon about leadership that concluded; "So the last will be first, and the first will be last." In another, the good shepherd left the rest of the flock in safety to go in search of the lost sheep, so that none would be left out. In yet another, the poor widow's last copper coins were deemed a treasure greater than the offerings of the rich from their plenty.[63] These are hard lessons for the ego. The intention is not to devalue the importance of high-profile skills and the resources or positions they may command, but to help the powerful not forget it takes the whole crew to keep the ship afloat.

And what of the ocean, the movement? Where the movement is based on love expressed as justice, the ocean always calls us back to life, to that fuller humanity. There is a "God of surprises" sense in spiritual teaching where we just don't know what hidden parts each other plays; even our adversaries. A sense, in the end, of a grand reconciliation of justice and the resetting of injustices in the mirror of the eternity. And so, says Kahlil Gibran in one of his short stories, two rivers one day met at a confluence in a gorge.[64]

"I've had such a good life," said the first river. "I started in the mountains where fishes, birds and children splashed amongst my pools. I coursed through the valleys, watering the almond trees as lovers kissed beneath the shade upon my banks. And now I meet you. Tell me, friend, how has it been for you?"

"I've had such a terrible life!" said the second river. "I started in the mountains just like you. But then I languished through a city where factories poured poison in my veins, and sickened all the life I tried to carry. Now I'm old and tired; but today, I have met you."

And both the rivers joined hands, and set off on their final journey, and sang to one another joyously; "To the ocean! To the ocean!"

Masters and emissaries

Even in light of the above, we must not be naïve. In busy organizations not every decision can be taken in a participative way. Accountability and the legitimate exercise of power is what is called for, not consultation constipation. It was the shepherd who went to look for the lost sheep, not another sheep that did so! Destiny played out differently for each river, notwithstanding their common destination.

We saw earlier how Nietzsche's story of the master and the emissary serves as a metaphor for brain functioning. Let us take it further. The master had long governed his state wisely and was beloved of his people, but the work was complex and needed attention to detail. He said to his emissary; "Look, I'll hold on to the big picture and you go and attend to the detail." The emissary faithfully fulfilled this role, but after some time, hubris set in, and he began to believe he could manage without the master. He usurped the throne and governed with an iron fist, focussing exclusively on material prosperity. Eventually the state collapsed. The emissary understood some things very well, but couldn't hold the bigger picture.

Such can often be the tension between visionaries and managers in our organizations. Sometimes the divide runs through individuals too. The story is a reminder of the danger of wanting to take over without having sufficient understanding of complexity. Had the emissary waited, the master (if a true master) would probably have invited him to step forward when he was ready. The problem was that he didn't wait to serve out his apprenticeship, and we all know the story of the sorcerer's apprentice.

The language of "masters" and "emissaries" does not map appropriately on to today's activist world, but the point of principle has to do with finding our place, as we will see later, with discernment. This is very different from being ordered to know your place or climbing sharp-elbowed over others to usurp a place. Ironically, the word "hierarchy" came from the Greek *hieros-arkhein* meaning sacred leadership. In its original context, it implied the "golden mean" with its sense of middle-way, proportion and right-relationship within the greater ecology of the whole - hence the etymology of terms that relate to the intrinsic structure of things, like "architecture" and "archaic". The meaning of hierarchy has changed too much for the word to be used with comfort in its original sense today. However, from *hieros-arkhein* we can perhaps be reminded of the dream of connecting to the implicit sacred ordering of life. To flow with the Tao and find our place in a continuous flux, like dancers, stepping in and out to the music. Here's a much needed skill for servant leadership in spiritual activism: to develop a good ear for the rhythm of being.

A movement operates upon a long front, not all of which is visible from our particular vantage point because none of us has a God's-eye-view. In Jungian terms, a movement is a psychological complex. It is rooted deep in the unconscious and only partly conscious as a symbol, or process, of growth and change. That tip-of-the-iceberg intangibility can vex the positivist and managerialist mindset, which doesn't get the visionary's insistence on working at the boundary of what mystics call "the cloud of unknowing".

This - where it is not merely down to attention-seeking eccentricity - is why movers and shakers are often at odds with more ordered ways of doing things. The true visionary is compelled by a force that can feel like a repeated pumping, pressing feeling from within; one that can distract the waking life, trouble sleep and intrude in to dreams. When destiny calls, its demands should be tested, preferably in community with others, as we will later see. However, it cannot be left untended for too long without resulting in a displaced expression such as a neurosis - perhaps an anxiety disorder, or depression.

The prophet Jonah tried to duck the issue when called by God to go to Nineveh - present day Mosul in northern Iraq - and bear witness against violence and corruption. He jumped on to a ship and ran away to sea, but a storm arose and the reluctant prophet was tossed in to the belly of the whale. Only after three days, deep beneath the rolling waves, languishing in the archetypal realms of the unconscious, was he spat back out into the restored ego-identity of dry land. To cut the remarkable story short, he took up his calling and in due course, the Saddam Hussein of Nineveh and all his people gave up their wicked ways; but it took a storm to get him there.

Fire in the bones

How does an activist become an activist? How did you? Some people are "rebels without a cause", seeking an issue around which they can construct an ego identity. That may be part of our journey, especially when we are young and trying out, as it were, differing configurations of identity. This book, however, is about the issues that arise once motivation has hopefully progressed beyond this. We want to speak to those who might feel, or have felt, *gripped* or *driven* by a cause. People who feel as if their inner voice is saying to them; "I know it's crazy, and it means dropping other important things, and maybe putting my own nose out of joint: but this is what I should be doing now!"

In the early 1990s Alastair was five years back from Papua New Guinea and had started work - he didn't know it at the time, but long-term work - on land reform in Scotland. One day he chanced to catch a television news item about a company that wanted to make a "superquarry" - a massive hole to take out road stone - on the Isle of Harris that adjoins his home Isle of Lewis (the two, being separated not by sea, but by a mountain range). Something grabbed him in that moment. It was a mixture of discomfort and excitement; a sense of suddenly sitting up and becoming hyperalert, as if responding to a small electric shock.

He had recently witnessed the social and ecological disruption and civil war caused by the Bougainville copper mine in the Pacific. People there had said it was a spiritual issue. Alastair realized that the same was true at home. He took part in a massive campaign that ran from 1991 to 2004. His highest-profile role was to testify to the spiritual value of the land at the government inquiry, together with the Mi'Kmaq war chief who he had brought over from Canada, and a professor of the island's Calvinist theology.

The company that had initiated the scheme, Redland, got taken over by Lafarge, the biggest cement company in the world. Backed by a network of environmental groups and local leaders, Alastair negotiated their dignified exit. What followed and was not high profile, is that "pull" replaced "push". For a decade, he served (unpaid) on Lafarge's corporate responsibility panel. He had the joy of seeing them shift their business model towards "sustainable construction solutions", cutting carbon emissions per ton of cement by a third, and becoming the first major extractive corporation to recognize the UN Declaration on the Rights of Indigenous Peoples.

Those stories have been told elsewhere, and the details need not trouble us here.[65] What does need to trouble us is that this involved a calling that was, with a small p, "prophetic". For Alastair and key local colleagues, it meant speaking from a not-always-comfortable place to reach the parts that other forms of discourse couldn't reach. It added backbone to the wider campaign.

Even to invoke a term like "prophesy" is uncomfortable. We do so because spiritual activism can sometimes thrust us into this realm. Where that is the case, it can be helpful to know that there is a body of knowledge and experience out there that offers assistance with discerning and testing such a vocation, and learning how to *bear* it in all three senses of carrying it, enduring it, and (to take liberties with the spelling), sometimes to feel nakedly exposed by it.

Prophecy only makes sense with a spiritual worldview. Put simply, the prophet is a visionary who gives outward witness to an inner calling. That calling comes from a level in the psyche that is beyond the more self-centred concerns of the ego, from a level that is grounded in the collective unconscious. This source might be expressed in terms of revelation, profound inspiration, and even God or the Spirit.

Are we, then, suggesting that we go about calling ourselves prophets? "What is your profession?" as you sign on for unemployment benefits. "A prophet," you reply. "Well," says the polite lady behind the desk (as she once said to Alastair when he gave his profession as "activist"), "our computer doesn't seem to have a box for that one." Is that how we're suggesting we portray ourselves? Of course not. But we do need to understand what prophetic work is and what it entails, without having our egos inflated by some notion that we are God's gifts to history.

Like all power, prophetic power has its learning curve. Unmoderated, it can inflate the ego with invidious results.[66] The biblical Elisha asked for a double dose of power or "spirit" from the elder prophet Elijah, which went quickly to his head. On his way to Mount Carmel he was teased by a group of boys about his baldness. Offended (offence as distinct from hurt is always of the ego), he called down a curse. Two she-bears came out of the woods and mauled the little miscreants – all forty-two of them![67] Sometimes when we ask to bear new powers, they can at first exceed our safe weight limit.

A giveaway with Elisha is that he solicited power. How easily some of us get ahead of ourselves and then trip over our shadows! Most of the Hebrew prophets were reluctant. Their call was unexpected and unwanted. Isaiah tried to plead unworthiness by telling God that he was "a man of unclean lips". Moses tried to wriggle out by complaining; "I have never been eloquent... I am slow of speech and slow of tongue." Jeremiah despaired at his vocation. He felt that God had overpowered him and even used a Hebrew term that implied a sense of being raped. In what has been described as the most blasphemous part of the Bible, he cursed his own God-given life and asked to die. Yet, he concluded; "there is something like a burning fire shut up in my bones." In the end he could not help himself from denouncing such idolatries as violence and injustice, even though he was locked in the stocks and dumped down a well for it.[68]

These stories teach that the true prophetic function is rarely glamorous. It's not a path to win a popularity contest. As a young woman, the 9th-century poet Kassiane was publicly lashed for supporting exiled and imprisoned monks whose practices were forbidden. Others have suffered martyrdom or, more usually, just the gut-wrenching frustration of being marginalized and denigrated. Our readers will notice that this is no sales pitch. We are not writing to recruit. We are writing to help others who may, wittingly or, more likely, unwittingly, have found themselves recruited.

Prophetic justice

The prophets of our times may not have a well-developed sense of the divine, but in their work for justice some may find themselves on paths that gravitate towards it. Often these hang out in activist circles that can offer a measure of support, encouragement and understanding. Radical religious groups can be helpful. As we write, the Iona Community is considering a training programme in spiritually-based activism for leadership in the world church and secular movements. In America, Father Richard Rohr's Center for Action and Contemplation has a similar mission, as does the progressive Jewish network, Tikkun, under the leadership of Rabbi Michael Lerner. Some Islamic movements can be read through a prophetic lens, even though Islam recognizes no official prophets with a capital P since Muhammad. That said, the prophetic register sounds loud and clear in the voices of such activist liberation theologians as the deeply humane Ali Shariati of Iran, or Muhammed Abduh of Egypt.[69] In Thailand, the Network of Engaged Buddhists was co-founded by the Siamese activist, Sulak Sivaraksa, and other notable teachers of our times include Starhawk and Joanna Macy, whose websites and books are shaping a new generation of spiritually aware activists in the West.

The Quaker tradition has nearly four centuries of experience in understanding and supporting prophetic testimony. The late Christine Davis, a Scottish "Friend" (as Quakers call themselves) used to say; "To be a prophet is not a fixed designation in our tradition, but a role into which we step, and step back out of once no longer called."[70] That kind of whisper in the ear is tremendously empowering. It both encourages and moderates. In Quaker tradition, anybody can experience prophetic calling and "minister" accordingly. Neither is this a heretical notion within the Judeo-Christian tradition for, as Moses famously exclaimed when his activism was being thwarted by those who hankered back to the relative comforts of slavery in Egypt; "Would God that all the Lord's people were prophets, and that the Lord would put his spirit upon them!"[71]

Alastair was helped to understand these ways of thinking by his Quaker friend, Professor Gary Trompf, a historian and anthropologist of religion who was based in Papua New Guinea. He seeks to clear up the unhelpful confusion between prophecy and prediction - particularly of an apocalyptic, end-of-the-world nature. He points out that none of the Hebrew Bible's apocalyptic writing has the name of a prophet attached to it and he also stresses the centrality of justice in prophetic calling:[72]

> What is a prophet? The answer does not come so easily. A hundred years ago most scholars would have quoted from the relevant parts of the Old Testament and sown up the matter from there; today the great wealth of ethnographic commentary makes the

task of definition so much harder. Probably the most useful way of defining prophets and prophetesses is in terms of their message... the procuring of a just society by warning about the future consequences of unrighteousness. Thus in our day many of us are inclined to call great social critics by the name of prophet, just because they demand change for the better and lament the perpetuation of existing human ills.

His inclusion of the word "just" in that last line is because secularized expressions of prophecy miss the spiritual underpinning, and therefore miss the point. That, however, can be work in progress. Alastair's experience with the Harris superquarry was that he started off with a light touch on spiritual testimony and with a slight cringe, but soon found himself on a journey of spiritual growth. Now he's not even embarrassed by it!

The pioneering sociologist Max Weber thought that the distinguishing mark of the prophet was "the economic factor", namely, that prophetic work is unremunerated, propagating principles purely for their own sake. He cites the early Christian Church and Buddhist monasticism as examples. Prophecy normally arises in times of social turmoil, which often go hand in hand with empire expansion and what we would now call the consumerist mindset that supports it. As Weber saw it, the social conditions at the time of Elijah were, in many respects, strikingly similar to the present era, these having been "...the growth of great world empires in Asia, and the resumption and intensification of international commerce after a long interruption."[73]

Weber also defines the prophet partly in terms of charismatic authority. We will address that in the next chapter, but for now, let us note that Gary Trompf is not alone in drawing attention to the fact that "the shaman has emerged as something of a substitute-figure for the prophet in recent literature". He points out that prophets and shamans often stand apart from the formal priestly or even sorcerer castes. A caste hands on tradition by heredity or training. The prophetic and shamanic functions usually stand outside of established authority structures. These people are born, not made; or rather, they are made though conscientisation on the grindstone of emergent circumstances.

Shamanic calling

If spirituality is an innate part of being human, we should expect to find prophets spread across many different cultures and through history. We do, and as we see it, the prophet who testifies in the name of God is a special category of the wider shamanic function. These days, however, many folks who might be called to prophetic witness do so in societies where religion no longer plays a strong social role. Often, these prefer to understand their calling in terms of shamanism, rather than through the language of prophecy with its religious baggage.

In his classic work, *Shamanism*, the Romanian folklorist Mircea Eliade evokes the subtitle, *Archaic techniques of ecstasy.* By "ecstasy" he means the Greek *ek-stasis,* to stand outside of, or apart from, one's usual state. "Archaic" also conveys two senses: both shamanism as the primal root of religion, and connection to the archetypal realms. Eliade writes:[74]

> Now, shamanism is precisely one of the archaic techniques of ecstasy - at once mysticism, magic, and "religion" in the broadest sense of the term... Shamans are persons who stand out in their respective societies by virtue of characteristics that, in the societies of modern Europe, represent the signs of a vocation or at least of a religious crisis. They are separated from the rest of the community by the intensity of their own religious experience. In other words, it would be more correct to class shamanism among the mysticisms than with what is commonly called religion... This small mystical elite not only directs the community's religious life but, as it were, guards its "soul". The shaman is the great specialist in the human soul; he alone "sees" it, for he knows its "form" and its destiny.

Jean Houston, a psychologist and philosopher renowned for her work on human potential, points out that all religions begin as spiritual experiences, which become politicized and bureaucratized. But in shamanism; "hierarchies are reserved for levels of experience rather than for priests and bishops, so the shaman can have their spiritual experience and revelation direct and unmediated by structures ordained by church or doctrine."[75]

Superficially it could be argued that the prophetic role differs from the shamanic in that the one is usually called and pushed, while the other seeks out experience by such exercises as prolonged drumming, fasting or drug use to induce altered states of consciousness. It could be argued that shamanism is ego-driven while prophecy is God-inspired, but this distinction wobbles on closer scrutiny. On the one hand, the exploration of our own states of consciousness can be a calling, indeed, it is one that many people avoid. On the other hand, Elisha did his share of pushing, and Jesus had his encounter with the Devil "after fasting forty days and forty nights."[76]

Notice how the gospel writer rubs it in – both days and nights – just to make sure we don't miss the point. The shaman is the walker between the worlds, their feet both choosing to step forward and being guided. One foot walks within the outer world of "day", the other, through the inner realm of "night". Connection is maintained with both realities, thus distinguishing a functional shamanism from dysfunctional psychosis. And why? To serve as physician to the soul. In many indigenous societies illness is interpreted as a "loss of soul". Jung suspected this to be the case with some disorders in our society too. Lost souls need calling back and nourishing. Jesus called back the soul of Jairus' daughter who was taken for dead with the words; "Little girl, get up", and then told her parents to feed her – presumably with soul food as well as bread.[77] Such spiritual calling back can be both individual and, as we will see with the bardic tradition, collective. Houston surmises:[78]

> For the shaman, however, the vision is never the goal. He or she must bring back from this other reality knowledge and power to heal the body and regenerate the social order. Without this humane and practical application, the shaman is merely crazy at best and unworthy at worst.

In short, the shamanic function is to step outside of ordinary reality, encounter transcendent realities and powers, and step back in again to heal and minister to the people's needs.

Shamanic elements

The Oxford Dictionary gives both open and closed "a" pronunciations for "shaman" – as in "apple" or "ace". Some academics dispute whether it is meaningful to apply the Tungusic word šaman outside of its original Siberian context. Others, while recognizing the attempt to respect cultural distinctiveness and shun "one size fits all" classifications, suggest that shamanism has many elements that occur cross-culturally. It seems to be archetypally constellated, thus the preponderance of shared patterns, rhythms and motifs. By nature, these women and men are often activists who normally play a healing role but extend this to a prophetic one if their communities come under threat. Among indigenous peoples across the world it is often shamans, or people with shaman-like qualities, who either lead the campaigns or give courage to others in opposing damaging developments like mines, dams, and logging. Expressions like "I speak for this land" - where it can be carried with authority and not just bluster - are typically shamanic.

Some key elements of shamanism include:

- **Initiatory Sicknesses and Facing Death:** The onset of shamanic calling is often an illness, accident or some other premature brush with death that opens an expanded awareness of mortality, possibilities, values and sense of purpose. It is as if one worldview gets blasted off its normal tramlines and hurled towards a parallel Otherworld.

- **Consciousness change:** Altered states of consciousness may be experienced either spontaneously, or induced by fasting, drumming, chanting, experiencing extreme weather or places, or the ingestion of psychoactive plants.

- **Spiritual Freedom and Wildness:** Shamanism usually stands outside of, or on the edge of, formal religious structures. It is the psychological equivalent of walking out of the church and into wild nature. This permits both freedom of thought and consciousness, as well as giving opportunities for the restoration of the soul.

- **Movement Between Worlds:** The shaman often feels themselves to be an intermediary between this world and the spirit otherworld. As Eliade and others show, the connection is often expressed as being through an *axis mundi* - an axis of the cosmos such as the world tree, Jacob's ladder, or the stem of the lotus. The latter is elegantly pictured by the Glasgow artist, Vic Brown, in her cover image for this book.

- **Visions and Dream Interpretation:** Waking visions, shamanic journeys and powerful dreams may be experienced, and shamans often help others to interpret their experiences, frequently in connection with a need for healing or in addressing interpersonal conflicts.

- **Paranormal Experience:** Most indigenous communities believe in paranormal phenomena, especially telepathic and precognitive experiences. These may be linked to a worldwide body of beliefs that the spirit can travel out-of-the-body and gather veridical information.[79]

- **Totemic Allies:** Natural features such as mountains, rivers, plants and animals may be held in special relationship as "allies" by a shaman. The Western mind would ask whether this is a projection of wishful thinking. The pre-modern mind and that of deep ecologists would say that we, the wolf and the mountain, are one, and infer meaning from the remarkable encounters that they often describe, especially with animals.

- **Shamanic Allies:** Shamans can recognize one another and do so cross-culturally. This charismatic recognition helps to distinguish friends from adversaries and sham shamans. Connection might be through a fleeting look directly in the eye, a warmth of handshake, or a brief but penetrating few words. These marks stand out in a modern world that is often characterized by superficial relationships. The shadow side that equally needs recognizing is the potential for sexual and other forms of power abuse. Like all spiritual gifts, shamanism is a flame that must be tended if it is to burn clean. Native American teachers warn, sometimes from experiences of tragic betrayal, that the greatest abuse comes from those who have betrayed the greatest gifts.

Bardic calling

Let us take stock for a moment. The spiritual worldview that we are outlining sees life as love made manifest. All is interconnected, thus the human self is ultimately the ecological self of a living universe. As St Paul put it; "All things are created by him, and in him... and in him all things have their being."[80] Or the opening lines of John's gospel; "Through him all things were made... In him was life, and that life was the light of humankind." Or as the Chandogya Upanishad of Hinduism put it nearly a thousand years earlier; "There is a Light that shines beyond all things on earth, beyond us all, beyond the heavens, beyond the highest, the very highest heavens. This is the Light that shines in our heart." It is the being of our being, therefore, *Tat Tvam Asi* – "Thou art that".[81]

Theologians call this fullness of the outer and inner worlds "the Creation". This should not be confused with "creationism" that misses the poetry of the scriptures, reading them in a way that spurns the revelations of science. Rather, Creation reminds us as activists that our inner and outer realities emanate from divine *creativity*. The Jewish idea that humankind is "created" – both female and male – "in the image of God" can be seen as very rich if this is thought of creatively, as meaning both in *the likeness* of and in *the imagination* of the divine.[82] As a campfire song puts it – one that liberates the divine gender – "We all come from the Goddess/ and to Her we shall return."[83]

If reality is the Creation, and if we are "participants in the divine nature",[84] then where does that leave the status of human creativity? The implication is that when we participate in creativity, we position ourselves on the cutting edge of the ongoing unfolding of divine reality. Here we glimpse how profound may be the old claim that the deepest art is sacred. It places a special responsibility on the shoulders of those whose activism invokes the arts; upon the bardic function.

We define the bard as one who works with the arts to conscientise their community in ways that liberate the flow of life. As such, the bard is a category of shaman and often their work is prophetic, testifying to justice and the Spirit. Bardic poetry, for example, is not the poetry of pretty ditties, of cleverly crafted words. Rather, as Scottish folklorist Hamish Henderson said, it expresses "when poetry becomes a people" (double meaning intended). Many contemporary lyricists, Kate Tempest for example, have traction because they function at the bardic level. Protest lyrics that raise consciousness and activate conscience are a case in point, but also ones that open up the heart to the beauty of the world and one another.

All the arts can express this bardic function of testifying to the people's condition. In the late 1940s, the Ministry of Defence announced its intention to build a rocket-testing range on the island of South Uist in the Outer Hebrides. The local priest, Canon John Morrison – a surname that, in Gaelic, means "Mary's son" – was resolutely opposed to this intrusion on an ancient way of life, earning him the moniker of "Father Rocket". The MOD got its wicked way, but only after scaling down the plans so that local residents could stay. As part of his campaign the good priest commissioned his own rocket in the form of a huge white statue. Our Lady of the Isles – *Moire ro Naomh nan Eilean* in Gaelic – now graces the slopes of Ruabhal: the Madonna, with her child raising two fingers in the direction of the base to signify, of course, the incarnational unity of the human and divine in the Christian blessing of peace.[85]

Other well-known examples of what the New York human rights artist, Tom Block, calls "prophetic activist art" include Picasso's *Guernica*, Alice Walker's novel *The Color Purple*, Alan Ginsberg's epic poem *Howl* and Radiohead's album *The Bends*.

In coming to understand all of this it helps to appreciate that "myth" is one of those words that's best applied in its original, and not in its demeaned colloquial sense. It is Greek for "story", but stories that touch us at archetypal levels and therefore open us to new realties. The *Mythos* is the deep context of story that hosts the *Logos* of the cosmic mind's reason.

Om mani padme hum is how the most famous of all Hindu-Buddhist mantras distils it. *Om* is the cosmic vibration or sound of the Creation, a sound – often pronounced *aum* – that intones the entirety of Being. *Mani* is the jewel that refracts light into its component parts, symbolizing the mind and its search for Truth. *Padme is* the many-petaled fragrant lotus blossom, representing the heart and its capacity to hold love. And *hum* means "undivided". Whole volumes of Eastern theology have been written about each of these words. We might sum them up as saying that *Reality is when the jewel of the mind rests in the lotus of the heart*.

The bardic function finds its power because it establishes what Ginsberg called "the ancient heavenly connection to the starry dynamo in the machinery of night". Mythic images are symbols of transformation because they mediate between the worlds. Far from the rational mind cleverly *constructing* realities out of the meaningless detritus of existence as in the postmodern vision, the true artist has to *find and discern* the patterns of a profound shared reality. The deepest art is gift, not manufacture. For us, *Logos* has to settle back into the *Mythos* rather than the other way around. The longest journey is from the head down to the heart, from the jewel to the lotus.

The stories woven by the bard, whether through poetry, music, drama, visual art or dance, therefore help to weave our lives together. They serve the functions of creating, sustaining and regulating community. Such arts transform the social world in the same way as the lotus that has its roots in the mud of everyday messy life, its stem in the waters of the unconscious and the blossom in the full blaze of sunshine. Activists are therefore storytellers and story makers. Such is their "faerie" magic and so, as Starhawk writes; "Magic can be very prosaic. A leaflet, a lawsuit, a demonstration, or a strike can change consciousness [because] magical techniques are effective for, and based upon, the calling forth of power-from-within."[86]

What distinguishes the bard's use of such power from that of the war propagandist, or the marketing executive trying to push a product? By what criteria can we condemn one as being manipulative and praise the other as transformative? For that matter, what distinguishes mainstream politicking from spiritual activism? What are we to make of the tome, published in 2015, highlighting Margaret Thatcher's profound conviction that her work was rooted in God's will?[87]

Bardic shamanism suggests that the distinction between healing magic and sickening sorcery is that the bard is, as they say in the Hebrides, "terribly strong on the truth". Thus in the Scottish Borders ballad, True Thomas returns from Faerieland with *a tongue that could not lie*. To lie is the greatest abuse of bardic power: an utter betrayal of vocation. To be strong on the truth is a divine gift.

In their study of bardic traditions in Celtic and African countries, Morton Bloomfield and Charles Dunn point out that a bardic satire; "could cause a king to waste away; it could cause a victim to melt; it could raise blotches on his face." But equally, "it could recoil on the satirist himself, if he uttered an undeserved satire, and at the least raise blotches on his face or even cause his death."[88]

If one agrees to act "vicariously" – as a "vicar" or intermediary; as a "pontiff" or bridge – between the world of narrowed perceptions and the expansive transcendent world, one takes on a huge but invigorating responsibility. To be an artist in this sense is to carry a spiritual vocation. It requires spiritual discipline. Anything less, and we'll face the music. Many an artist who has been less than true to their calling has found their gift cave in on them. Artists must cultivate humility, not pride, in an ever-deepening commitment to truth and integrity. Inevitably, the more we try to live a discipline of truth, the more we see our own shortcomings. That is something we must learn to live with. It is part of "carrying your cross".

All of us in part are children of the lie, and this is very challenging, but the upside is that it invites forgiveness of both self and others. Without that, spirituality corrupts to harsh religiosity and sheds its nascent beauty. As activists we rail against the blindness, denial and dishonesty of "The System", but we can only do so with integrity if we also acknowledge our own complicity. In various senses of Adrienne Rich's expression, "I stand convicted by all my convictions". One could almost say – "I have seen The System and it is we!" This mandates us to try to work *with* others for change wherever possible, rather than *against* them. We must, then, be gentle.

The sharpness of the jewel must be held within the petals of the lotus heart. As Tom Forsyth of Scoraig would often say in mentoring Alastair: "Speak truth to power in love." There is a lyric of John Martyn's that reaches to such tenderness: "I won't be fancy/ But I will be free/ ... / Oh, my lover, we can go down easy/ Oh, my darling, we can go down easy."

CASE STUDY

Anne Hope & Sally Timmel: Training for Transformation

Anne Hope and Sally Timmel of *The Grail*
Training for Transformation.

Since the 1960s, Anne Hope from South Africa and Sally Timmel, an American, have built up an internationally renowned approach to community development called Training for Transformation (TfT), based upon the liberation theology and conscientisation pedagogy (approach to education) of Paulo Freire. The programme is taught through four handbooks expressing complex principles in grassroots language, making extensive use of comic strip drawings, discussion points, listening methods, reflection, theatre, poetry and even prayer.[89] It has been used in countries as far apart as Indonesia and Scotland, but it is in Africa that its impact has been greatest where, through Anne's and Sally's connection with an international ecumenical women's movement called The Grail, it now runs a one-year in-service diploma course.[90]

TfT gets people to ask questions about their lives, starting with the personal, and widening out in concentric circles to family, community and world. A sense of why the programme has had such impact can be glimpsed from Sally's and Anne's description of an encounter with Steve Biko and Bokwe Mafuna in June 1972.

The two the South African freedom campaigners said:[91]

> "SASO (the South Africa Student Organization) is planning to run a national literacy campaign all over the country... We have heard about this method of Paulo Freire's that combines reading and writing with conscientisation, and... we would like you to teach it to us."

> "It isn't really something that can be taught," Anne said. "It involves a lot of research, preparing, and testing materials, trying them out with pilot groups, and then training facilitators in all the principles of this approach, before one can even begin such a campaign."

> "That's fine," they said. "That's exactly what we want to do, and we can do all that, if you are willing to work with us..."

Here were two white women being asked to lead training for the black consciousness movement that involved community building, ethical leadership, spirituality, gender, local economic development, organizational development and strategic planning.

Africa today is changing very fast. Behind the headlines, much is happening that gives life and hope. Sally and Anne have now "retired". Be that as it may, their work rolls on and on "like a mighty stream". It must, by now, have watered the lives of millions.

CHAPTER SIX

Understanding Cults and Charisma

Why study spiritual failure?

We have been exploring movements for social, environmental and spiritual change, and the kind of people who move them. Underpinning that, is a worldview that sees power as resting ultimately on spiritual foundations. In theology, a spiritual power, gift or grace is known as a *charism,* thus spiritual movements are technically described as *charismatic.*

In the Christian Bible the seven gifts, or charisms, of the Holy Spirit attributed to the servant leadership of Christ are wisdom in the sense of discernment (Latin: *sapientia*), understanding (*intellectus*), counsel (*consilium*), strength (*fortitudo*), knowledge (*scientia*), piety in a sense that includes conscientiousness (*pietas*) and the "fear" of God in the sense of awe and reverence (*timor Domini*).[92]A charismatic individual should correctly be understood as somebody who bears some or all of these qualities and does so as grace-conditioned gifts. In the spiritually-rooted sense that we explored in the previous chapter, the functions of the prophet, shaman and bard are all charismatic and as such, sacred responsibilities. In this chapter we want to explore the downsides: the misuse or faking of charisma such as when it degrades into the pursuit of celebrity for its own sake, and the setting up of cults that, unlike authentic spiritual movements, delude and exploit vulnerable followers.

These are not side issues in spiritual activism. It was not for nothing that we devoted chapter two to exploring the validity of a spiritual worldview.

Some people would argue that all talk of spirituality deludes and exploits the vulnerable and is therefore, by definition, cultic. Each of us has to weigh up that point of view and consider where we stand in the balance of positions about what constitutes reality.

However, so does the other side of the debate! The atheistic modernist or post-modernist thinker might dismiss charisma and cults as a "religious" problem, a gone-wrong search for meaning in a meaningless world, but the sacred and the secular are not so easily compartmentalized. Science too can take on the characteristics of a cult. So can postmodern philosophy. Hitler was a case in point where politics was driven by a dark psychology and messianic calling. The truth is that many of us, given half a chance, can be vulnerable to the ego blandishments of power and celebrity. If as activists on the spiritual path we value our integrity, there is no alternative but to look the heart of darkness in the eyes.

What is a cult?

So, what does the word *cult* mean to you? Consider this description:[93]

> An 18-year-old girl decides to go off and join a movement. She's given a new name, maybe even a male name. She has her beautiful long flowing hair shorn off; she wears old-fashioned clothes which, among other things, completely desexualise her. In fact, she'll never know the joys of sex, or of having children; she's gone through a bizarre ritual in which she's symbolically married the founder of her movement, even though he's long dead. She gets up before dawn every day. She spends long hours every day chanting and praying. She's cut off from the outside world. Her family will rarely, if ever, see her again.

> And her family are proud of her because, of course, they're a traditional Catholic family and their daughter has become a nun.

As Michael Barrett concludes after giving this example in his book, *The New Believers*; "It's all a matter of perception." Etymologically, the word "cult" derives from the Latin for *worship*. When the French talk of going to *le culte*, they mean going to a mainstream church service in order to "cultivate" their spiritual "culture" - these words all have the same root.

What we English speakers call a *cult* they call *le secte,* whereas to us a *sect* is usually a small non-mainstream or breakaway religious group, perhaps a bit wacky but not malign.

Cultural norms and historical eras matter in this debate. Mainstream religious activity has become, often after much historical persecution, normalized in society and therefore the Catholic nun of an enclosed order in the example above is not seen as belonging to a cult. New religious movements find more variable degrees of social acceptance. Much has to do with the degree to which they are felt to serve wider society. Happy clappy bead-wearing Hare Krishna devotees are probably felt to be "not very British", but modest red-robed converts to some of the more established Buddhist orders get invited onto the BBC to do *Thought for the Day.*

What rightly freaks people out is where a new religious movement seems to take over a devotee's psyche and results in bizarre behaviour, occasionally with tragic consequences.

In November 1978, US Congressman Leo Ryan of San Francisco flew into the remote village of Jonestown, Guyana, to check out family complaints about the Rev. Jim Jones's *People's Temple.* Jones had first built up his following in San Francisco after training in the Methodist Church and undertaking well-respected social work among the poor. However, it had gone off the rails and was going further wrong while decamped out in the jungle. While Ryan and his entourage were visiting, four cult members opted to defect from the movement. It had become authoritarian and violent, with punishment beatings, humiliation and polymorphous sexual abuse by Jones. Unable to accept the defections, Jones had Ryan and his entourage killed as they boarded their aircraft home. This, of course, turned prior paranoid fears of an attack by the CIA into a self-fulfilling prophecy. Jones accordingly persuaded his followers to commit suicide. They were told to "step over quietly - because we are not committing suicide - it's a revolutionary act", as they drank fruit juice laced with cyanide, measured out by the camp's qualified physician. As far as is known there was little resistance. 914 people died, including 216 children.

In 1997, 39 members of *Heaven's Gate* committed suicide in San Diego because Marshall "Bo" Applewhite, their charismatic leader and the son of a Presbyterian minister, persuaded them that it was time to leave their "earthly vessels" and progress to the Next Level – courtesy of a flying saucer that awaited in the icy tail of Comet Hale-Bopp. Many of the dead had been members since 1975. Apart from strictly enforced celibacy, bizarre diets, and an obsession with enemas for "purification", they were otherwise "normal", middle-class and well-educated people. Applewhite and a few others had had themselves surgically castrated to ensure conformity with the cult's sexual taboo and to help Applewhite deal with his own suppressed homosexual leanings. Those who died appear not to have seen their drinking of vodka and barbiturates as suicide. Rather, given the paranoid fear that their movement might be broken up by Christian fundamentalists or the government, they believed that to stay on Earth would have been suicide.[94]

Most cults are not lethal but, depending on one's definition, they harm in lesser ways. The London-based Cult Information Centre defines the phenomenon as a group having *all* of the following 5 characteristics:[95]

1. It uses psychological coercion to recruit and indoctrinate potential members.
2. It forms an elitist totalitarian society.
3. Its founder leader is self-appointed, dogmatic, messianic, not accountable and has charisma.
4. It believes "the end justifies the means" in order to solicit funds or recruit people.
5. Its wealth does not benefit its members or society.

This serves as a useful guide for relatives and friends who are not sure how worried they should be about loved ones involved in strange religious sects. For Arthur Deikman of the blue vase experiment, people join cults for two main reasons: they want to find a meaningful spiritual life and they want the guidance and protection of an ideal parent figure. The trouble is, they hook in to a level of universal tribal behaviour where the law says; "Be one of us and we will love you; leave us and we will kill you."[96] Literally or, more commonly, metaphorically.

In her studies of the Nazi era, Hannah Arendt observed that what most characterized group evil was its "banality". A broader definition of a cult might therefore be helpful; one that allows for greater ordinariness, but also, Deikman's search for connection. We might say that a cult offers;[97]

1. a deeper meaning in life,
2. in ways calculated to enhance the position of cult leaders,
3. whilst damaging alternative ways of a person becoming themselves,
4. with the predatory effect that life's goodness is degraded.

Cognitive Dissonance and Cults

As far back as 1912, the pioneering sociologist, Émile Durkheim, pointed out that secular academics often have difficulty in seeing the depth of religious subject matter because they limit themselves to examples which fit their preconceptions of religion.[98] While that is true, social psychology has widened understanding with some fascinating studies. The classic one was published as a book, *When Prophecy Fails,* by Leon Festinger and colleagues in 1956. In it the researchers document how they infiltrated an American flying saucer cult in which a devastating flood had been predicted by the group's medium, Mrs Marian Keech. At the appointed hour, cult members gathered in a house in Lake City, Illinois, and waited for the UFOs to come and carry them away to safety. No spacemen came and no flood followed, so what happened next?

Counterintuitively, the cult grew in size as believers redoubled their missionary zeal. Rather than admit that they'd been deluded, most searched for alternative explanations that reinforced their beliefs. Disaster had been averted, they held, because "the forces of Light predominated", or "the space people just told us there would be a disaster as a... test of our faith".[99]

Based on such fieldwork, Festinger went on in 1957 to publish his influential theory of *cognitive dissonance.* This posits that a basic human need is "cognitive consistency" – agreement between our beliefs, values, attitudes, intentions, behaviour and perceptions of reality. When these are not aligned we experience psychological discomfort, or dissonance, that we try to ameliorate.

Once dissonance has been aroused, the coping strategies that we adopt are very revealing.[100] These include the urges to:

- *Reduce Ascription of Responsibility to Self*: ("I never really believed in Mrs Keech's channellings anyway – I was just a neutral interested observer.")
- *Deny Consequences*: ("Yes, I did give up my job to join Mrs Keech, but I didn't like that job anyway.")
- *Alter Moral Norms*: ("OK, so Mrs Keech got it wrong about the space-men. But the party was great while it lasted. In any case, why get so hung up on 'the Truth' all the time? Truth is only relative, and her teachings were spot on about the state of the world today.")
- *Shift Perception of Reality*: ("Actually the spacemen did turn up, but it was all in Spirit. It was our mistake to have thought that Mrs Keech's predictions applied to the low-vibration level of the physical plane.")

Festinger's theory of cognitive dissonance is one example of how widely elements of cult psychology can be observed in everyday life. Earlier we saw that in the Peg-turning Test (which Festinger conducted with Carlsmith) those who were paid little for doing a menial task reported most job satisfaction. In this way, they arguably reduced their cognitive dissonance at having spent so long doing so little for next to nothing. Similarly, studies of consumerism show that a customer's product satisfaction will generally

increase once a purchase decision has been made.[101] Evidence suggests that people will waver over making a decision between, say, two makes of car, but once they've paid their money they'll play up the features of the one they've bought and play down those of the other. This is called *post-decisional cognitive dissonance reduction*. It probably applies to religious affiliations every bit as much as it does to consumer ones.

One implication is that harmful religious movements have a built-in defence system against followers' reasonable and compassionate reactions. Like gang members who have to break a moral code to earn acceptance, followers may even reinforce negative belief systems as part of their own commitment. For example, authoritarian Christians may be "tested" on their willingness to buy into teachings that marginalize women, homosexuals and divorced people. Another example is the doctrine that a supposedly loving Father God required Jesus' torture and death to recompense for human sin. Such Christians - perhaps mindful of Dorothee Söelle's critique of authoritarian religion as what she called "Christofascism"[102] - can often see the problem with the paradox, but maintain; "We can't let that go, or too much else would go with it."

They might almost have a point. Transcendental insights can be alogical or nonrational rather than illogical and irrational. Divine mystery outclasses human reason. Yet mystical insight deepens reality by adding to it new dimensions of perception and cognition; not by forcing cognitive square pegs into round holes in ways that might be justified by certain "scripture proofs", but which miss the greater scripture proof of love.

The problem with cults and cultic ways of thinking, is that these are not concerned with discerning the truth about reality in the way healthy religion, philosophy and science try to do. Cults are concerned with maintaining their own cognitively consistent and self-serving worldview. Such is why their teachings become dogmatic. Authoritarian religion is therefore nearly always the hallmark of a cult, even when it is well concealed behind an avuncular or laissez-faire persona.

Marc Galanter, Professor of Psychiatry at the New York University School of Medicine, agrees with others that rigid social cohesion is the crux of generating a cult following.[103] He highlights the following characteristics among those which bind people in cults together:

- Shared beliefs, including predictions, healings and other remarkable real or supposed occurrences used to cement strong social cohesion.
- Altered states of consciousness used to validate spiritual reality and progress.
- System boundaries that control belief, and define "in" and "out" groups.
- Celibacy, and other libido-sublimating or loyalty-testing forms of renunciation.
- The "relief effect", or "pincer effect", whereby "the group acts like a psychological pincer, promoting distress while at the same time providing relief".
- Punishments, using physical, sexual or psychological intimidation, often administered in public and with group sanction, to control deviance from cult norms.
- Identification with cult values, and reinforcement of the group's deviant identity by cognitive dissonance reduction mechanisms including, in worst-case scenarios, seeking relief from ontological and physical fear by "identification with the aggressor" (otherwise known as the *Stockholm Effect*).

Cults are therefore the antithesis of authentic spiritual organizations because they revolve around spiritually empty individuals who use others to feed their extreme and even psychopathic narcissism. Sexual abuse, financial fraud or psychological or physical violence are par for the course. At the same time, many people will say that a period of being caught up in a cult was part of their spiritual journey, not least in helping them to wise up. There can be many shaky steps up the stairway to heaven. What matters is not to confuse the steps with destination.

An analogy might be drawn here with the use of drugs to induce mystical or emotionally positive experience. There is evidence to suggest that this can be a life-changing part of the spiritual journey, not least in demonstrating that powerful altered states of consciousness do exist, thereby blowing off the cobwebs of intellectual inhibitions. Yet, as Deikman points out, care must be taken not to over-estimate such fast-food enlightenment. Other evidence suggests that once the feelings of loving everyone wear off, people may have no stronger an emotional base than before with which to put their newly-felt intentions into action.[104] As with shamanic experience in general, it is one thing temporarily to illuminate the jewel of the mind, but quite another to ground it in the social context of the lotus heart.

Pseudoscience

An everyday manifestation of cultic thinking – one to which most of us are vulnerable if lacking either training in the philosophy of science, or long-in-the-tooth common sense – is pseudoscience.

Pseudoscience is any belief system that dresses with the language and appearance of real science, but which makes claims in excess of its evidence base. Often this is down to what philosophers call the "misplaced concreteness" of "attribution errors" caused by a "confusion of categories" of thought. For example, a person who falls ill with a mild infection and gets better the next day might categorize their improvement as having been caused by a friend's wonder-remedy, but actually, it may have had more to do with the natural action of their immune system, or the placebo effect, or just the emotional uplift of receiving tender loving care. While not wanting to be closed to that which might lack conventional explanations, reason has its reasons, and if we are to avoid gullibility it is important to keep our bullshit detectors turned on.

When Alastair was an undergraduate in the 1970s, he founded the Aberdeen University Parapsychological Society. It invited well-known scientists of the time to give lectures about anomalous phenomena, drawing audiences of up to 300. However, being a student group and still learning how to attune the said detectors, the odd guest speaker got through the gate who ventured on the wackily but instructively pseudoscientific.

One such occasion came to pass because a student member of the society had a great aunt who, he assured the committee, was an authority on "radionics". This claims to be an alternative therapy that heals the body by radio waves through "radiesthesia". It sounded fun and worth a hearing. The great aunt duly made her way up to the Northern Lights from southern England, bringing with her a wooden box covered in radio knobs. These she twiddled mysteriously, this way and that, as she delivered her lecture to an increasingly puzzled audience. Apparently, by suitably combining differing wavelengths and frequencies to the condition of the patient's aura, the medicinal effect could be - to borrow from *Lily the Pink* - "most efficacious, in every case".

Unfortunately for the science of radionics, the majority of those present were BSc students. They wanted to know: *what was in the box?* The answer was: *precisely nothing!* This did not in the slightest disturb the grandiloquence of the guest speaker. She believed the knobs themselves conveyed a power that warranted no explanation. The evidence was there in her experience for those with eyes to see and ears to hear. The committee members cringed with embarrassment. The hapless nephew sunk slowly through the floor. One could imagine undergoing a course of such a treatment and proclaiming - *yes, I'm cured!* - just to beat a retreat.

To this day, there is still a "professional body for qualified radionic practitioners". While the emphasis seems to have shifted onto dousing (which has a different and a stronger evidential basis), the association's online shop still sells the knobbly boxes. There's the "16 Dial Copen Broadcaster" on offer at £70. The HUDET - Holistic Universal Distributor of Electrical Transmissions - at £170. Or you can go hi-tech with the "Radionic Analytical Computer ASLD 95 design AK 12" (made in Mexico). Albert Abrams, the American doctor who "invented" these machines in the early 20th century, made a mint from leasing out such "rheostatic dynamizers" for $200 a month. The contracts, however, contained a strict restrictive clause. On account of the boxes' highly-strung contents, *on no account must they be opened!*

A parallel to such pseudoscience today - whether well-meant or as profit-turning charlatanism - is the plethora of claims to variations on the perpetual motion machine. One such inventor is "Professor" John Searl. His website, with its persuasively impressive graphics of revolving magnets, informs would-be investors that the physics behind his Searl Effect Generator "is evidently beyond basic academic and mainstream comprehension". However, "patience in learning with an open mind will reveal [how to harness] unlimited renewable energy... in complete accordance with the laws of thermodynamics". The happy outcome will be an end to "ever-increasing greenhouse gas emissions of epic and catastrophic proportions" - this, with anticipated revenues to investors in excess of

$12 million per day – "to the future of the people of planet Earth... and bless you all for your interest".[105]

Here is the perfect investment for those who believe that "money's just another form of energy"; those who, perhaps embarrassed by the sources of their unearned wealth, can hope to wash their riches clean by having helped to save the world. One Irish company, *Steorn*, has reportedly raised millions of euros, not least thanks to a full-page advertisement that it took out in *The Economist* in 2006. Yet, not a single one of these machines has withstood independent scrutiny. If any ever did, it would headline every newspaper and turn the world's oil-driven economy on its head.

Alastair knows a green-aspiring heir who sunk several tens of thousands into one of these investment companies. But hey! When the dividends don't come through, who wants to draw attention to themselves? Who wants to tell the local cop shop – and have it in the papers – that they lost their fortune on roulette? With a perpetual motion machine!

"Professor" John Searl's entry on *Wikipedia* has been "archived for deletion" by moderators. Reason? "The sources just don't stack up."[106] And that's the problem. Pseudoscience works by spinning threads of scientific jargon, cherry-picking information, triggering confirmation bias and citing authorities in ways that conjure up a chimera of reality. It lays claim to knowledge and techniques that exceed its evidence base. It's Wizard of Oz, its traction found by flattering the egos of the greedy, the gullible or, more sadly, just the innocently uninformed.

All this is of more than merely passing interest to the activist. Consider climate change. Pseudoscience permeates both ends of its spectrum of contested discourse. At one extreme, the self-styled "sceptics" or deniers, such as Lord Christopher Monckton, apply a *Daily Mail* level of science to support their claim that global warming is a scam. Similarly, in the *Daily Telegraph,* the likes of Christopher Booker and Lord Nigel Lawson minister to the denial needs of a more scientifically and business-literate clientele.

At the opposite extreme, "hard green" activists, like the retired American professor, Guy McPherson, put out the message that we're all doomed to "near-term human extinction". That's not the mainstream consensus scientific position, but it could be just within the bounds of possibility. What starts to stir a deeper unease are the indications of social nihilism within McPherson's communications. At the time of writing, all the main pages on his website have a suicide warning. He counsels against such a course of action and gives links to suicide hotlines. At the same time, he prominently states that suicide "can be a thoughtful decision, as illustrated by Martin Manley".[107] Manley was the US sports analyst who "necroblogged" the taking of his own life.

That kind of flag should twitch the dials on any well-attuned cult detector. The danger, at McPherson's end of the green spectrum, is that the science gets cherry-picked to say: *The state of the planet is so apocalyptic that it justifies apocalyptic rhetoric to ward off an apocalypse that cannot be warded off.* McPherson himself concedes; "I'm often accused of cherry picking the information... I plead guilty, and explain myself in this essay... My critics tend to focus on me and my lack of standing in the scientific community..."[108] Well - point taken!

What about a book like this? What about our discussions, between these covers that, centrally, give spirituality house space? Is that not pseudoscience, too? One response would be to lean upon the evolutionary biologist, Stephen Jay Gould. He argues that science and religion can co-exist with mutual respect because each universe of discourse is compartmentalized, as it were, by an impermeable membrane:[109]

> No such conflict should exist [between science and religion] because each subject has a legitimate magisterium, or domain of teaching authority - and these magisteria do not overlap (the principle that I would like to designate as NOMA, or "non-overlapping magisteria"). The net of science covers the empirical realm: what is the universe made of (fact) and why does it work this way (theory). The net of religion extends over questions of moral meaning and value. These two magisteria do not overlap.

Such, however, is at the heart of the destruction we witness today. By dividing values and meaning from the world of matter, the modernist mindset turns poverty, or climate chaos, into endless intellectual wordplays to be debated at arms length on public radio. This keeps God safely in "his" box in heaven. It sets up a transcendent realm to be approached, if at all, by thinking harder: or, by cultivating an obsession with personal salvation that is possessively based on "my" spirituality, or "my" religion, as if the Spirit's gift is bankable.

Our reading of the mystical traditions of the world's great faiths is that such a one-sided emphasis on transcending this world – whether by religion or by rockets – is a misinterpretation of life's meaning. Wilfully or otherwise, it overlooks God's immanence; the presence of the transcendent in the here and now.

A theology of immanence frees the flow of life from the disastrous dualism that Stephen Jay Gould wants to sound so reasonable in promoting. It recasts private spirituality into its proper context of full community, or interconnected relationship, with life on Earth. In Christianity, this unity of spirit with matter is spoken of as "incarnation". God starts becoming visible as the aliveness of life itself, life that runs inherent in everything, a universe that is alive – mountains and rivers, friends and enemies, all. Anything less would make a pseudoscience of theology, traditionally "the Queen of Sciences". It would reduce religion merely to the cult of God. And a book like this? We invite our readers to keep open minds and bullshit detectors turned full on!

At Climate Camp in 2007, Matt attended a workshop with the writer, Jay Griffiths. She told of an Inuit woman who had said to her; "If the snow melts, the Earth will break." Matt broke down in tears and had to leave the workshop. This woman's personal connection to her natural environment told her everything that his extensive Western education was telling, except in a more human way. Such an anecdote can have a power to move people far more than the recounting of statistics. Scientific evidence is of very great importance, but it is not the only source of human wisdom.

Secular cults

What happens when cultic elements derive, not from new religious movements, nor from the extremes of activist debate, but in close alliance with the mainstream structure of a state? There is now abundant evidence that a spiritual mission of redemptive violence bolstered the wars in Afghanistan and Iraq. In his masterly review, *Chosen People: The Big Idea that*

Shaped England and America, Clifford Longley of *The Times* and *Daily Telegraph* explores the theology behind the "Special Relationship" between the United States and England, arguing that the key is an anachronistic understanding of themselves as God's "chosen people".[110]

Put very simply, the Jews considered themselves to be God's chosen people. They blew it when they colluded with the Roman Empire to crucify Christ. The Roman Catholic Church took on the mantle, but they blew it when they persecuted the Protestant reformers. The English Protestants then took on the mantle of being the chosen people, but they too blew it when they persecuted the Puritans. These headed off on the *Mayflower* and took the mantle of the chosen people to the New World, there to be cemented in place by figures such as John Winthrop, an early governor of the Massachusetts Bay Colony. Winthrop's words, which likened America to "a city on a hill" watched by all the other nations, are quoted to this day by US presidents whenever patriotic ginseng is required.

For Longley, New York's mayor Rudi Giuliani summed it up in December 2001 when he chose St Paul's chapel next to the destroyed World Trade Centre for his farewell address. "All that matters is that you embrace America and understand its ideals and what it's all about. Abraham Lincoln used to say that the test of your Americanism was how much you believed in America. Because we're like a religion really. A secular religion." [111]

On the one hand, today's world can be portrayed as secular or devoid of spiritual meaning. On the other, we might ask whether this portrayal is deceptive in a way that suits corrupted powers. The sociologist of religion Richard Roberts warns that New-Age techniques currently being assimilated into the business world are appropriating religiosity into the globalized capitalist system; "Management training is now a drill square on which economic warriors, fully primed with spiritual awareness and techniques, are prepared for campaigns of endless conquest."[112] *Guardian* journalist Madeleine Bunting documented one example when she discovered that Microsoft were using Abraham Maslow's ideas to tap into employees' deepest motives, in the service of corporate profit. Using corporate rather than religious or psychological language, they pretended to offer spiritual fulfillment (as a substitute for higher wages) in exchange for years of extreme devotion to the company. Fast forward a decade to

2014, and Microsoft's CEO, Satya Nadella, hit the headlines for suggesting that it was not "good karma" for women employees to ask for pay rises. Instead, it should be about "knowing and having faith that the system will actually give you the right raises as you go along".[113] Nadella quickly withdrew this remark, but shortly afterwards, in a separate sign of the times, Facebook was reported to have begun a scheme to offer female employees up to $20,000 to freeze their eggs and defer having children. As reader comments on the *Daily Telegraph* website put it; "Starts as a perk, becomes an obligation... like women are livestock."[114]

In biblical theology, the worst plight for a human being is idolatry because it cuts one off from true life. Figures like Richard Roberts and Madeleine Bunting infer a prophetic point: namely, that the downside of a secular age is that it puts the soul in jeopardy to false gods. We must press deeper in our examination of charisma.

Authority and charisma's downside

Max Weber distinguished between three types of authority. *Traditional authority* is the right to rule as passed down by others, for example, royal families, the hereditary peers of the House of Lords, or perhaps the Kennedy or Bush dynasties. *Bureaucratic* (or *legal*) *authority* is the rational, rule-structured set of protocols that channels power in most modern societies. Tony Blair's New Labour was a good example. Most interesting for our purposes, is *charismatic authority,* that je-ne-sais-quoi or "X-factor" that allows certain individuals or groups to inspire and influence others. It operates by direct influence upon the community and generally does so without a job remit, without training, and without a formal structure or mandate. Weber wrote:[115]

> The term "charisma" will be applied to a certain quality of an individual personality by virtue of which he is considered as extraordinary and treated as endowed with supernatural, super-human, or at least superficially exceptional powers or qualities. These are such as are not accessible to ordinary persons, but are regarded as of divine origin or as exemplary, and on the basis of them the individual is treated as a "leader".

Weber observed that since charisma is "extraordinary", it is "sharply opposed to rational, and particularly bureaucratic authority", as well as to lineage-based "traditional authority".[116] As such, the bureaucrats feel threatened with disorder and try to take over and regulate the show through the co-option and patronage that he called the "routinization of charisma". Here, charisma is "captured by the interest of all economic and social power-holders in the legitimation of their possessions by a charismatic, and thus a sacred, source of authority".[117]

Authority, like power, is one of those spectral words, the semantic range of which can stretch from authority over, to authority with, to authority as the fruit of authenticity. Those who lack charismatic authority may envy and try to appropriate it. Thus in trail-blazing NGOs, it is common to see the charismatic founder, after a few years, knocked off their pedestal by the bureaucratic authority of a management team concerned with the routinization of charisma. This may be self-seeking or it may be for good reasons of accountable governance and long-term effectiveness. Ideally, charismatic authority needs to work in a symbiotic and appreciative relationship with bureaucratic authority and, in some social contexts, with traditional authority. Charisma without the good management of outward affairs is a flash in the pan, but bureaucracy on its own without charisma is a dead hand on the tiller. Charisma's role is thus to legitimize and energize political authority. Here the Powers that Be need God more than God needs the Powers that Be.

It is not for nothing, therefore, that US dollar bills carry the inscription; "In God we trust", or that all British coins are embossed with the letters, DG and FD, subtly to remind their bearers that, by divine grace, the sovereign is Defender of the Faith. It may seem like a bizarre anachronism, but the evidence rattles in the pockets of us all. Charisma, with its pomp and circumstance, is the halo with which the medieval church crowned the monarch. It stands in leaden silence each November at the Cenotaph. It is why, in olden times, the bard was deemed more powerful than the clan chief; and the court jester could tweak the whiskers of a king and get away with it. It is also why, in our times, politicians love to touch the cloak of celebrity endorsement, why the outlandish Russell Brand got to tweak Paxman's whiskers on *Newsnight*, why UK governments have to accommodate unruly London mayors and why, even in a largely secular society, the questioning of government policies by the Archbishop of Canterbury can provoke such furious debate.

These observations, however, will stir unease in many activists and especially those committed to participative and egalitarian ways of doing things. Corporations like Apple and Facebook may be charismatic, so might the comedian Russell Brand or London's Boris Johnson, but where are they coming from within themselves? Is their charisma gifted to them by grace of the Holy Spirit - if we might invoke such language to make the contrast - or is it something more self-serving? It is perfectly possible for a power to be innately "spiritual" without being healthy.

The American anthropologist Charles Lindholm worries that we live today in a world where all charisma has become dangerous. In the early days of Tony Blair's rise to power, a controversial Conservative party political poster depicted him with demon eyes and the caption *New Labour; New Danger*. Was it just a visual slander, or did it touch on something? Something that maps on to cultic psychology? Lindholm happens to be a scholar of romantic love and sees distortions of love as the essence of the charismatic hypnotic swoon that accrues to celebrity. He writes:[118]

> The powerful attraction of the beloved in the first flush of romantic love is also portrayed in Western popular culture as "charismatic". The beloved, in romantic imagery, is understood as having the same sort of intrinsic magnetic quality, outside the range of ordinary thought and logic, and is believed by the lover to be special, extraordinary, remarkable in every way.

The love in question that Lindholm depicts, though, is that of a sadomasochistic relationship. His focus is on the lover that wants to *obey* the beloved, and the follower who wants to obey the leader. A charismatic movement to Lindholm is one where the leader offers love and the followers desperately yearn to believe that he (usually he!) really does love them. Thus in the rock opera *Tommy* by The Who, Sally Simpson "knew from the start/ Deep down in her heart/ That she and Tommy were worlds apart". Yet she rushes up onto the stage, is hurled off by a uniformed man, and it all ends in blood and tears. "Little Sally was lost/ for the price of a touch/ and a gash across her face!" Tommy, the trumped-up celebrity, never knew her. In contrast, when the bleeding woman touched Jesus in the crowd he knew immediately, notwithstanding all the jostling. She was made whole, went in peace, and there lies the difference between a cult and an authentic spiritual movement.[119]

Cultic evil is the inevitable result of an unreal co-dependency collapsing inwards on its own vacuity. This is the mass psychology of the crowd by which flimsy ego boundaries collapse into that which gives an impression of greater meaning. Even though the members of the cult are lost in slavishness, says Lindholm, they *feel* immersed in love. Hitler understood that the bigger a crowd, the more easily it could be placed "under an hypnotic influence", and mass rallies were meticulously staged to maximize this effect. Usually at night to exaggerate lighting and set design effects, people were deliberately pressed together to heighten the excitement. A third of the crowd had to be undercover party members, with "emotional" women at the front. Thus, concludes Lindholm; "he achieved grandiose masterpieces of crowd manipulation where the audience was both a prop, and a participant, in a cosmic magical theatre."[120]

Hitler's childhood resembles that of a typical "narcissistically" disturbed individual – that is to say, one with arrested ego development – in which family problems distort the child's core identity.[121] Likewise, Jim Jones's childhood was lonely, so his own needs were served by telling his followers what they wanted to hear; "You'll never be loved again like I love you."[122] However, while adulating their charismatic leader, followers will always feel ambivalence stemming from their counterpoint of deficiency in charisma. Such love is therefore matched only by its jealousy. The danger for group cohesion is that the followers' gaze may drift from the leader to each other, so the successful cult leader typically scapegoats a third party – be it Jews, the CIA, the other church down the street, or lapsed cult adherents. This directs negative emotions outwards and away from their real target.

So we arrive at Lindholm's sorry bottom line. To him, both charismatic leadership, and charismatic following, are forms of socially expressed madness. In Lindholm's view, there is no escape from this gloomy analysis that leaves little choice between bland managerialism on the one hand, and mass insanity on the other. Modern society, he suggests, is too far removed from its roots for spirituality and neo-shamanism to find benign expression. The way he tells it, there is no social framework of support by which these forces can safely be contained. As *Tommy*'s self-satisfied Rev Simpson tells Sally, as he goes on cleaning his blue Rolls Royce; "don't say I didn't warn yer."[123]

Love's charisma can go right

Lindholm, as a major figure in the field, has offered a salutary appraisal. However, what are we to make of his seeking, like many of those whose work he cites, to analyse charisma almost exclusively through the lens of a modernism that has lost touch with the spiritual? Could it be a scape-goating; a displacement of authentic spirituality? His book starts with the confession; "After I graduated from college my idea was that in a different society, surviving without the baggage of my own identity, I could live more intensely and escape the alienation I felt from American culture." This led him into fieldwork in the intensively patriarchal communities of the Swat Valley of Northern Pakistan, where it seems the bubble burst. He became one of those for whom the dream of the counterculture genera-tion (he was born in 1946) got ahead of itself. He acknowledges "that there is a deep human desire to escape from the limits of the self", but goes on to tame that self same "potent desire for transcendence", ending with the constricted conclusion that; "Romantic love, because it is so powerful and so involving, and yet so harmless, is the best and most efficient safety valve for the intense emotions that might otherwise be channelled into dangerous charismatic social movements."

While romance may or may not prove harmless, it sidesteps the wider spiritual question. Lindholm intuits transcendence but chooses to cast it in a dark light. He quotes Hitler; "I'm now and then aware that it is not I who is speaking, but that something speaks through me"; but in so doing, fails to offer any counterpoint that offers life-giving potential.[124]

Other equally respected researchers are more at ease. For example, Marc Galanter cites Alcoholics Anonymous as an example of a "positive" char-ismatic movement.[125] Arthur Deikman concludes that while many utopian spiritual groups are counterfeit, the authentic ones "assist the student in making the shift from a self-centred life to one that is centred in ser-vice."[126] He reckons that Freud had it right when he defined a healthy individual as someone who is reasonably able to work and to love, since these twin attributes require an ability to relate fully as a human being; something that a lack of authentic grounding denies.

The Trappist activist monk, Thomas Merton, reminds us that living from the principle that "God is love" is no easy path.[127]

> Love means an interior and spiritual identification with one's brother, so that he is not regarded as an "object" to "which" one "does good"... Love takes one's neighbour as one's other self, and loves him with all the immense humility and discretion and reserve and reverence without which no one can presume to enter into the sanctuary of another's subjectivity.

There, Merton nails the downside of unhealthy spirituality. It violates the sanctuary of others' innermost depths. Perhaps that is what lies at the bottom of Lindholm's fear, albeit to a degree that limits his vision?

Yes, there are pitfalls, but they too can be teachers on the spiritual path. The great but troubled Glasgow psychotherapist, RD Laing, who wrote *The Divided Self* said; "True sanity entails in one way or another the dissolution of the normal ego, that false self competently adjusted to our alienated social reality." Through archetypal mediators in the unconscious, healing brings the emergence "of a new kind of ego-functioning, the ego now being the servant of the Divine, no longer its betrayer."[128]

In this chapter we have focused on that which betrays. We have done so because working with the gifts of the Spirit entails special responsibility and therefore special awareness. If we have put any of our readers off, it is probably just as well. What excites us is not the many things that can go wrong, but what can go right. To help one another to build on rock is our objective, but to do so, we have had to map the shifting sands.

As Stanislav and Christina Groff say in their important edited collection, *Spiritual Emergency* (which includes the paper by Laing), the process of spiritual emergence in itself can readily provoke a spiritual emergency, an acute psychological crisis. That's OK, but it helps to understand what might be happening.

CASE STUDY

Mama Efua: Shifting Religion's Shadow Side

UNICEF estimates that, every year, nearly four million girls are subjected to female genital mutilation (FGM). It considers that the incidence would be fifty per cent higher were it not for powerful campaigning in recent decades.[129] This has been led by African women. "Mama Efua" as she was affectionately known, was one of the foremost.

Born in Ghana in 1949, Efua Dorkenoo was educated at Wesley Girls' High School. She left when she was nineteen and studied nursing at the London School of Hygiene and Tropical Medicine. Working as a midwife made her aware of the enormity of suffering caused by FGM. In

Efua Dorkenoo by Lindsay Mgbor, DFID
Creative Commons

the 1980s, she shifted gear to campaigning. She founded FORWARD - the Foundation for Women's Health, Research and Development - working to bring closure to the practice at levels that combined medical, legislative, cultural and religious approaches.

Religion is often used in a semi-cultic manner to mask what is really a cultural practice, thereby lending FGM a spurious legitimacy. For example, Christian history tells of individuals who mutilated their genitals to suppress sexual desire. Within Islam, certain *hadiths* or oral traditions have been used to support FGM on grounds of "modesty". In facing up to these shadow sides of religion, Mama Efua drew heavily upon the pioneering work of the Egyptian Muslim feminist Nawal El Saadawi, and the Sudanese physician Asma El Dareer, who wrote *Woman, Why do you Weep?*

Efua worked sensitively with religious authorities. She opened eyes and won respected figures over, leading to a widespread withdrawal of any sense of religious blessing. For example, FORWARD co-publish a leaflet with the Muslim Council of Britain.[130] This states that; "One of the basic principles of Islam comes from the Prophet (PBUH) when he said: 'Do not harm yourself or others.' Accordingly, it quotes Imam Abu Sayeed, Chairman of the Islamic Shari'a Council, as stating:

> In Islam it is forbidden to mutilate the body, in this sense Female Genital Mutilation is condemnable as it irreversibly harms the woman. It is also prohibited to compel an individual to undertake this operation.

Efua became a friend of Alice Walker, author of *The Colour Purple*, who said that she would agree to becoming *patron* of FORWARD, "only if we called her matron".[131] In 1992, Walker had published a novel about FGM, *Possessing the Secret of Joy*. In an interview about it on British TV, she described her conclusion that the colonizer's mind appropriates everything that it values from the colonized. Only the unpalatable aspects of a culture get left alone. Harmful practices, from which an indigenous culture might have moved on in its own good time, thereby become potentized. They take on new meaning - albeit dysfunctionally so - as markers of a threatened residual identity; even, as symbols of resistance.

Where can joy be found amid such heavy histories, where even tradition has been warped by the psychopathology of colonization into a kind of cultural self-harming? Walker beamed her interviewer an enormous smile, and said; "*Resistance* is the secret of possessing joy."[132]

When Efua died from cancer in October 2014, at the age of sixty-five, the "matron of FORWARD" penned a eulogy. It was read out by Meryl Streep.[133] Walker's words situate Mama Efua in the lineage of the world's great spiritual activists. These are the tribute's opening lines.

> To be great means to put our love to work for all of God.
> This means Everything.
> And so you are defined.

CHAPTER SEVEN

Nonviolence and the Powers that Be

Pussy Riot and liberation theology

When rock band Pussy Riot performed their "punk prayer", uninvited, in Moscow cathedral in 2012, it appeared at first sight to be an irreverent publicity bash. The state authorities prosecuted three of the young women for "hooliganism". Their "prayer", addressed to the Blessed Virgin Mary, was called *Mother of God, Chase Putin Away!* Only during the court case did the deeper basis of their action emerge.

It is risky from a Western standpoint to be certain how to assess Putin's role in the Orthodox Church, and the allegation that Patriarch Kirill of Moscow - equivalent to the Archbishop of Canterbury - was once a KGB agent. What is widely acknowledged, is that during the communist era Russian religion survived both by resisting and collaborating with the state authorities.[134] This limitation on freedom held back its social evolution. In contrast, the Roman Catholic Church of the 20th century was able to put itself through a major reformation.

In the early 1960s, Pope John XXIII - "Good Pope John" - established the council known as Vatican II that, among other reforms, gave explicit sanction to a gospel of the poor. This legitimized the rise of "liberation theology", especially from within Latin America where land rights, bloody dictatorships and American corporate imperialism were burning issues. Liberation theology advances integral (all-round) human development centred on "the preferential option for the poor" - the idea that God is

Mammon versus God – Financial sector billboard outside
Christ the Saviour cathedral, Moscow, 2000 © Alastair McIntosh,

always on the side of those who suffer.[135] Not to be confused with the
more recent "integral" grand theory of Ken Wilber,[136] it achieves this by
reading the Bible in ways that liberate theology itself from suppression
and co-option in the interests of the powerful.

Whether it was because of collaboration or out of brute necessity, the
Orthodox Church in Russia slept through most of the 20th century. It
lacked the opportunity, even had it so wanted, to update its theology from
that of Tsarist feudalism to a progressive social gospel. The members of
Pussy Riot saw themselves as taking an explicitly prophetic stand. The
battle line lay between the charismatic authority of the young women and
those they represented on the one hand, and the routinization of that
charisma by the state, the state-embraced Church and wealthy oligarchs
on the other. When Alastair was a guest of the Russian Academy of Sciences and the Holy Trinity Sergyev Monastery to lecture on land reform
theology in 2000, he couldn't resist snapping a picture of an advertising
billboard outside the cathedral that captured this contrast of God versus
Mammon with the words; "The Wall Street in Moscow."[137]

The closing defence statements and other writings of the three young women who went on trial for their punk prayer reveal a remarkable and unexpected theology of liberation. The performance was, as they saw it, a ritual of delegitimization; a removal of blessing; even an exorcism.[138]

Prior to being handed down a sentence of two years, Masha Alyokhina said; "Speaking about Putin, we first of all mean not Vladimir Putin, but Putin as a system created by him." In other words, she saw power in systemic terms that went beyond individual persons into the transpersonal backdrop. This was further emphasized by Nadia Tolokonnikova's assertion; "People can sense the truth. Truth really does have some kind of ontological, existential superiority over lies and this is written in the Bible." Complementing this, Katja Samutsevich said; "The fact that Christ the Saviour cathedral had become a significant symbol in the political strategy of our powers-that-be was already clear," when Kirill Gundyaev (who the band understood to be Putin's former KGB colleague) took over as head of the Russian Orthodox Church and used it "openly as a flashy setting for the politics of the security services." Pussy Riot's protest was not to reject the Church, but to reclaim it for the people and civic protest.

Naming, unmasking and engaging the Powers

In Chapter Two we saw that Walter Wink, an activist American theologian, understood spirituality to be the inner dynamic of outer realities - the *meta* or "beyond" that lies behind the *physical* to comprise the *metaphysical*.[139] He would have seized on Masha's statement; "not Vladimir Putin, but Putin as a system created by him," as epitomizing the biblical sense that sees the "Powers that Be" as transpersonal constellations of spiritual force.

Thus, when the New Testament, the Christian Bible, speaks of "Mammon" as the God of money, it doesn't mean a golden image set up for idolatrous public worship. More powerfully, it means the innermost spirit of greed that seizes human hearts and sucks dry their treasures. Newspaper cartoonists understand this intuitively. They are in touch with the political unconscious, which is why they pick up nuances that the rest of us might miss. In Jungian terms, Masha's "Putin" is not Vladimir; it is a complex of the collective unconscious - a feeling-toned libidinal field within the Russian people. It might be said that Vladimir is himself possessed by Putin's archetypal presence, and that configures a certain type of social behaviour and Russian society.

The Powers that Be, says Wink, "be" because they *are*. Those who see power only in its outward forces would dismiss this as magical thinking, but they fail to take account of consciousness and the unconscious; how inner forces, through a sense of meaning, purpose and lived-out story, constellate outer realities. This is why, if we respond to violence in kind by cutting off its Hydra head, others spring up and only violence wins. We've not dealt with the underlying psychodynamic, and the bulk of human history is the tale of such violent cycles. Marx saw these cycles as the material embodiment of Hegel's dialectics: the privileged wrest control of resources from the proletariat, who in turn organize to get them back. Despite repeating the same mistakes again and again, the story loops round endlessly because, from *Tom and Jerry* to *Batman* to *Inglourious Basterds*, we are continually indoctrinated with what Wink calls the Myth of Redemptive Violence.

The Myth of Redemptive Violence enshrines the belief that "violence saves, that war brings peace, that might makes right." It persists because it serves the interests of those in power and fuels the hopes of those who are not. Its character, says Wink, is religious, albeit idolatrously so, thus; "If a god is what you turn to when all else fails, violence certainly functions as a god... It demands from its devotees an absolute obedience-unto-death... This Myth of Redemptive Violence is... the dominant religion in our society today." Our very blindness to the spiritual interiority of power leaves us susceptible to its pervasive influence.[140]

To respond to violence in kind is tempting, even instinctual, but it brings with it many drawbacks. In many circumstances it is impractical simply because of the overwhelming might of the oppressor. A military coup can also take decades to organize, dumping ordinary citizens with the enervating psychology of submission for long periods. Most seriously, though, responding in kind deprives the oppressed of yet more of their dignity by demanding of them the same behaviour they so hate in their oppressors. In almost every case the result, should the oppressed succeed, is that the spiral of violence simply tightens as oppressed become oppressor. One domination system replaces another, just as George Orwell's pigs morph into humans at the end of *Animal Farm*. Orwell was writing about Russian

Communism, but he came up with an archetypal image that describes the French Revolution, the English Revolution, the Chinese Revolution, American imperialism, Rwandan involvement in the war in the Democratic Republic of Congo, and any number of other historical and contemporary situations. As Wink surmises; "Violent revolution fails because it is not revolutionary enough. It changes the ruler but not the rules".[141]

Violence serves what Walter Wink calls the Domination System, which is hierarchical, authoritarian, legalistic and usually patriarchal in nature. He suggests that power is intrinsically good because all power is God given. However, just as the law of entropy in physics says that all energy degrades, so spiritual power in human hands degrades. However, this corruption or "fall" is not a terminal catastrophe. The ultimate purpose of power is to serve God. For this, the Powers must be called back to their higher, God-given vocation (or calling). Thus our slight caution at the start of this chapter, about presuming to push Vladimir Putin too much into a corner. And so Wink's triptych:

- The Powers are good
- The Powers are fallen
- The Powers must be redeemed.

This redemptive understanding can be applied to people (including ourselves), to institutions and even nations. In the Hebrew texts, the "angels of the nations" - the inner collective spirits of nationhood - wrestle with one another and even do battle. And yet, the story of Jacob wrestling all night with the angel at Peniel makes an interesting point.[142] He gets hurt - struck in the hip and left limping - but is granted blessing. And what is the hip, we might ask, but that by which we stride out into the world? Psychologically, the ego. It challenges the ego to try to see the soul in the "enemy".

Wink continues. It follows that:

- The Nations are good
- The Nations are fallen
- The Nations must be redeemed.

None of this should be misunderstood as suggesting we should appease evil. The partner of an abusive spouse - to bring it back down to the level of individuals - does not help to advance their potential for redemption by grinning and bearing the beatings. Our part is not to be confused with the greater work of God, and even Jesus said that there come times when you have to shake the dust from off your feet and leave the household or the town behind you.[143] You can't force good, but neither give up on the potential for another's redemption. That's all. It's not for us, metaphorically speaking, to throw other people into an inescapable hell. By the same token, it's arguably not for us to kill and take away their opportunity, in this life, to find redemption. We all have a right to self-defence but, if the exercise of that right means killing, we also have a right to choose to renounce our right.

Joanna Macy's language is helpful here. She distinguishes between *power-over* and *power-with*. The Domination System's rules embody power-over - the leader's power over their subjects, the colonizer's power over the natives, the natives' power over immigrants, the power of the rich over the poor, or of men over women, and sometimes, the other way around. Perhaps power-over is part of the natural order, but if that is the case, so is power-with. Life systems evolve flexibility and intelligence, not by closing off from their environment and erecting defensive walls, but by opening to sensory information with sensitive, vulnerable protuberances like eyeballs, lips, tongues and fingertips. Neurons allow themselves to channel currents from their neighbours, and every part of an ecosystem is dependent on every other part. Here, power requires openness and readiness to change. It is not a power one can own, but which all are invited to participate in by life itself.[144]

How can we as activists move with the rough and tumble of life, but in ways that hold out the light of the redemptive principle? Furthermore, how can we do that from a place of courage rather than cowardice? For as Gandhi with good reason maintained, it is better to fight than to refrain because we are afraid. Here we reach the heart of Wink's activist methodology; it involves wrestling power itself towards conscientisation. We should proceed, Wink suggested, by:

- Naming the Powers
- Unmasking the Powers
- Engaging the Powers.

In having the courage to say that the cathedral of Christ the Saviour was being used to sanitize a corrupted politics and the security forces, Pussy

Riot were *naming* the Powers that Be; naming Putin, naming the Patriarch, naming the KGB, naming their perceived abuses of power.

In stating that this went beyond the individual person to a system called Putin, the women were *unmasking* the Powers that Be, and by implication (more explicitly in their other writings), revealing how such a system caused oppression. The tool by which unmasking takes place is, as Nadia rightly identified, a transcendent sense of Truth.

In conducting their crazy dance, knowing that this would force a confrontation with the authorities, Pussy Riot *engaged* the Powers that Be. Having themselves put on trial also put the system on trial. They wrote in response to criticism from Patriarch Kirill:[145]

> A fervent and sincere prayer can never be a mockery, no matter in what form it occurs, therefore it cannot be said that we jeered at, or mocked, the shrine... You were endlessly wrong in saying in your sermon that we do not believe in the power of prayer. Without belief in the power of prayer and of words, we would never have offered our prayers so desperately and fervently, in anticipation of the severe persecution that could be dealt to us and our loved ones.

The lyrics of the punk prayer did not use accepted theological language. Appeals to gay pride and lines like; "Patriarch Gundyaev believes in Putin/ Bitch, better believe in God instead", shocked many Russians and limited the women's public support.[146] But when the prophet Isaiah stripped off his sackcloth at the Lord's request and walked naked and barefoot for three years "for a sign and wonder", he probably didn't manage to swing the Churchwomen's Guild onside either. Pussy Riot played the holy fool. Explaining themselves in a letter to supporters of 24th July 2012 they said:[147]

> Perhaps our behaviour is perceived by many as defiant and obnoxious. This is not the case. We are in desperate circumstances, in which indifference is difficult to maintain... We emphasize that we advocate for non-violence and hold a grudge against no one; our laughter is, in a sense, laughter through the tears, and our sarcasm is a reaction to the lawlessness.

We have used Pussy Riot to illustrate Walter Wink's schema because their case is high profile and it throws up the unexpected. So often in the work of nonviolence the unexpected – the serendipitous – appears from nowhere and transforms realities. Tim DeChristopher was a wilderness guide in Utah working with at-risk youth when the Bush regime opened up wilderness areas adjacent to national parks for oil exploration. At first he took part in all the usual forms of activism, standing with placards, leafleting and writing letters. Then one day in 2008, he gate-crashed an auction and, with an empty wallet, successfully bid for 22,000 acres. By the time they'd sorted out the mess, Bush was out of office. The politics changed, there was no re-auction, and the wilderness was saved.

Before deciding to engage the Powers, the position seemed hopeless. DeChristopher's standpoint felt pretty powerless. Later he told his trial judge; "This is what hope looks like. In these times of a morally bankrupt government that has sold out its principles, this is what patriotism looks like. With countless lives on the line, this is what love looks like, and it will only grow."[148]

After serving a two-year sentence, he signed up for studies with Harvard Divinity School. His activism had taught him that conscience is the only peaceful power that can engage the Powers and avert atrocity. "That's part of why I'm going to divinity school," he said to the activist magazine *Yes!* in 2014. "I see this question of whether or not we have faith in our own moral authority as a spiritual issue."[149]

Breaking the spiral of violence

Some hold that nonviolence is a misnomer because it's predicated on a negative. We don't see it like that. We see it as a direct challenge; a rebuke to violence. Nonviolence does not mean non-confrontation or pacifism in the weak sense of being passive. Rather, nonviolence is pacifism in Gandhi's sense of *ahimsa* – literally "nonstriking" or "without harm" – and *satyagraha* – "truth force", "soul force" or "God force". Thus he made statements like; "The badge of the violent is his weapon, spear, sword or rifle. God is the shield of the nonviolent."

Dom Hélder Câmara was the Brazilian archbishop who asked why when he fed the poor they called him a saint, but when he asked why the poor were hungry, they called him a communist. Living out liberation theology led him to write a powerful little book with a lovely spirit called *Spiral of*

Dom Hélder Câmara's 'Spiral of Violence'

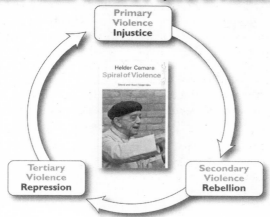

Violence, Nonviolence and Liberation Theology
Diagram: Alastair McIntosh; photograph: Dutch National Archives

Violence.[150] This showed how the Level 1 or primary violence of social *injustice* leads to the Level 2 or secondary violence of *rebellion* by the oppressed. That stimulates the Level 3 or tertiary violence of *repression* by the powerful, which further impoverishes the nation and thereby feeds back into further primary violence. The upside is that the spiral of violence can be broken at any one of these points.

We love the interfaith way in which this Roman Catholic leader cited Gandhi, a Hindu, and drew on the Buddhist teacher Thich Nhat Hanh, whose 1967 book - *Vietnam: Lotus in a Sea of Fire* - had a foreword by the Trappist monk Thomas Merton. Such is interfaith *appreciation* and not just heady dialogue. It means coming to appreciate one another's faiths from the inside, as they see and treasure things, rather than just through the perceptual planes of our own cultural projections. Such is one of many ways in which the spiral of violence is broken, and a virtuous spiral set turning in its place. Then, in the words of Martin Luther King; "The aftermath of nonviolence is the creation of the Beloved Community, so that when the battle's over, a new relationship comes into being between the oppressed and the oppressor."[151]

Nonviolence in action

Until the mid-20th century when Gandhi put it squarely on the map, the techniques and, more especially, the spirit of nonviolence were poorly understood. Most people had heard of it only in the limited context of First and Second World War conscientious objectors. Now there are a great many examples of nonviolence being applied around the world. Often, though not always, the outcomes have been positive.[152]

People often say; "Ah yes, but what about Hitler?" One response is that the idea of nonviolent civil defence was virtually undeveloped in Europe at that time. A more full answer is that it was work very much in progress, and there are a number of examples of nonviolence successfully challenging Nazi policies. These include the Norwegian teachers refusing to teach a Nazi curriculum and the story, until recently virtually untold, of the Danish systematic evacuation of Jews to neutral Sweden.[153] A breathtaking case study is the role of the Orthodox Church in Bulgaria, which prevented the transportation of most of that country's Jews to concentration camps.[154] The Patriarch himself threatened to lie down on the tracks if they were loaded in to trains, and a memorial to this wonderful act of witness now stands in the Garden of the Bulgarian People in Jaffa, Tel Aviv.

Central to nonviolence is the delegitimization of illegitimate power through choosing suffering in preference to the perpetuation of violence. Even Hitler understood the need for social support to give the regime coherence. He wrote in *Mein Kampf*; "In the long run, government systems are not held together by the pressure of force, but rather by the belief in the quality and the truthfulness with which they represent and promote the interests of the people."

Power that becomes disconnected from the people's will is thereby vulnerable to moral challenge. It becomes a political false self, draining energy from the real self and distorting human relationships and perceptions of reality. Just as Deikman, when writing about cults, remarks that; "authoritarian organizations are not usually advocates of psychotherapy,"[155] so authoritarian states fear actions or analysis that will lead to their examination and self-examination. Such is the power of unmasking and this, very often, falls upon the cartoonists, poets, playwrights, journalists, essayists and theologians. Thus censorship. Thus, too, why the campaign for land reform in Scotland has drawn heavily on exposing the psychopathologies of landed power, including the multiple poverties of wealth such as children being sent off to boarding schools that deprived them of family love.[156]

Some theorists view nonviolence instrumentally. Gene Sharp's influential *The Politics of Nonviolent Action* outlines a plethora of techniques justified as "a pragmatic choice", because they work. However, it sidesteps spirituality, giving just five words in the case study of India's independence to Gandhi's "philosophy or frequent religious explanations".[157] This surprising omission leaves unanswered why, very often, it is religious people or organizations that spearhead nonviolent direct action and civil defence. Examples include Quaker mediation in the Biafran war, the leadership of Cardinal Jaime Sin in ousting Marcos in the Philippines, the Buddhist monks in Burma, Muslims and Coptic Christians in the Arab Spring, Archbishop Desmond Tutu and now his daughter Mpho teaching the "cycle of forgiveness" in South Africa, the Peace Women in Northern Ireland, and Presbyterian clergy being arrested *en masse* while protesting at the Faslane nuclear submarine base in Scotland.[158]

We do not have space for detailed case studies here, and in any case, these are amply documented elsewhere.[159] However, when nonviolence comes up in conversation, what grips people most are personal situations into which they could imagine themselves being caught up. Here's one.

Back in the early 1980s, Alastair attended a week at Iona Abbey run by the Iona Community's then justice and peace worker, Helen Steven. It was the night of the weekly healing service. Not feeling comfortable with the hocus pocus that can surround "healing", he sat at the back of the ancient building near the exit. Just as the service was starting, two guys came in the door and sat down near him. One was a burly white Glaswegian. The other was a black American with an intellectual's demeanour. Half way through the first hymn the Glaswegian started singing erratically. When silence fell he started hurling obscenities, including some pretty spot-on abuse about hypocrisy within the institutional Church.

"Ye'r all a pile o' fuckin' hypocrites," he snarled, through the dim lighting. The service carried on, as people acted as if they had not noticed. "If Jesus fuckin' Christ could see you the now, he'd be ashamed of you."

The embarrassed friend remonstrated and managed during the second hymn to draw the unruly Scotsman outside. Meanwhile, Alastair had all of a sudden become interested in the fact that this was supposed to be a *healing* service! He followed the men outside into the Hebridean starlight, went up to the heckler, and said; "Look, if you've come for the healing, then come on right back in. There's people in there who'd help you."

It seemed a reasonable enough suggestion. After all, Jesus never seemed too put out by the Gadarene demoniac's profanities. Why should the Iona Community - if it was any good - worry about a few f'ings and b'ings rattling around the Abbey?

"And who the *fuck* d'ye think *you* are?" said the man, spitting venom as he measured Alastair up. Then he threw his fists up and laid down a challenge to fight. "I'm going to fix you," he said, "put you six feet beneath the peat," and he took a swing, shadow boxing to within a shave of Alastair's face to try to provoke an instinctual reaction.

"You can hit me if you want to, but I'm not going to hit you back."

It might sound good in print, but truth be told, the knees had turned to jelly and shook so uncontrollably they knocked against each other. At this point, something very strange happened. Alastair was scared, well aware of being out of his depth, and suddenly it was as if a blissful force field swept down from the stars above. It was as if a great scooping hand cupped him into a space of transcendental calm and with it, the conviction that all was well no matter how the conflict might end.

By this time the church service was ending. Helen Steven slipped straight out to see what was the matter. She took over with a cheerful touch, defused the tension, and Alastair promptly made himself scarce.

The next day, Helen said she'd sat up late into the night making tea and toast as the man played exquisite Bach on the Abbey piano. Before leaving the island the next morning, he'd come back. He said he'd "never known such love" as that night - presumably the kindness she'd provided - and that he'd decided to join the Church.

"And do you know who he was?" Helen concluded. "It was RD Laing, the great but crazy psychotherapist."

Some years later, his obituary in the *Guardian* reported; "There is disagree-ment over Laing's religious beliefs, and a clergyman at his funeral claimed that he joined the Church in his last four years, which rather surprised his relatives." John Clay's biography, subtitled *A Divided Self*, holds that during this period he was dragged under by the demons of his alcoholism and, as a trained ex-army boxer, would sometimes walk into public venues and pick fights; not for nothing had Alastair's knees knocked.

Not all brushes with nonviolence end so happily. While Alastair can tell of other positive encounters, there's also one from his less artful days from which he emerged bloodied. A valuable talisman given to him by a Belfast shipyard worker is; "Never show fear; do show respect." People, of course, get hurt and die in nonviolent confrontations, but not as much as in violent ones and with less of the smouldering aftermath from which violence can rekindle.

The main argument in activist circles against nonviolence is advanced by Derrick Jensen and Ward Churchill, who claim that nonviolence under-mines the resolve and tactics that are necessary to dislodge violent politi-cal and corporate systems. Thus the title of Churchill's book: *Pacifism as Pathology*. We would just ask whether, by feeding the spiral of violence, they begin to take on the likeness of that to which they are opposed?

Peace and Judeo-Christianity

The point of Ronnie Laing's protest in Iona Abbey at a time when he was wrestling to find a spiritual breakthrough in his own life, was that main-stream religion for him had fallen short; the trellis lacked the strength to carry the vine. Nowhere is this more apparent in world religions - even in supposedly peaceful Buddhism - than in the contrast between holy war and nonviolent spirituality.

As we have seen, political power very often needs the charismatic halo of religious sanction to feel legitimized, but in so doing, it lowers the spiritual tone. Terror in the name of jihad or crusade is a case in point. A key role of prophetic voices is therefore to expose collusion between systems of domination and religious authorities.

To borrow from Walter Wink, we might say that the religions are good, the religions are fallen, therefore the religions must be redeemed. How? Partly by returning to source documents and partly by discerning the ongoing unfolding of the living Dharma or Spirit. We will address spiritual discernment in Chapter Nine, but for now let us see how, in both Judeo-Christianity and Islam (to take examples that are often in conflict), a nonviolent spirituality is at the heart for those with ears to hear and eyes to see.

There are many hundreds of passages in the Hebrew scriptures - the Old Testament - in which violence is mandated by God or carried out in the holy name. At face value, the Bible is almost beyond redemption, until one looks at the trajectory. It is an historical set of books that reflects an evolution, if not in God, then certainly in the human understanding of God. The trajectory moves from the tribal war God of Joshua carrying out genocide to take back the Holy Land from the Canaanites - people like the Philistines who would be today's Palestinians - to a God who, more and more, stands in solidarity with the victims of violence or misfortune, especially the alien, the widow, the orphan and the poor.

The rules of war laid down by Moses in Deuteronomy 20-21 are draconian. It's OK to take the vanquished as slaves, to take conquered women as "booty", and genocide has its place. That said, many commentators interpret Moses' "an eye for an eye..." as the beginnings of placing limits on retribution.[160] This trajectory develops until the later Jewish prophets anticipate a world beyond war. Both Isaiah and Micah therefore prophesy that:

> In days to come... they shall beat their swords into ploughshares, and their spears into pruning hooks; nation shall not lift up sword against nation, neither shall they learn war any more.'[161]

Jesus followed in these footsteps with a mission that repudiated both Roman imperial power and the Jewish temple authorities' collusion.[162] Jesus never taught "just war" theory; he taught nonviolence. This included nonviolent direct action such as turning over the tables of the money-changers who propped up the temple's exploitative economic system - fashioning a whip for use not against people (as is often misinterpreted), but to drive out "both the sheep and the cattle" - thereby rescuing them from sacrifice and rebutting the lucrative sacrificial system.[163] Christian pacifists who break into military bases and hammer nuclear submarines and jet fighters tread this "ploughshares" path. These do not run away like terrorists would, but await arrest to take up further stands of witness in their trials.[164]

Jesus told his followers to love their enemies, to pray for (or do good towards) those who mistreat them, and to turn the other cheek if struck. He said; "...*until now* the kingdom of Heaven has suffered violence, and the violent take it by force." In other words, a new and nonviolent world order is to take ascendancy henceforth. When the brothers James and John - *Boanerges*, or the Sons of Thunder, as they were nicknamed - asked Jesus to draw down "fire from Heaven" to burn up their enemies, he refused. Instead of sending in squadrons of angelic drones by prayer remote control, he rebuked them, saying that they didn't know themselves, and that he had not come to destroy people's lives but to save them.[165]

His dalliance with the sword was explicitly symbolic, serving only to fulfil prophecy, and he therefore told Peter; "Put your sword away. For all they that take the sword shall perish with the sword... No more of this!" He also healed the severed ear of Malchus, the high priest's official, thereby symbolically restoring the enemy's capacity to listen - the prerequisite for peace.[166] At his trial he told Pilate; "My kingdom does not belong to this world; if my kingdom belonged to this world, my followers would fight to keep me from being handed over..." This is the context of his prayer, "Thy Kingdom come." It was God's realm of love and justice and not what people were used to: Caesar's violent empire. Even the gendered feudal language of monarchy he questioned. When Pilate asked; "Are you a king, then?" Jesus replied; "King is your word."[167]

Later Christian theology, which is not present in the gospel stories, developed the idea that the cross was God's punishment for human sin.[168] This projects human vengeance on to the divine heart. It obscures the meaning of the cross as God's suffering with a learning, growing world; the cross as the supreme symbol of nonviolence, a dynamic symbol of transformation. Here is love that refuses to join violence, but absorbs it. Here is love belonging to a God of activism, in spite of all the world. Here is love to which resurrection from death is not an adjunct, coming after the event, but intrinsic: because it is outside of space and time, its greater part has never in the first place been "born". Here, indeed, is the fire of love that melts the violent spiral and starts to end its never-ending knock-on self-perpetuation. As the great Hindu-Christian theologian Raimon Panikkar said; "Peace is participation in the harmony of the rhythm of Being. Only forgiveness breaks the law of karma."[169]

Peace and Islam

Islam is closely related to Judaism and Christianity because all three trace their genealogies through the patriarch Abraham, thus the term, "Abrahamic faiths". The stories and characters in their respective scriptures have important differences but also considerable overlap, thus Jesus and Mary are also revered in Islam, but in the sense of prophetic rather than divine or quasi-divine figures.

The central text in the Qur'an that relates to war is Surah 2:190:[170]

> Fight in the cause of God
> Those who fight you,
> But do not transgress the limits;
> For God loveth not transgressors.

This is pure "just war" theory, however the *Hadiths* go further. These are authoritative oral traditions of the Prophet (pbuh). They include injunctions not to kill women and children, to treat POWs humanely, not to kill anyone by burning, and not to mutilate the dead. As Philip Stewart points out:[171]

> If the Islamic rules were followed today, much of modern warfare would be impossible, and terrorism would be unthinkable. There would be no attacks on civilians, no retaliation against innocent parties, no taking hostage of non-combatants, no incendiary devices.

The problem with "Islamic" terrorism is therefore the same as the problem with "Christian" terrorism. It is a problem of militant (in the sense of military) religion. They let down the richness of their own fundamentals.[172] Most striking and least widely known is the Qur'an's explicit endorsement of *nonviolence* in Surah 5:31 (or 5:28 in some editions). In telling its version of the story where Abel is murdered by his brother,

Cain, the former says to the latter:

> If thou dost stretch thy hand
> Against me, to slay me,
> It is not for me to stretch
> My hand against thee
> To slay thee: for I do fear
> God, the Cherisher of the Worlds.

To this and its surrounding verses, the leading scholar Abdullah Yusuf Ali publishing in Jeddah, gives the commentary; "Abel's speech is full of meaning. To the threat of death held out by the other, he returns a calm reply, aimed at reforming the other."[173] The Surah goes on to say (verse 35, or 32 in some editions) that if anyone kills unjustly, it is as if they had slayed a whole people. Even the root of the very name *Islam* links to *salam*, meaning peace, as in the Islamic greeting, *Assalamu alaikum*.

Pashtun resistance to the British Raj

The theory is all very well, but what about the practice? We in Britain and some other European countries are not taught our colonial history objectively. We therefore do not hear stories that might change our perceptions about those we conquered and colonised. Here is one such story about Islamic spiritual activism.

Throughout most of the 19th century and into the 20th, the Pashtun (or Pathan) peoples – the backbone of today's Taliban – were caught in the "Great Game" buffer zone of the British and Russian empires. In 1893, Britain's drawing up of the Durand Line, to delineate what is now modern Pakistan's north-west frontier with Afghanistan, sliced through Pashtun territories. British efforts to suppress unwelcome political ideas that arose in resistance to such intrusion included collective punishments against whole communities and a gross neglect of social measures, including education.[174]

Ghaffar "Badshah" Khan (1890-1988) was a devout Muslim landowner who used his influence to open schools (*madrassas*) that would raise popular political consciousness. When his father came under pressure from the British Chief Commissioner to rein in his son, the young Khan replied that; "educating the people and serving the nation is as sacred a duty as prayer." So began a series of prison sentences for the youth, some lasting years, during which time he discoursed with prisoners of other faiths and became inspired by the teachings of Mahatma Gandhi. He concluded; "It is my inmost conviction that Islam is *amal, yakeen, muhabat* [service, faith and love] and without these the name *Muslim* is a sounding brass and tinkling cymbal."[175]

Badshah Khan's subsequent work for Indian independence as "the Muslim Gandhi" led him to establish the *Khudai Khidmatgar* - the Servants of God. These were a pacifist Mujahedeen who chanted slogans such as *Allah-O-Akbar* (God is Great) and were derogatorily called "red shirts" by the British on account of their uniform. The membership oath included, "I shall always live up to the principle of nonviolence," and, "All my services shall be dedicated to God; they shall not be for attaining rank or for show."[176] Khan told them:[177]

> I am going to give you such a weapon that the police and the army will not be able to stand against it. It is the weapon of the Prophet, but you are not aware of it. That weapon is patience and righteousness. No power on earth can stand against it.

In close co-ordination with Gandhi, the *Khudai Khidmatgar* invoked a spiritual *jihad* of civil resistance including refusal to pay taxes, noncooperation with the Raj, boycotts and pickets, general strikes and the mass commemoration of iconic events. By 1938, Pashtun membership exceeded 100,000. Nonviolence had held fast even in the face of imprisonment, torture, and at the Kissa Khani Bazaar massacre in 1930. Here, the British killed more than 200 civilians who were protesting the arrest of leaders, including Khan, who had just been sentenced to three years for fomenting civil disobedience. Some of the *Khudai Khidmatgar* sustained as many as 21 bullets in the chest as they stepped forward, peacefully, to interpose their bodies between the troops and the crowd. Gandhi subsequently told Khan; "The Pathans are more brave and courageous than the Hindus. That is the reason why the Pathans were able to remain nonviolent."[178]

Notwithstanding the later tragedy of ethnic cleansing that resulted in the partition of India, Khan's pacifism never faltered. In 1983 he told his biographer; "The present-day world can only survive the mass production of nuclear weapons through nonviolence. The world needs Gandhi's message of love and peace more today than it ever did before."[179]

Redeeming leadership

When we see nonviolence managing to bridge such cultural gulfs as that between Islam and Hinduism, and with such revolutionary effect against a domination system as powerful as the Raj, we start to glimpse a power the world has hardly yet begun to comprehend. In explaining the immensity of *satyagraha* - "truth force" - Gandhi showed that spirituality is not an optional add on. It is foundational to reality itself, thus:[180]

> The world rests upon the bedrock of *Satya* or Truth. *Asatya* meaning untruth, also means non-existence: and *Satya* or Truth also means that which is. If untruth does not so much as exist, its victory is out of the question. And Truth, being that which is, can never be destroyed. This is the doctrine of *Satyagraha* in a nutshell.

There, too, we see the immensity of spiritual activism. The relatively small struggles in our lives are with the symptoms of oppression. The greater struggle is our individual and collective birthing of and in to reality itself. That is the redemptive light at the end of the tunnel.

The main practical difficulty with nonviolent direct action is the unavoidable spiritual depth it demands. To work in ways that might mean giving up one's life rather than taking life - and even harder, to try to live the whole of one's life in ways consistent with that principle - makes little sense to those for whom love is only a set of electrochemical processes in the brain. But if love is the sign of the myriad wider connections that link us all in the web of life; if individual consciousness is just the fingertip of the divine consciousness in which we all partake, then renouncing the option of killing one another starts to add up on a scale that raises our sights on what it means to be human to a level that is nothing less than cosmic.

Those who might grant the benefit of any doubt that consciousness and love extend beyond what we know of this life; those of us who feel even a hint that the greater part of our selves, far from being vulnerable to death, have never been fully born in the first place - we, surely, do not need to grasp so tightly to physical life as to deny the need of it to others. We, surely, might be the first to reject violence and try to live in a way consistent with the greater dream, in which all are members one of another.

Nonviolent direct action lives on its wits, using every ounce of creativity to turn the domination system against itself to redeem itself. When Jesus advised carrying a Roman soldier's burden "the extra mile", he was probably playing on the fact that soldiers could be harshly disciplined for requiring Jewish subjects to carry their loads beyond the distance stated in the rules. By insisting on going further, soldiers would be placed in a quandary.

Matt experienced playing with such humour when he joined the political comedian Mark Thomas on a demonstration march around the perimeter of the American military base at Menwith Hill. The police sat menacingly in their vans filming the protesters as they arrived. Then Mark's lawyer advised everyone that they had a right to copies of all footage of themselves. Reasoning that the police were going to use the footage to identify them anyway, the group decided to volunteer their personal details to fill in forms demanding their films. They hoped that the administrative headache would put the police off filming. It turned out to be even easier than that. They didn't have copies of the form and therefore had to discontinue filming.

Even if we adopt a nonviolent standpoint, we will be left with many quandaries. These are par for the course - material for the praxis of action, reflection and more action; and for continuous conscientisation of both others and ourselves. Is it right or wrong to throw a tear gas canister *back* into a line of police? Is it okay to break a transnational corporation's window? Is damaging property nonviolent or does it harden the heart? Does lecturing a police officer about their role in the domination system achieve anything? None of these questions is resolved by the principle of nonviolence in the abstract. But that's the point. Attempting to live with love or "in the Light" is not a theoretical proposition. It is Truth expressed experimentally, often imperfectly, in a series of sacraments of the present moment. Such is *satyagraha*.

In our view, the idealist vision of a world without leaders and the hope for "leaderless" movements panders too much to those who think they can chew before they've cut their teeth. It can be childish, even narcissistic. Equally, though, the top-down forms of leadership to which we are often exposed are no longer acceptable. Indeed, we have wrestled in this text even with having to use the word "leader" because of some of its connotations, but alternatives such as "coordinator" or "facilitator" lack the sense of drive and direction that is often necessary in activism, and terms like "eldership" or even "stewardship" need too much explaining to use as shorthand in the modern world. Such is the reality of working with fallen powers, but we're left with the question; if "leadership" is the best available term to describe the flow of charisma through individuals and groups and out into the wider world, what would its "redeemed" form look like?

We suggest that it would look like people who are not attached to leading for its own sake, but who can step in and out of roles according to their skills and calling to the benefit of the community. It would look like people who are prepared to give their lives and sometimes risk their reputations in order that others might learn to participate and live fully, for as the African proverb has it; "If you want to walk fast, walk alone; if you want to walk far, walk with others." It would look like people who will speak out uninvited to save the group from itself - practising tough love that might risk their own place in the group - yet doing so with the grace and the knowledge that discernment does not play by hard and fast rules. It would look like people who help one another to discern that which they already know within their hearts, and who can laugh at themselves with that twinkle-in-the-eye rascal quality of kindness and connection. It would look like people who can stand at a sink with the washing up and not just on a podium. Or who might ask not to stand at the sink or on the podium because they need to cut themselves some slack. It would look creative, feel natural and be wholesome.

We are minded of Native American groups where the young braves will argue out the issues and the elders mostly sit in silence, but now and again, throw in something that gathers folks back around the vision, or maybe reminds them of the boundaries. You know those moments, because everybody perks up alert and listens. We are also minded of the leader who will take the tiller, issue urgent orders, and steer the ship out of trouble. All these can have their place. What matters is the intention and its legitimization; power with rather than power over. Such is how the Powers can be redeemed; not by getting rid of power but by resting ego down into the deeper self, the jewel into the lotus, violence to nonviolence.

CASE STUDY

Muhammad (pbuh): Spiritual Revolution

Muhammad (peace be upon him) was the founder (or restorer) of Islam. At a time when media representations of Islam are ubiquitous, it is remarkable how little attention is afforded to the historical figure of the Prophet himself. A focus on extremism and corrupt or belligerent governments has distracted attention from the inspirational spark of spiritual fire that first ignited the new religion.

***Muhammad* crafted in Arabic Script**
www.freeislamiccalligraphy.com

The violent society Muhammad was born into was dominated by the proud Quraysh tribe, who controlled religion and trade to their own advantage. By the end of his life, Muhammad had founded the city of Medina on radically egalitarian principles, and staged a classic nonviolent direct action to neutralize the Quraysh in Mecca.

After a series of transforming spiritual experiences, Muhammad started attracting followers, teaching that there was only one God in whose eyes all people are equal. Tribalism, with its inherited hierarchies, could no longer be the foundation for society. This was symbolized when he left his own tribe to take up residence with another - a deeply provocative and totally original act. It led him into direct conflict with the Quraysh, who planned to kill him. He escaped Mecca with his followers, but not before ensuring that all had paid their debts.

In Medina he guaranteed freedom of religion for Pagans, Jews, Christians and Muslims. He raised the status of women,[181] freed slaves and encouraged public debate. He established the rule of law based on principle rather than privilege. He appointed Bilal, an African slave freed after brutal treatment in Mecca, as the first *mu'ezzin* and founded the first mosque as a place for community renewal and education, open to all.

His success threatened the Quraysh in Mecca even more, resulting in a series of military exchanges. Muhammad was no pacifist, and the consequences of the violent episodes he sanctioned echo down the ages. However, there is no doubt that in his context he raised the ethical bar where conflict was concerned by setting ambitiously strict rules. These included a requirement to accept any terms the enemy offered to bring a halt to violence, however disadvantageous. Throughout the decade when his community faced the constant threat of annihilation, he never lost his focus on reconciliation.

In 628 CE, a dream inspired him to exploit the Meccan religious traditions and bring hundreds of his followers, unarmed and defenceless, into Mecca on a pilgrimage. This placed the Quraysh in a quandary. If they let him in, they would be humiliated. If they didn't, they undermined their own cultural authority. They could not decide, and Muhammad staged a sit-in just outside the city. The Quraysh imposed apparently crushing conditions for a truce, which Muhammad accepted gracefully, risking his own allies' trust. These very conditions proved to be the undoing of the Quraysh who could not live up to the bargain themselves. Within two years Muhammad's army was able to enter Mecca unopposed. This proved his unassailability and he promptly returned to Medina, without humiliating any of the Meccan authorities further, showering some of his fiercest enemies with gifts.

In ten years he had irrevocably transformed the culture of Arabia. He had established peaceful relations between the groups who lived there, convincing most that his new Islamic ways were better, but insisting that those who continued to practise their traditional religions should be respected.[182] The Holy Qur'an that was communicated through Muhammad is difficult for non-Muslims to follow without a good commentary, for example, that of Abdullah Yusuf Ali. As we have seen, the Qur'an, like the Hebrew Bible, conveys an assortment of positions on violence and nonviolence. Although little known in the West, some of the world's most inspiring examples of nonviolent witness have come from oppressed but devout Muslims. These range from Badshah Khan's self-abnegating Servants of God to stories, both reported and unreported, from the Arab Spring.

CHAPTER EIGHT

The Psychodynamics of Campaigning

Waking up

To transcend ego you must first develop an ego. Such is "growing up". The Buddhist teacher Jack Kornfield says; "There are two parallel tasks in spiritual life. One is to discover selflessness; the other is to develop a healthy sense of self. Both sides of that apparent paradox must be fulfilled for us to awaken."[183]

As an example, Alastair's friend, Djinni, lives in a small alternative community in the north of Scotland. On one occasion pending what threatened to be a heated public meeting, she stood at the entrance to the hall with a large cardboard box marked, *Egos*. As each person arrived she cheekily called out; "Do you need one, or would you like to leave yours here?" That's an example of empowered leadership. It might have annoyed a few people, it will have encouraged and reassured others, but either way, it probably provided a stimulus to waking up and, in the meeting, to being more self-aware.

Father Richard Rohr, founder of the Center for Action and Contemplation, describes spiritual development as a process in which we first "build a strong 'container' or identity" by becoming who we truly are, then "throw our nets into the deep"[184] to fill with divine gifts to share with the world. In the first half of life, who we are - our identity - is largely a working out of what we have been patterned to be by genetic, family and cultural determinants. In the second half of life, the task of this ego awareness is to settle into the universality of the deep Self in community with others.

This means coming to see that all nature is Buddha Nature. We are simul-
taneously utterly insignificant and of the utmost significance or, as Rohr
puts it with a twinkle in one of his recordings; "You're important, but not
that important."

The process of awakening from out of the scripts of the consensus trance
to a greater whole often causes considerable psychic pain. It is not comfortable to face up to the reality that who you have become - or who in
counterpoint reaction you have forcefully decided *not* to become - has
been patterned by absent, smothering, domineering or indulgent parents,
or by a religion or other "formation" (as the French call training) that has
constricted you. These comprise powerful social forces, which may have
made us who we are in an ego sense, but equally blocked us from what we
might have become. Such denied authenticity sets up dark shadow
dynamics.

Of course, for many people, these issues are either never addressed, or
work themselves through in "normal" patterns of dysfunctional relationships and ego-driven choices. Thus the consensual trance is maintained.
For the activist it can be a little different. Hopefully, we only become activists once we develop sufficient awareness to be able to see that something's wrong, and the confidence to name and act upon it. That can
trigger reflection on who we are and how we came to be thus. Being an
activist (as distinct from an egotist who uses activism to bolster their own
narcissism) implies an ability to reflect on values and feelings. It implies a
degree of psychospiritual awakening. The more we go with this and
become "involved" (notice that we use the same word when we fall in
love!), the more we find ourselves pushed to reflect on our authenticity,
identity, values and integrity.

This awakening is inevitable for all who act decisively in the world and are
not doing so from a position of manipulation for selfish ends. It applies to
any person who finds themselves having to ask; "Where do I really stand
in relation to this matter?" It is a function not so much of what we do or
don't do, but of the awareness with which we do it. As such, activism is
active meditation, a form of spiritual practice.

Ego inflation versus karma yoga

Campaigning work can get heady. In part, that feeds the energy. To feel blown away by the power of what you're working with can be a thrilling experience. However, notice how this happens more with punch-the-air successes than with failures. There is a trap in headiness. An obsession with success, or the blind expectation of it encoded in a wearing degree of "positive thinking" are all signs of ego inflation. It's like a ship that's overloaded with deck cargo. It may reach its destination if there's plain sailing, but give the slightest storm and there'll be not sufficient ballast down below to sustain stability.

Failure has the spiritual advantage of keeping the feet on the ground. At the same time, when failure is so often our lot, we risk moving from one doom-laden and perhaps self-fulfilling prophecy to another. This, too, is a trap; that of the nihilism sometimes present at gatherings of gloomy environmentalists and depressed leftists. Yes, we are up against huge

bulwarks of what has been called "structural evil"; but also, one some-times gets the sense that the wellheads of a deeper joy have not been tended, and this causes the oil in the lamp of life to run low.

Rudyard Kipling's poem *If* has at times been voted the most popular in the English language. It speaks of success and failure and counsels; "treat those two imposters just the same." Kipling was influenced by an India where a lynchpin of Hindu thought is karma yoga - the *yoga* (or "union with God") of *karma* (or "work", and its consequences). The *Bhagavad Gita* - Hinduism's most sacred text - says that karma yoga is the highest path and describes it in terms that could be an activist's credo:[185]

> Set thy heart upon thy work, but never on its reward. Work not for a reward; but never cease to do thy work.

> Do thy work in the peace of Yoga and, free from selfish desires, be not moved in success or in failure. Yoga is evenness of mind - a peace that is ever the same.

> Work done for a reward is much lower than work done for the Yoga of wisdom... In this wisdom a man goes beyond what is well done and what is not well done. Go thou therefore to wisdom: Yoga is wisdom in work.

Buddhism speaks of the same principle as the practice of *equanimity*, or even-handedness (not to be confused with indifference or lack of effort). Jesus similarly said to act so that you "do not let your left hand know what your right hand is doing" - in other words, do the right thing without being motivated by hope of reward.[186] In that way we reduce the dangers of self-righteousness - of spiritual pride as the fastest way to warm the fires of Hell!

One consequence of this for Alastair has been sometimes taking on campaigns that seemed to be no-hopers. Particularly when speaking in America, he's had people say; "How could you do that? In this culture, winning is everything. Losers and loser philosophies suck." But such is a way that misses the distinction between hope and optimism. Optimism is no more than an emotional wager on a good outcome, but hope endures in dark times, rooted as it is in spiritual principles. As Gandhi said; "When I despair, I remember that throughout history the way of truth and love has always won." At one level of consciousness this sounds absurdly naïve, but at another it is self-evident. Most campaigners who are motivated only by optimism have yet to cope when the ego crash of a serious failure hits them, as it likely will. Seeking to find equanimity in success and failure brings the opportunity for spiritual growth.

At issue is how to follow the Dharma without tripping up on the karma. The *Gita's* approach is that this is possible only by giving over our works – "sacrificing" in the sense of "making holy" to the divine ground of being. At the level of human relationships this is the spiritual psychology of forgiveness – "for-give-ness" – a yielding over of the demands we make upon others and thus Panikkar's "only forgiveness breaks the law of karma".

How do we find this cosmic release? Christian spirituality sees a symmetry between asking to be forgiven, or freed from the debts of another's karma, and being able to forgive and set free. As a modern translation of a line in the Lord's Prayer beautifully puts it; "And set us free from our debts, as we set free our debtors."[187] However, we have to ask for this ability from within. Both the capacity to be set free and to set others free are gifts of grace and not achievements of willpower.

All that said, it has to be admitted that success now and again is nice, and it would be a dull world that cracked open no champagne bottles! Honest pride at honest achievement makes a prettier sight than false humility, which is one of the ego's most twisted inflations. We do need to be careful about ego when undertaking heady work, but equally, let's be careful about the narcissism of getting too uptight about controlling our egos! The ego has a vital part to play in our outward presentation to the world. Perhaps the most human thing of all is to accept our own humanity, foibles and all for then, like a ship with ample ballast, we can roll with – and not be rolled over by – the waves.

False selves, inversion and shadowstrike

The problem with ego is when we become inwardly attached to it as the outward representation of ourselves. Narcissus did not fall in love with his true self; he fell in love with an image of himself as reflected in water. A well-functioning ego needs to be able to meld and flow as we move through life. If we get attached to our physical appearance at a certain stage of life, or to professional acclaim at the peak of our careers, or to our possessions that might be taken by a thief, we set ourselves up to be miserable if these things fall away. In fact, we never fully find satisfaction because we're always after what was or has yet to be.

When the inner self identifies with the ego, a person becomes materialistic and dissatisfied. This is because to live from the ego, as distinct from healthily living with the ego, is to place faith in a false self. One of the areas where RD Laing's (of the Iona incident) insights were very helpful was his understanding of the consequences of living with a false self. As our diagram redrawn from his *The Divided Self* suggests (overleaf), when we relate to others from our true self, others will find our actions meaningful and we are able to perceive them in ways that are real, which is to say, unfiltered through our falsehoods. However, when the true self is intermediated by a false self, our actions become futile and we therefore perceive others in ways that are unreal. As the folklorist Hamish Henderson once put it; "The non-genuine person cannot believe that the genuine exists."

Not only that, but the true self within shrinks because psychological energy is consumed by the voracious false self that has to keep on propping up the lie. This generates more and more emptiness inside. In Laing's view - and this is contested by those who see the mind only as a product of brain chemistry - symptoms like neurosis, psychosis, addictions and depression usually come about when the relationship between the true self and false self can no longer be sustained and one collapses into the other. He often said that mental illness is about the need to "break down in order to break through".

What we earlier described as the "shadow" is the realm of the self that we hide from others. It includes all the undeveloped and wounded parts of ourselves as well as our hidden potential. Shadowstrike, as we saw, is when an aspect of the shadow lashes out and hits another person. The whip crack is all the louder when a person glimpses in another the hint of something that they harbour in themselves. That irritation with oneself energizes the reaction to others. Thus, when Ronnie Laing threatened to hammer Alastair, the shadowstrike he threw may have found a lightning

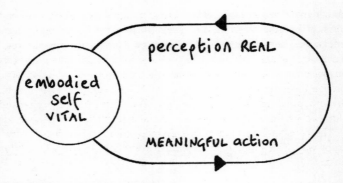

Healthy relationship between self and others

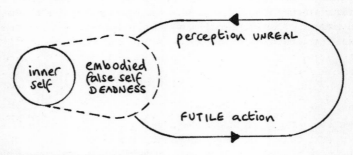

Relationship distorted by a false self

Redrawn from RD Laing, *The Divided Self*, Penguin, 1990 (1960), p. 81

rod of resonance within Alastair; perhaps, for example, a hint of self-righteousness in Alastair's suggestion that Ronnie might have liked to re-join the Abbey service.

It often takes a bit of shadow for a shadowstrike to find traction, which is why the most artful mediators are people of deep self-awareness. In pre-modern thought, such as in the sayings of the early Christian ascetics, shadow dynamics are described in terms of "demons". These may find expression through the seven deadly sins - the idolatries of the ego: anger, greed, laziness, pride, lust, envy and gluttony - to which Muslims would add despair, for that is to lose faith in Allah. Buddhism similarly has its three poisons, or *kleshas*, of ignorance, attachment and aversion. The ignorance in question is unawareness of the spiritual truths of reality. Such *maya*, or cosmic delusion, underlies all else that clouds the mind and muddies action through attachment or aversion to whatever life sends our way. The consequence is insatiable dissatisfaction and all that follows. Thus, by way of an antidote, the rejoinder from the Hebrew Psalms; "This is the day which the Lord hath made. We will rejoice and be glad in it."[188]

To personalize the things that bug us and cause us to bug others in terms of demons or the *djinn* may sound quaint, but spiritually it can be surprisingly helpful, just like those old teaching stories about the Devil are helpful. What would we do without him? Gender intended! To think of one's demons is useful shorthand. It protects from too much psychobabble that can lead to the avoidance strategy of taking distance in intellectual abstractions. Ironically, it can stop us from psychologizing our psychological issues away. One of the problems with treating psychology as an academic discipline is that its very study can be an ego foil to keep one's own issues at arm's length. Instead of such displacement activity, we need to get acquainted with our demons. Ram Dass has a lovely line where he says; "Oh, hello old neurosis. Hello sexual perversion! I've not seen *you* for a very long time."

Activist organizations frequently experience high levels of interpersonal conflict because they're made up of people who yearn for a better world but who may not yet have come to grips with their own complicity in how things are. You can see how RD Laing's insight applies here. When trying to convince yourself and others that you are ethically blameless or morally superior to the masses, or even to your fellow activists, you have to do a lot of denying. You can't face the complexities of others' lives, which lead to their choices, so you become judgmental. Your ego is on high alert for anything that might expose you, and things that were not about you become about you. You can't take a joke that implies imperfection. A corporation at least has the goal of making money to focus energies. In NGOs it gets more complicated because people's motivations are usually more involved. In the worst situations, a failure to resolve – or to come to partial terms with – one's shadow, can lead to a psychological inversion where a person flips over into what they previously deplored – a kind of Dr Jekyll and Mr Hyde condition of inner collapse into that which they had previously managed to keep at bay. The environmentalist who gets fed up with low pay and no recognition and joins the board of the logging company can be (though is not always) a case in point. The evangelical "gay cure" campaigner who gets caught out seeing rent boys is another. Creating an awareness of shadow dynamics and learning how to recognize and process conflict is therefore vital for interpersonal health and sustainability. This is why many people make use of training offered by psychotherapists, counsellors, mediators, meditators and approaches like Nonviolent Communication (NVC) and the Alternatives to Violence Project (AVP) to try to chart their way.

In this book, we are not able to tackle this range of skills, even if we possessed all of them. We can, however, briefly flag up a few more of the psychodynamic issues that most commonly arise in campaigning.

Madness versus craziness

There is a danger in the foregoing discussion of "pathologizing" normal, healthy behaviour. For sure, we need to be aware of the extremes because we will encounter them in activist work. At the same time, a distinction can be made between going mad and merely being crazy. The one is destructive ego inflation. The other, a cracking out of one's shell, like crazy paving on a wild pathway.

We also find it amusing to toy with the popular designation of a psychotherapist as a "shrink". It's as if to suggest that part of what it's all about is shrinking (though occasionally, expanding) the ego into right relationship with the rest of the psyche.

Transference and countertransference

In classical psychoanalysis, the analyst may try to adopt a shadowy persona on to which the person being analysed can project (or "transfer") their "stuff" – particularly that relating to a parent or authority figure. The idea is to draw out such "transferences" to bring them into awareness.

However, the analyst is also a human being. Often, the person being ana-lysed will trigger off the analyst's own psychodynamic process in the course of the transference. The therapist then becomes the unintended object of the therapy! Such is countertransference.

As activists, we need to hold awareness that our campaigns will engage with our deepest needs and that these will kindle transferences and coun-tertranferences. Some activists are like mousetraps who go off at the slight-est touch of authority. It's one thing to question authority and to read Kropotkin and profess anarchism. Quite another to do so without examin-ing the extent to which there might be a disturbingly close fit between the personality of one's trigger figures and the "personality" of the govern-ment, or capitalist system, or whatever is the object of one's protest. We are reminded of a newspaper cartoon that showed a procession of placard-bearing protestors. "Save the Whales", read one. "Stop Logging", said the second. "Down with the Corporation", another. Finally, right at the end of the line, "I hate my Dad!"

Psychological honesty is the toughest kind of honesty because it is the foundation on which all other honesty rests. Unless we commit to it, our activist work will only result in further entanglement between causes and effects - the endless "wheel of karma". Thus the adage; "The truth shall set you free."

Compartmentalization, splitting and projection

Linked to all of this, there is a strong propensity for groups to organize themselves into "insider" and "outsider" dynamics, including splits within the group. Put simply, we tend to compartmentalize our own inner con-flicts to reduce the cognitive dissonance that exists between behaviour and values. We then, as a group and not just as individuals, project these out-wards as a process of "othering" or alienating.

Thus, for example, we hate the corporations and their sweatshop labour, but by wearing fatigued clothing we turn a blind eye to that and like to think we're somehow expressing solidarity with those who have to wear ragged clothes. Poor becomes *chic* in the eyes of those who have the choice. We're really wearing fatigued clothes because they're in vogue, and we want to be "with it". Plus, it might be one in the eye for dad. We split off ownership of our own consumerism, but the lie becomes a psychological complex - a charged constellation of feeling-toned energy that autonomously bounces around in the unconscious. Sooner or later it will make its presence known. If we still fail to own it, to resolve the issues it presents us with, the way the psyche works can be to exteriorize such energies on to others. This is the projection, scapegoating or demonization mechanism. We come to hate the very trappings by which our unacknowledged weaknesses hold us trapped. You only have to look around at the fashion labels being sported at many an anticorporate gathering and see how many people so unconsciously make the point!

Projection focuses on some greater "sin", but blinds us to our own. This is not to say the greater sin is not real. Neither is it to deny its structural qualities that go beyond the personal. But it does invite reflection on our own complicity, otherwise our witness becomes bad witness where the flame does not burn clean.

Many radical organizations are highly schismatic because they fail to understand the holier-than-thou dynamics of compartmentalization, splitting and projection. Added to this is the distinction between vertical and lateral violence. Ideally, oppression from above should be dealt with vertically, tackling injustice at the top of a system of domination. Where that is not possible, because what's at the top is too strong, the pressure lower down readily breaks out sideways.

Such lateral violence, driven by unresolved vertical violence, typically finds expression in self-harming, victim blaming and the crippling sense of shame that so often afflicts those who suffer. Its like-on-like sideways expression shows as crime that is poor-on-poor, black-on-black, and other forms of kick-the-dog displacements of angst and anger that afflict many hard-pressed families and communities.

Protestant churches are particularly noted for their schisms because it is challenging to match spiritual freedom with an adequate depth of psychological awareness. There was once a mariner from the Outer Hebrides of Scotland who got shipwrecked and spent twenty years on a remote coral island in the Pacific. Eventually he was spotted by a passing ship and picked up. Before leaving, the ship's captain said; "I'd be fascinated to know how you survived. Will you show me around?"

"Well," said the mariner. "I made it just like the village back home. You see, there's my vegetable patch, there's my fishing boat, there's my croft house, there's my church..."

"But tell me," says the captain. "Why have you built two churches?"

"Ah! That's very simple," says the mariner. "The one at this end of the village is the one that I attend every Sabbath day. The one down the other end? Well that one is where I'd never in my life set foot!"

Love and anger

Anger is a normal response to hurt and injustice. Holding on to it, "nursing one's wrath", and shunting it down into the psyche's shadow department does not deal with it. Eventually it seeps back out as slow poison or sharp shadowstrikes.

Feminist theologian, Beverly Wildung Harrison, addresses this in her essay *The Power of Anger in the Work of Love*. Her concern is with the deadened nature of institutional religious life. She says anger is not the opposite of love. It is "a feeling-signal that all is not well in our relation to other persons or groups or to the world around us. Anger is a mode of connectedness to others... a vivid form of caring..."[189] In her view, it is not anger that subverts community but the *denial* of anger, because it forces human relations onto a footing of psychological dishonesty.

As activists we work with things that often cause anger. We must respond to it or be ruled by it. How? Most spiritual teachers hold that while eminently understandable, anger is destructive. Often, their counsel is to observe the flow of such negative emotions, bringing them to consciousness, and trying to find compassion in their causes.

Can we find compassion for those who destroy life in all its forms, or does that neuter us from action? The veteran Quaker mediator, Adam Curle, said that when he would sit down with warlords he'd usually find that underneath the brutalization they were usually seeking justice for their people. To work up from there was the basis of building reconciliation.

Our struggle as activists is to try to hold compassion even in the face of atrocity. It means pushing with one hand and supporting with the other. It means, wherever the distinction can be made, trying to go heavy on the issues but gentle on the people. This is never easy, often riddled with apparent contradictions, yet how else can we proceed without feeding the spiral of violence?

The work of peace, being on the long wave, requires very great patience, even to the point at times of having to take on suffering. We're sorry, but that's as good as we can answer.

A family affair

In the *Bhagavad Gita*, the battle fought by Arjuna is against his own kith and kin. Jesus, likewise, had his own family trying to take him home because they thought he had gone too far. He said that he had come to bring "not peace, but a sword" and to set a son against his father, a daughter against her mother, because "a man's enemies will be the members of his own household".[190]

Often it is those closest to us who are most disturbed by our activism. They may worry for us. They may worry that they'll be held accountable as we trouble the peace of others. They may be spiritually envious. The "sword" Jesus refers to cuts through the Roman peace of complicity with the Powers that Be and this unsettles. For younger people – that is, people at any time during the psychological first half of life – conflict with family members is often part and parcel of their individuation. Typical responses to having an activist in the family are:

- "Charity begins at home."
- "I can see there's a need for what you do, but why does it have to be my child?"
- "Don't you ever think of us when doing all your good works?"
- "How can you keep drawing attention to yourself when you know it upsets us?"
- "We didn't make all these sacrifices just so that you could..."
- "If you're not a socialist at 20 you've got no heart; but if you're still one at 40 you've got no head!"

- And the old standby; "When are you going to grow up and get a real job?"

Such statements can embody genuine home truths. We have to be careful not to become telescopic philanthropists like Mrs Jellyby in Charles Dickens' *Bleak House*, who gave generously to distant causes and neglected her own family. We also have to guard against what Chögyam Trungpa called the "spiritual materialism" that turns a disembodied "spirituality" – the bells and smells but little else – into addictions in their own right. Equally, though, we need to guard against family dynamics that would keep us sleepwalking.

In some ways, the distinction between wrestling with your dad and wrestling with walls of authority in the wider world is not so clear-cut. In part, one builds and is built by the other. Rock music is full of allusions to needing to break away from family conditioning to enter or engage with the world. We saw it in the "Sally Simpson" lyric from The Who. It's a dominant theme in *Sgt. Pepper's* where "she's leaving home after living alone/ for so many years". Radiohead's second album, *The Bends*, trawls through the paranoia, self-loathing and alienation of modern life with searing honesty to discover that you can try to heal the world by force, but "it will stay stung... everything is broken". A malcontent tries to "bite through the big wall but the big wall bites back". and the narrator tells her that her sulks and rages make her "just like your dad". How does this album conclude? With its only imperative as if Thom Yorke, or some other angel, is breaking through to address us directly; "Immerse your soul in love."

Studies in child psychology have demonstrated that what an infant needs more than anything else is love – unconditionally. When we don't get it a part of us closes down. We cauterize the need and so build emotional barriers – upright and uptight as the heart's flesh turns to stone. Ordinary everyday neurosis is made up of these various hard or cold spots, hard-to-specify anxieties, and lingering moods. We all need love but screw up in how to get it, and together we created from these hard barriers the wall that is a screwed up world. Coping strategies or ego defence mechanisms that do this variously include:[191]

- repression (denial of reality),
- displacement (deflection or scapegoating to elsewhere),

- sublimation (re-channelling of energy),
- rationalization (reasoning it away),
- reaction formation (overegging one's response),
- projection (seeing in others what's denied in ourselves),
- dogmatism (over-simplification of reality),
- authoritarianism (control-freakery),
- money-grubbing and accumulation (more control-freakery),
- workaholism and other addictions (running away from it),
- hypochondria (excessive self-protection), and,
- energy vampirism (clingy or "needy" attention seeking).

Each of these can often be traced back to dysfunctional family psychodynamics, or to other kinds of rejection or trauma. However, each also compounds and normalizes the wall. It almost gets too much to comprehend or cope with. Yet this is the deep work of spiritual activism and other approaches to healing. It means learning and teaching how to love and be loved. It is why nonviolence should have a growing part in our work. Yes, the activist's "sword" disturbs the peace of those who have closed down, but such is truth, as much for their awakening as for those they keep asleep. We're all in this together; it's a family affair.

CASE STUDY

Sojourner Truth: Ain't I A Woman?

Isabella Baumfree was born in New York State to Ghanaian slaves in 1797. By the time of her death in 1883 she had become a legend of the burgeoning abolitionist and feminist movements.

Sold aged nine as part of a lot along with a flock of sheep for $100 and treated brutally by a series of slave owners, when "Belle" fell in love with a neighbour's slave he was beaten to death because his owner did not want him to have children by another man's slave: their children would be the slaves of Belle's owner, not his. After Belle's owner reneged on his promise to free her in 1826, she escaped with her infant daughter and found work

Sojourner Truth, taken about 1864
Public Domain

as a servant. During this time she won the custody of her son from his white slave-owner, a landmark victory in the history of abolition.

Today, this uneducated, illiterate genius is remembered as a preacher and activist, but the completely idiosyncratic nature of her faith is usually overlooked.

Belle had a lifelong habit of going into the countryside and praying to her mother's God "in the sky", making deals and demands reminiscent of Abraham bartering for Sodom. This was a great comfort to her but she had never been taught any form of religion. Then, in 1828, a sudden vision of God transformed her understanding. Instead of a man in the sky, God was suddenly an all-powerful, all-pervading spirit. Her immediate reaction was to feel unworthy and insignificant, cut off from God. She could no longer approach God with her wishes, but thought that "if someone, who was worthy in the sight of heaven, would but plead for her in their own name, and not let God know it came from her, who was so unworthy, God might grant it." In this state, a friend appeared before her, praying on her behalf, making her feel "as sensibly refreshed as when, on a hot day, an umbrella had been interposed between her scorching head and a burning sun."

When she asked who it was, the very concrete vision replied audibly; "It is Jesus."

She had heard vaguely of a Jesus but had no idea of his significance and thought of him as a wonderful friend, hoping that she might meet him again. She thought no-one knew Jesus but herself, and when she heard him spoken of she felt a sort of jealousy, thinking she might be robbed of her new friend! Gradually she gleaned enough Christian theology to avoid being labelled an infidel, but she never bowed to religious authority. Her own study of the Bible (read to her by children because adults always tried to give her their interpretations as they went along) led her to a conclusion that academic theologians would not reach for another century: namely, that "the spirit of truth spoke in those records, but that the recorders of those truths had intermingled with them ideas and suppositions of their own."

On June 1, 1843 Isabella changed her name to Sojourner Truth and became an itinerant preacher and activist, saying; "The Spirit calls me, and I must go." She would not receive money for her work, saying she worked for "the Lord", and supported herself through other forms of labour. She tried to persuade ministers of the church that God's work should not be paid. For the next four decades she spoke at hundreds of radical gatherings, including the first National Women's Rights Convention in Massachusetts in 1850. She dictated articles for the Ohio *Anti-Slavery Bugle* and in 1865, in a kind of foreshadowing of Rosa Parks' direct action, she rode in the Washington streetcars to help force their desegregation. She also spoke against the death penalty and in favour of prison reform, dispersed rioting mobs and recruited troops for the Union Army in the Civil War.

Records of her words reveal an entirely original use of religious authority. In one address, she compared the struggle for women's rights with the biblical story of Esther. In the best known, Frances Gage's version, she explains her own theologies of the Fall and Nativity:

> Ain't I a woman? Look at me. Look at my arm! I have plowed and planted and gathered into barns... Ain't I a woman? I could work as much and eat as much as a man, when I could get to it, and bear the lash as well... Ain't I a woman? That little man in black there [a clergyman] say a woman can't have as much rights as a man cause Christ wasn't a woman. Where did your Christ come from? From God and a woman! Man had nothing to do with him! If the first woman God ever made was strong enough to turn the world upside down all alone, together women ought to be able to turn it rightside up again.

CHAPTER NINE

Tools for Discernment

Truth and the opening of the way

We have been treating truth as more than just a category of logic, but as spiritual essence and with it, essential meaning. Whereas logical truth works at an analytical level, ontological truth - truth with a capital T - is concerned with relationships of Being. It can only be discovered through wisdom, authenticity, courage and a feel for the paradoxes of poetry by which the opposite of one great truth is very often another great truth.

In the East, such truth is seen through the lens of the Dharma or Tao - words that are poorly translated by such renditions as "the law" or "the way". Jesus, similarly, said; "I am the way, the truth and the life." These "I am" statements in John's gospel are thought to link deliberately back to God's self-description to Moses at the burning bush; "I am that which I am."[192] Set in that context, they do not have to be read in an exclusive manner that renders Christianity the one true faith. Rather, the "I am" can be seen in its mystical light as universal; what is sometimes called the Cosmic Christ. If by circumstances of birth, culture, choice, or grace, we happen to consider ourselves Christian, we should be careful of making our Christ too small. Equally so if we happen to consider ourselves, say, Buddhist. From Sanskrit the term that is usually translated as Buddha Nature is *Tathagatagarbha*. This means the Buddha that is beyond space and time (*tathagata*), that is the essence, the dynamic embryo, or womb (*garbha*).[193]

As such, Truth might be understood as the ongoing *birthing* of reality, the opening of the Way. We might say; *Seek ye the opening of the way!* Islam, too, can be seen in similar light. At the risk of being misunderstood, it is worth observing that the *Sharia* - again, often poorly translated as "the law" - has an Arabic etymology that means, "the pathway to the watering hole". Our spiritual work in life is to seek out the good water, that which is the water of life. Too often, the problem with outward expressions of religion is that we have poisoned our own water, or as God complained to Jeremiah (in what can serve as a cracking critique of the idolatry of consumerism); "They have forsaken me, the fountain of living water, and dug out cisterns for themselves, cracked cisterns that can hold no water."[194]

How, and how in our many walks of life, can we seek out the good water, that which gives life? The spiritual terminology for such a searching and testing process is *discernment.*

Discernment and humility

By this late hour, our readers will have observed that we are obsessed, maybe overly so, with etymology. That's what you get from a lover of bards and an English teacher! To push on regardless, the etymology of "discern" is from *dis* (to cut through) and *cernere*, (to separate). Discernment is thus a progressive process of deepening by sifting for the truth, like digging down through the gravel and panning for gold.

There's some lines in *Four Quartets* by TS Eliot that borrow from Dame Julian of Norwich; "All shall be well and/ All manner of thing shall be well/ By the purification of the motive/ In the ground of our beseeching."[195] There we see it. We must wrestle constantly with the psychological honesty of purifying our motive. We must "beseech". We must inwardly *ask* to be given the spectacles of in-sight, just as we might ask an optician for the spectacles of out-sight.

The Majorcan scholar, Juan Mascaró, translated both the *Upanishads* and the *Bhagavad Gita* for Penguin Classics. His interfaith introductions are as important as his translation, which, said the Bengali poet Rabindranath Tagore, "has caught... the inner voice that goes beyond the boundaries of words." Mascaró translates the *Gita's* opening line as; "On the field of Truth, on the battlefield of life, what came to pass, Sanjaya..."

In reverse order, "what came to pass" denotes the everyday ground of events. That nests within the greater "battlefield of life". And that in turn nests within the *Dharma-ksetre*, the Truth-field that is the cosmic Dharma.

But who is Sanjaya? Who is doing the discerning? The answer is that Sanjaya was the eagle-eyed charioteer to the blind king, Dhritarashtra. There we see the lesson that distinguishes spiritual activism from ordinary activism; political power on its own - politics within a spiritual vacuum - is always blind. We too must find Sanjaya's eagle eyes.

How?

The Desert Fathers of Syria and northern Africa had a tale that, one day, as Abbot Macarius headed back to his cell from gathering reeds in the marshes, he met the Devil on the path wielding a reaper's sickle.[196] The Devil started taking swings at the holy man, trying to scythe him down, but Macarius was too agile, and every stroke missed. At last the Devil said, exasperated; "I can do all the things you can do. You fast, and I eat nothing at all. You watch, and I never sleep. But there is one thing alone in which you overcome me."

"What's that?" asked Macarius.

"Your humility," the Devil replied, "for because of it I cannot overcome you."

That's how.

"Blessed are the pure in heart: for they shall see God."[197]

A young rabbi said to an old rabbi; "In the past the wise saw God. Now nobody sees God anymore. How come?"

Said the teacher; "Because these days, nobody stoops low enough."

Mind you, it is best not to get too cocksure. Like the flaw in the otherwise perfect Persian carpet that reminded its maker that they were not in competition with Allah, it's no bad thing to have the odd foible.

As Golda Meir quipped when she was the prime minister of Israel; "Don't be so humble; you're not that great."

Working under concern

Both the Quaker and the Jesuit traditions within Christianity have developed very strong traditions of discernment.[198] Here is how the former, the Friends describe it:[199]

In our meetings for worship we seek through the stillness to know God's will for ourselves and for the gathered group. Our meetings... in which we conduct our business, are also meetings for worship based on silence, and they carry the same expectation that God's guidance can be discerned if we are truly listening together and to each other, and are not blinkered by preconceived opinions. It is this belief that God's will can be recognised through the discipline of silent waiting which distinguishes our decision-making process from the secular idea of consensus. We have a common purpose in seeking God's will through waiting and listening, believing that every activity of life should be subject to divine guidance.

This giving of oneself to the divine Spirit - "thy will be done", not necessarily "my will" - is a question of *surrender*. We prefer to use that term rather than *submission*. To submit (*sub*), suggests going under, or being dominated; whereas to surrender (*sur*), suggests a yielding, the way that lovers do it.

Even terms like "God's will" are much too hard-edged when it is an opening of the way that is being described, the harmonizing of one's own heart with the cosmic pulse. The Quaker experience is that this quality of presence to the "movement", "leadings" or "prompting" of the Spirit has led many of them into spiritual activism in such fields as black, sexual and women's civil rights, peace and mediation work, mental health and prison reform, care for nature, simple living, tackling poverty, climate change advocacy, business ethics and "truth and integrity in public affairs".

If such forms of witness came easily, the world would be a very different place. They don't come easily - not when they can involve putting our own noses out of joint. One example was the Quaker purveyor of chocolate, tea and coffee, William Tuke (1732-1822). He was so moved at the inhuman conditions in which mentally ill people were kept at the York Asylum that he used his wealth to found The Retreat. Set in beautiful grounds on the edge of the city, The Retreat to this day pioneers dignified care. However, Tuke's efforts were not universally appreciated. Mental illness at the time was enmeshed with fears and prejudices. He remarked, with great sadness; "All men seem to desert me."

The gift from such loneliness of the long-distance activist is that Friends have come to recognize, and develop collective expertise, in what they call "working under concern". A culture has been built up of recognizing that when a person feels moved to do something because of a concern, it can help them to have an empathetic context in which to test that concern and to purify the motive. Also, they may need support in carrying their burden of awareness. The central committee of British Quakerism continues to be called by the magnificently antique name, "Meeting for Sufferings", precisely because, especially in the past, Friends sometimes suffered grievously for standing by their beliefs and standing up for others.

The support given to those working under concern can range from helping a person to become more aware of psychological issues – such as shadow and ego entanglements – to helping with the practicalities like training needs, strategy, ethical dilemmas, fundraising and childcare.

Recognition of the need for support in activism is by no means an exclusive preserve of Quakers! That said, through Friends' involvement with justice and peace movements in particular, their core approaches have filtered out, modified to more secular settings, and thus found wider traction.

Meetings for clearness

One example of that wider traction is the notion of seeking "clearness", and specifically, having "meetings for clearness" or "clearness committees".[200]

In this, a person might ask friends in their faith or other affinity group to help them thresh though an issue, such as a sense of calling in activist work. Typically, a group of perhaps half a dozen people will gather, and perhaps after a pot-luck supper, the person seeking to refine their sense of clearness around an issue will open by stating their situation and their questions. For example; "My dilemma, is whether to give up my well-paid job and wholly follow this sense of calling, or whether to stay in my job, but support the cause by giving money." Or; "I am wondering how to handle the fact that I am totally engrossed in this crucial work, but am I neglecting the children?"

The clearance group shouldn't be like an interview. Allowing space for silence, and what might gestate in the darknesses of silence, is preeminently important. Questions should not be prepared, leading, or judgemental. They should be open; questions like:

- Could you share with us why this calling stirs you so strongly?
- What makes you feel so alone in your concern?
- In what ways would you love to be supported?
- How might others have been seeing the situation differently?
- Is now the right time, or might you want to let it sit for longer?

Parker Palmer is a Quaker spiritual teacher who speaks of clearance committees as "circles of trust". Such a group, he says, "is not just a place where we learn to ask honest, open questions. It is a focused microcosm of a larger circle of trust, a setting in which we have an intense experience of what it means to gather in support of someone's inner journey."[201] This relies upon a capacity for "creative listening" in the assembled group. It is the soul that is being drawn "into the light" of clearness; the soul not just of one, but of all involved. This is why, although clearness can be sought in secular contexts, the seeking of it cannot be instrumentally reduced to a technique. At the deepest level, it is a sacred trust. Here is Palmer's lovely description:[202]

> Like a wild animal, the soul is tough, resilient, resourceful, savvy, and self-sufficient: it knows how to survive in hard places... Yet despite its toughness, the soul is also shy... It seeks safety in the dense underbrush, especially when other people are around [and], unfortunately, *community* in our culture too often means a group of people who go crashing through the woods together, scaring the soul away... Under these conditions the intellect, emotions, will, and ego may emerge, but not the soul: we scare off all the soulful things, like respectful relationships, goodwill, and hope.

> A circle of trust is a group of people who know how to sit quietly "in the woods" with each other and wait for the shy soul to grow up. The relationships in such a group are not pushy but patient; they are not confrontational but compassionate; they are filled not with expectations and demands but with abiding faith in the reality of the inner teacher and in each person's capacity to learn from it. The poet Rumi captures the essence of this way of being together: "A circle of lovely, quiet people/ becomes the ring on my finger."

Support groups and avoiding burnout

A meeting for clearness that gathers regularly, may not have a sharply focussed question and may be much more laid back rather than formal in its holding, is a support group. Finding support is what follows on from seeking clearness. Many activists find that it is helpful to have either an individual to whom they can regularly go to "chew the cud", or a group for what Tova Green calls "reflection, challenge and affirmation".

People use lots of different terms in their own ways for different kinds of group, but we would suggest that a support group is not quite the same as a steering group. It is not there to tell or direct a person as to what to do. Rather, as one activist told Green for her chapter in a wonderful little book about these matters, *Insight and Action*, a support group is; "...a safe place for me to have feelings about what is happening in the world, and the opportunity to feel and heal helps. When I do that I feel better and can keep working for the world."[203]

As with a clearance group, a support group is ideally made up of a circle of what are sometimes called "critical friends". Here "critical" is meant both in the sense of playing a critical role in our lives, but also being critical in the sense of questioning, challenging, educating and encouraging - and sometimes suggesting when we need to stop. It's one thing to try to "walk in the light". Quite another, to suffer "burnout", of which Katrina Shields writes:[204]

> Burning-out is a downward spiral. When we cut ourselves off from sources of nourishment, be they the natural environment, loved ones, or from inner spiritual sources of renewal and inspiration, the problems compound. We get more and more caught up in the delusion of separateness. Like a ring-barked tree, we are surrounded by nourishment but unable to let it in. We can lose the sense of wonder at what is still unspoilt in this world and the daily miracles before our eyes. In our quest for a better world, we may be failing to take action on the one thing we can really do something about - our own lives.

Support groups, as Shields puts it, can help us "to spark without incineration". However, care should be taken that the group does not itself become a burden, either to the person (or people) being supported, or to the critical friends who give their time. It is wise to build in clear limits to what is expected, including what Quakers call "the ministry of laying down" - the recognition that winding something up is every bit as much a service to the cause, as getting it going was in the first place. In fact, probably more so given the lack of glamour.

Mentoring and eldership

Many of the forms of activism for social and environmental change that are so familiar today took shape in the counterculture of the 1960s. The spark was a heady combination of pollution, racism, sexism, sexuality, global poverty and the Vietnam war. Part of what made all this possible was the youth, and young of spirit, finding the courage and seeing the necessity to break with the past. The "generation gap" and its product, the "rebel without a cause", needed to happen. Yet as we saw in Chapter One, this all too easily yielded to the narcissism of the "rebel without a clue".

Now that we have made it to the 21st century, many activists are rethinking the value of eldership - of valuing and drawing upon people who stand out not so much because of their age - because they can be chronologically young - but for their skill as mentors. A mentor is a "wise advisor". Originally in *The Odyssey*, Mentor was an advisor to Telemachus; in fact, often the goddess Athena in disguise, the companion of heroes.

The mythologist Joseph Campbell says that all of us are heroes in the making. All are on a sacred journey that begins with the *departure* when our boat of life is pushed out upon the river, and most of who we are was made by the family and community that brought us into being. That moves on to the *initiation,* when we hit the rocks and rapids of life and need to find our courage. Finally, as we reach the ocean, is the *return.* Here, as navigators of the soul, we help restore the flow of life back into our communities.

What is critical to understand is that this is not about being "heroes" in the way the mainstream world uses that word: often, a form of grandstanding. This is a heroism of the karma yoga that we touched on earlier. Of Kipling's "two imposters" - success and failure - to be treated "just the same". This is about the ego dying, or rather, settling into the great self. It is, as Campbell puts it, the completion of a movement; "Full circle, from the tomb of the womb to the womb of the tomb."[205]

Why is that so hard? Precisely because we confuse the ego with the soul and fear its death. We therefore cling to outer things, to cracked cisterns, unaware that, as that Hebrew God-man-shaman Jesus put it; "Whoever finds their life will lose it, and whoever loses their life for my sake will find it."[206]

To take on a mentor, or to be one, or both at once, is not easy. Our individualistic culture is not well geared for it. As Richard Rohr says; "The current older generation of men in the United States has, to a great extent, not been mentored by their own fathers", resulting in overgrown teenagers, and "neither gender is ready for the work and adventure of a full life."[207]

To seek a mentor, or to serve as one, is no evening course. It runs the risk of crucifixion. All that we want to suggest to end this chapter is that such eldership in spiritual activism merits a fresh eye of understanding. We speak from the experience of having benefited in these ways more than we could describe, and from many helpers.

In his short story, *The Poet*, Hermann Hesse tells of Han Fook, who yearned to learn the poet's art, yet was so riddled through with contrary yearnings, that he became frustrated with and jealous of his teacher.[208] After many years he grew to feel overcome with bitter hatred for this man who, by setting him on a spiritual trajectory, had "cheated him" of an ordinary life.

One night he decided he would kill him. Talk of a shadowstrike! As he was about to throw himself upon his sleeping grey-haired teacher, the old man awoke. He smiled "with a sad sweetness and gentleness that disarmed his pupil."

"Remember, Han Fook," said the master softly. "You are free to do what you like. You may go to your home and plant trees, you may hate me and kill me, it makes very little difference."

"Oh, how could I hate you?" the young poet cried, in the breakdown of breakthrough. "That would be like hating heaven itself."

CASE STUDY

Desmond Tutu: Truth and Reconciliation

Archbishop Desmond Tutu of South Africa, by Rémy Steinegger
Creative Commons

Bombs had been going off left, right and centre. There had been explo-sions at the international airport in Johannesburg. Anything could happen. Up to the proverbial eleventh hour, Chief Buthelezi's Inkatha Freedom party had threatened to stay out of the election and we were all bracing ourselves for the most awful bloodletting. Mercifully he was persuaded to abandon his boycott. The country breathed an enormous sigh of relief.[209]

And so, on 27th April 1994, South Africa did what had been thought impossible. It held a peaceful democratic election, and Archbishop Des-mond Tutu thought he could look forward to a quiet retirement in 1996.

Life for an activist is rarely so straightforward. Soon Tutu found him-self at the forefront of a question that could hold the key to lasting peace in his country - that of how to deal with the past. The negotiated settlement, which had enabled a peaceful transition, ruled out a South African version of the Nuremberg trials for war crimes, but scope remained to bring individuals to trial. Some Afrikaaners suggested letting bygones be bygones, albeit forgetting how impossible that sentiment had been to achieve in their own bitter history with the British.

So it was that a process came about under which, for three years, the Truth and Reconciliation Commission considered 7,112 applications for amnesty by perpetrators of violence on all sides. The price of such amnesty was "full disclosure" of the truth. High standards were set, and only 849 amnesties granted. The process was controversial, being opposed by Steve Biko's family and defied by the former president PW Botha.

In general, though, it is credited as a remarkably successful attempt not to bury the past, but to come to terms with it. Tutu explains the spiritual principles underlying the idea in his account, which also acknowledges many of the limitations of the process. It is perhaps surprising that an archbishop should consider the chief principle to be not a Christian one, but one derived from indigenous African spirituality: *ubuntu*.[210]

> Ubuntu is very difficult to render into a Western language. It speaks of the very essence of being human. When we want to give high praise to someone we say he or she has ubuntu. This means they are generous, hospitable, friendly, caring and compassionate. They share what they have. It also means my humanity is caught up, is inextricably bound up, in theirs. It is not "I think therefore I am." It says rather: "I am human because I belong." I participate, I share. A person with ubuntu has a proper self-assurance that comes from knowing that he or she belongs in a greater whole and is diminished when others are tortured or oppressed, or treated as if they were less than who they are. To forgive is not just to be altruistic. It is the best form of self-interest. What dehumanises you, inexorably dehumanises me. Forgiveness gives people resilience, enabling them to survive and emerge still human despite all efforts to dehumanise them.

CHAPTER TEN

Into the Deeper Magic

Magic and redemption

We want to conclude by nodding towards some of the outer edges, or perhaps, inner arteries of spiritual activism, recognizing that these may impinge on the comfort zones. The further reaches of spiritual work have always been difficult to talk about. It riles those of a militantly atheist disposition and equally riles the conventionally religious. This is one reason why spiritual paths have often been treated as "occult" (hidden) or "esoteric" (belonging to an inner circle). True spirituality, though, being the practice of love, can never be sustained as an elite exercise.

When Carl Jung examined alchemy in the Western mystery tradition, he concluded that, like astrology, its chief importance lay in summing up archaic Western psychology. He believed its underlying intention was to transform the alchemist. Trying to change base metals into gold was, to an extent, a foil, which made it more acceptable to the world. Alchemy in its psychological sense was the work of transforming the base lead of an unreconstituted ego self into the spiritual gold of a realized self able to integrate the psyche and thereby be made whole. The philosopher's stone was a symbol of such transformation. The "magic" in question concerns inner realities, thus Starhawk, the American feminist and pagan activist witch, defines magic as; "the art of changing consciousness at will", and says it is a word that makes people uncomfortable because it puts them back in touch with power from which domination, and especially patriarchy, has estranged them. It restores stunted capacities to full responsiveness. Such magic is political. It shifts shapes and sets in course change. As such - to quote her again, more fully than before:[211]

Magic can be very prosaic. A leaflet, a lawsuit, a demonstration, or a strike can change consciousness... Those techniques, like any techniques, can be taught in hierarchical structures or misused in attempts to gain power-over. But their essence is inherently anti-hierarchical. As a means of gaining power-over, magic is not very effective - hence its association with self-deception, illusion, and charlatanry in our society. Magical techniques are effective for and based upon the calling forth of power-from-within, because magic is the psychology/technology of immanence, of the understanding that everything is connected.

As Jung looked back on his life he observed; "The experiences of the alchemists were, in a sense, my experiences, and their world was my world." Where alchemy had worked with matter, he worked with psyche, but with an *incarnate* spiritual understanding where the distinction between matter and psyche breaks down. Jung's last major dream was to see a huge stone high on a plateau - a philosopher's stone, as it were. At its base were carved the words; "And this shall be a sign unto you of Wholeness and Oneness."[212]

If spiritual reality is for real, we are invited to be "disciples" or followers of a "discipline" not in any blind cultic sense, but in that word's original meaning of *dis*, "to go through", and *capere*, "to take hold of". On such a path we can only ever be amateurs. A true amateur is not a dabbler, but a lover, with all the responsibility that entails. If we are not to wall our "enemies" into hells of our own making we have to try to love, recognizing them at some deep level as *worthy adversaries*. To imagine that we can kill another, literally or metaphorically, is one thing, and some people choose that path. However, if we are to limit our exercise of power to that of a sub-lethal martial art, then we must carry a duty of care towards others. How else can the spirals of violence be replaced with circles of forgiveness and reconciliation? That care can be frighteningly far-reaching.

Consider the following from Mikhail Bulgakov's classic of Russian magical realism, *The Master and Margarita*. Here Satan - humorously depicted as a foreign professor - is surrounded by all his "guests". Enter a recently beheaded newcomer. Says the host by way of welcome:[213]

You have always been a fervent proponent of the theory that when a man's head is cut off his life stops, he turns to dust and he ceases to exist. I am glad to be able to tell you in front of all my guests - despite the fact that their presence here is proof to the contrary - that your theory is intelligent and sound.

"Magic can be very prosaic" – Starhawk
This was the conclusion to a quiet Quaker meeting in Glasgow one sunny summer's Sunday afternoon. We even phoned Lynx to confess. They said; "But that's illegal!" We said; "Yes, so we'd like you to report us." End of story. *Alastair with Mary Roslin (seated) and Rosemary Milne, 24 July 2005.*

The wit shifts to chill if one sets such imagery in the context of real-life testimonies by psychopathic killers and wartime torturers.[214] Bulgakov's alchemy conjures up the spectre of living death. "With a shudder Margarita saw that the eyes in that dead face were alive, fully conscious and tortured with pain."

We who see ourselves as being in the business of trying to make a better world might be among the few who can reach out to those who made it worse. Again, *if spirituality is for real*, who is to say where stop the limits of our activism?

During the motorway protests of the 1990s, Alastair remembers standing around the fire on sub-zero night-watch at the Pollok Free State M77 protest in Glasgow. Earlier in the evening his companion, the protest's leader, Colin Macleod, already nursing stab wounds in the chest from a gang attack on the camp, had almost been assaulted for a second time by a former IRA protection racketeer who'd come down to join the protest, but wasn't fully settled within himself.

With everybody else asleep in their tents or tree houses, the two found themselves reflecting on the totemic symbolism of both the eagle and the bear. "See the eagle," Colin said. "It's often mobbed by smaller birds, but keeps on flying straight ahead. If it got distracted, it would never get a chance to find its food." Likewise the bear. The bear is the totem of clan Matheson, the IRA man's mother's name. "You can use or abuse that power," somebody had gently suggested to him when fists were raised. "You can live up to the name you carry, or you can let it down." And the tension defused. It was beautiful, but then, behind Colin's tough persona he was a man of greater substance, in Desmond Tutu's sense, of *ubuntu*.

"You know what, Alastair?" said Colin, quietly.

Sufficient time has elapsed since he passed away to directly quote him.

"This place is a fuckin' redemption centre."

"Redemption" is what Paulo Freire taught when he urged that the pedagogy of the oppressed is about universal liberation; including the rehumanization of oppressors; including those trapped in their tortured deadness, such as Bulgakov depicts.

Non-spiritual activism usually sidesteps or ridicules this point. Spiritual activism cannot do so. At a certain level, we are each other's keepers. Love is community. If we even slightly hope to change the world, we have to work with the many manifestations of living death.

"Do what you have to do with others," says Ram Dass. He had once been a Harvard psychiatrist and perhaps sometimes had to medicate people against their will. "But keep your heart open to them." Never close down another's possibility of redemption. As such, spiritual activism may entail pushing our adversary in the chest to make them fall with one hand, but with the other hand ready to catch them from behind.

To bless, to curse or to withhold?

To bless is a spiritual art, fine brushwork with a paint that flows less from us than through us. It can be as simple as a nod, a wink, a comment, a card, or a fleeting tap to the shoulder. In healthy societies the elders know how to pass the touch of blessing to apprentice walkers on the path. Such can be the lightest yet the most effective way to nudge the rudder of the ship.

Blessing is one thing, but to curse our adversaries - while tempting - is quite another. The early Quakers called the Devil "the Great Reasoner". It's never hard to make a rational case to call down fire upon the heads of others; politicians and soldiers do it all the time, but for spiritual warriors, a curse is a boomerang.

Straddled between curse and blessing, what options are open to us? One is to withhold blessing. Pussy Riot's protest in Moscow cathedral was a pronounced form of such delegitimization. To withhold blessing is to signal; "You may choose that course of action, but I (or we) cannot give my (or our) blessing."

If this sounds a little forceless, consider the alternative. To act harshly in spiritual work is harmful to us. It leads to our desensitization. That chips away at the lodestone in our spiritual compass. Experience also reveals a strange paradox; often, our adversaries will have a grudging admiration of us. They'll expect better of us and sense that we're pointing to a better way. This can be part of their journey of transformation.

We must never presume that our virtues render us assured of grace. Tom Forsyth of Scoraig, who founded the Isle of Eigg Trust for land reform, says that in the game of snakes and ladders; "You can fall down the spiritual ladder no matter how high up the board." That's another reason for having circles of trust comprised of people who are capable of, and have been given permission, to offer critical feedback.

That said, as our spiritual traction increases, so will our charismatic authority. We might keep in mind that a little goes a long way. As our voice deepens, so does its capacity to work magic with others. We might not always need to keep the volume set at maximum the way it was, back in the days of our suitably misspent youth! A few whispered words might be enough. It is more enduring to be a catalyst that's never used up than to be a force that gets spent; therein lies the alchemy.

Psychological honesty

To grow in awareness is to take on a *burden*. This is when, more and more, we start to glimpse our own complicity in some of the very things that we challenge. For example, we might deplore corporate capitalism, but how's the pension fund? The trick needs to be for the burden of awareness to become a *precious* burden; for our own ordinary humanity to point us towards that of God in others.

How can that happen? In part, by soul-searching honesty that nurtures a dignifying humility. For instance, Dr Martin Luther King Jr wrote about his debt to the Protestant anti-pacifist theologian, Reinhold Niebuhr. Niebuhr helped him "to recognize the illusions of a superficial optimism concerning human nature and the dangers of a false idealism". This opened up a way towards a "realistic pacifism" by which, King said; "I came to see the pacifist position not as sinless but as the lesser evil in the circumstances."[215] Outward honesty in life is one thing, but much more challenging is such inner psychological honesty, honesty with ourselves that is the foundation of authentic relationships with others. Far from avoiding points of view that might confront his beliefs, King sought them out and granted them house space in his psyche. It made him a better exponent of nonviolence, more able to dream the dream of rehumanizing even those who fell by the wayside of its standards.

Psychological honesty is both a personal and a cultural issue. Many of us live in cultures or subcultures, including families, that take for granted the lubrication of social realities with "little white lies". It can pass as "politeness" and "making people feel comfortable". But where this is the norm, even to try to live without white lies for just one day, or even for just one hour, can be hard going. It requires a discipline of mindfulness that asks: just how "little" are those white lies really? They distort the very fabric of reality and subtly erode community. They create a culture of what Scott Peck called "people of the lie", a syndrome that he saw as lying at the root of evil. He quotes Erich Fromm as saying:[216]

> Most people fail in the art of living not because they are inherently bad or so without will that they cannot lead a better life; they fail because they do not wake up and see when they stand at a fork in the road and have to decide. They are not aware when life asks them a question, and when they still have alternative answers.

Instead of answering the phone and saying, "The boss is in a meeting", why not be more mindful of the words used and say, with honesty; "The boss is not available right now"? Of course, that may have consequences. The boss may say, "Lying is part of your job description". Fine. Ask if you can carry that one forward when next you do your expenses!

Even such small things can become big things. Especially the small things! This is how spiritual activism works and how people can find that they have more power to change the world than they might ever have imagined. That's why God, on one of those thunderbolt days of old, could say to Jeremiah; "Run up and down every street in Jerusalem... Look high and low; search throughout the city! If you can find even one just and honest person, I will not destroy the city."[217] Just one person who is just and honest! It's probably best not to be naïve about such things, but it does stir the thought: could that conceivably be all it takes?

Meditation and mindful presence

In February 1980, Alastair was travelling overland back from Papua New Guinea and had reached Darjeeling on the Olde Hippie Trail. One morning, there was a knock on the guest-house door. There was a little old man. He had a birdlike face with lichen wisps of trailing beard and eyes of mountain blue that seemed to dream of far away.

He was a pedlar and explained, in broken English, that he hailed from over the nearby border with Sikkim. In his bag were all the usual tourist trinkets. One by one he emptied it out, displaying his wares and coming, lastly, to a silver Buddhist prayer wheel. He swung it round, uttering *Om mani padme hum*.

In experiments with meditation down the years, Alastair had sat for hours in the fug of incense-fumigated darkened rooms, trying to get high by interminably repeating those four words. Nothing had ever happened. His consciousness had remained resolutely locked in boring "normal" mode. Now, there was this little old man at the door.

"What do those words mean?" Alastair asked, playing the "daft laddie", already knowing about the *mani* diamond of the mind, and the *padme* lotus of the heart, with its roots deep in the mud, its stem in the waters of the unconscious, and its thousand-petalled blossom supposedly emanating the pure fragrance of being.

He knew, but he also knew he didn't know, and so he repeated the question; "What do those words *really* mean?"

The pedlar gazed with an intensity that remains etched to this day. "*Om mani padme hum*," he repeated. "God come to my heart."

If we don't at some level invite the divine into our hearts, it's probably not going to force an entry. The Qur'an says that if you take one step towards Allah, he will come running towards you; yet you must take a step. Meditation can be many things, but at deeper levels it's about more than just a quietening of the chatter of the monkey mind. It is the practice of *mindfulness*, of cultivating *presence* or awareness. It might be waiting for a passing pedlar to knock one day unbidden at the door. "When the student is ready, the teacher arrives." It might be the everyday mindful activism of walking down the street, looking to catch what might be thought of as *the activist moment* – those fleeting opportunities, gone if not immediately grabbed – to *see* another human being, to show them respect (*re-spect* – "to see again", or to see more deeply). Like Starhawk's sense of magic, it can be as simple as holding open a door, letting someone who needs it ahead in a queue, giving up a seat, smiling to a child, or greeting the Asian newsagent with *Assalamu alaikum.*

("Actually" - as we have both experienced - "We're Sikhs!")

Meditation can also be a formal practice: so many minutes a day, this *mudra* with the hands or that, one teacher or another.

Matt practises *Metta bhavana* meditation in the Buddhist tradition. He considers this especially valuable for enabling activists to perceive their opponents in their full humanity, but it requires regular practice to have any real effect. *Metta* means loving-kindness, or good will, and this form of meditation trains the psyche in the cultivation of *metta* in four carefully choreographed stages.

The meditator may spend some time settling the monkey mind in preparation. Then, in the first stage, *metta* is directed towards the self. This is not easy because of the distorted images we carry of ourselves. So, within this first stage particular qualities of *metta* are practised: the four "immeasurables" of friendship, compassion, joy and equanimity (or even-handedness). By bringing to awareness our own capacity to love, alongside our need for love and the conflicts and anxieties with which we struggle, it becomes possible to experience a form of self-acceptance that is free, at least to some extent, from the harsh evaluations we might otherwise place upon ourselves or adopt from others.

In the second stage, you call to mind someone for whom you have no strong feelings one way or the other, and direct *metta* towards them by going again through the four "immeasurables": friendship, compassion, joy and equanimity. You think of their good points and their faults, and with this real picture in mind, wish for them all the happiness and fulfilment that you desire for yourself.

In the third stage, you go through the same process for someone you positively like - a friend or family member, perhaps developing an awareness of the biases which can make your love less real, less true, less authentic.

Finally, in the fourth stage, you think of someone you actively dislike, typically a work colleague. Of course, it is more challenging to direct genuine *metta* towards them. You become aware of the subjectivity of your judgements, how limited your compassion can be. However, the mind is powerful enough to learn equanimity towards such a person. They have good points and faults just like you. They long for happiness too, and suffer like anyone else, perhaps in secret ways that would make a mockery of your judgments. With equanimity, it becomes possible to wake up to the reality of that person and to direct *metta* towards them without inauthenticity. It requires patience like any other skill, but it is achievable. As the religious historian Karen Armstrong puts it; "practiced over time, this meditation can make a compassionate groove in your mind."

The challenge she issues towards the end of her book on compassion is eventually to use the final stage of this meditation to direct *metta* towards an "enemy with a capital E".[218] In order to get anywhere in such a meditation, you have to get real to your true feelings of anger and resentment, and the reasons for them. For the activist, they may be particularly good reasons. But this is just the start; from here we may discover that this hatred has become grafted into our own identity, or that there are striking resemblances between aspects of our own character and something similar in our enemy. As Jung taught, if you want to know what your shadow looks like, think of the person you most despise. From here, we can move towards equanimity, and from there, compassion.

The power of this meditation is that it recognizes the importance of getting real to the work of love. Activists who wish love to be a gloss over the truth, or who think of peace as a matter of good manners enabling dialogue, are only burying bad news that will inevitably resurface another day. It's hard to stay alive to the reality of another's complex humanity when we find ourselves in conflict with them. The urge to reduce the other to fit our mental categories can be overwhelming. Other people, though, enemies included, are not just "text" that we have constructed in our minds (as some post-modernists would have it). Glorious and inconvenient as it may be, they are our brothers and sisters.

Ideally, this is where the spiritual activist starts. It's the starting point of the *Bhagavad Gita*: the question, how do I fight (or hold fast to my integrity with) my own flesh and blood? Sometimes it takes all our courage and tenacity not to be sucked back into the consensual trance where enemies are simply bad and the answer is to get rid of them - assassinating Hitler, Saddam, or the noisy neighbour.

Prayer on the interior battlefield

Prayer reveals a spectrum ranging from the formal and petitionary - such as set prayers with responses in a place of public worship - to free-ranging inner "conversations" with the divine in wordless contemplation. There is little to distinguish prayer from meditation. The one flows into the other, though in the contemporary West the mention of prayer can invoke the Christian cringe, just as meditation, amongst some Christians, can invoke a cringe and the New-Age put-down around free-range spirituality. No need to get so uptight. In Hinduism, all reality is *lila*, the "cosmic play" of the divine. We, too, are invited to the playground. It's said that religion is like a swimming pool: most of the noise comes from the shallow end.

Prayer also tends to be more cognitive, more word-based, and more "God-talk"-centred, while meditation is more likely to rest with ineffable principles such as *no-thing-ness* (which is not to be confused with the empty nihilism of "nothingness").

Like meditation, prayer is a bringing of awareness to the ingredients of life. It can be touchingly simple. A child's prayer at night; "God bless mummy and daddy, granny and granddad, and all the people that we love, Amen!" The notion of "talking to God" and of a "personal" God can seem weird, even regressive. Why should we have a problem with per-sonification, though? Consider: if human life emerges out of the divine, is it not conceivable that the same, or even greater depths, of love and inti-macy might be as possible, as they are with other human beings? Do we have to be so guarded about such potential intimacy? After all, a sense that the divine is somehow with us and in us - our friend of friends, as well as transcendently beyond us - can come in handy! There's the story of the little boy who took two cakes from a baking tray in the kitchen.

"*Johnny?*" calls out his mother, in *that* tone of voice.

"God said that I could take one," retorts Johnny, quickly.

"Then why did you take a second?"

"God said - *grab one for me too!*"

Joking apart, contemplative prayer - which is indistinguishable from meditation - is specifically pitched towards mystical intimacy. In the following exercise, Anthony de Mello SJ translates the *Om mani padme hum* mantra in to a Christian form. He calls such interfaith cross-fertilization, *God in my breath*.[219]

> Close your eyes and become aware of body sensations for a while... Then become aware of your breathing as described in the previous exercise and stay with this awareness for a few minutes...
>
> Now reflect that this air that you are breathing in is charged with the power and presence of God... Think of the air as of an immense ocean charged with God... While you draw the air into your lungs you are drawing God in...
>
> Notice what you feel at the thought that you are drawing God in with each breath...
>
> While you breathe in imagine God's Spirit coming into you... Fill your lungs with its divine energy...
>
> While you breathe out imagine you are ejecting all your impurities... your fears... your negative feelings...
>
> Imagine your whole body becoming radiant and alive...

At yet another level, prayer can be the heart's seeing - the exercise of the heart as an organ of intuitive perception - a *scrying* or inner discernment. The English Quaker, Roy Stephenson, speaks of "putting oneself in a place where one tries to see things with God's eyes". This entails "accepting great risk, because what a situation needs could mean self-sacrifice". Paradoxically, to be receptive to such a God's-eye-view is "[to] be our true selves, and yet enable something greater than ourselves".[220]

The implications for activists are far-reaching. Says Walter Wink; "Prayer is... the interior battlefield where the decisive victory is first won, before engagement in the outer world is even attempted". If unprotected by prayer, he concludes, "our social activism runs the danger of becoming self-justifying good works, as our inner resources atrophy, the wells of love run dry, and we are slowly changed into the likeness of the Beast."[221]

Of runes and dreams

It is not uncommon among radical activists for divination to be used in an attempt to guide difficult work. This rests on the ancient principle that, as Jung surmized; "Whatever is born or done in this moment of time has the quality of this moment of time".[222] In an interconnected universe, the microcosm and the macrocosm are held to reflect one another. According to

this way of looking at things, to throw an *I Ching* hexagram, lay out a tarot pack, draw up an astrological chart or cast dice such as the biblical *urim* and *thummim,* is to touch base with the divine patterning of reality.

While such practices might be ripe for self-delusion, it is probably fair to say that they can offer frameworks of symbolic meaning, the motifs of which can serve to bring unconscious processes into consciousness. As such, divination techniques could be seen as aids to imaginative visioning and akin to dream interpretation. Here we will confine our discussion to dreams, as these can speak to everybody's experience.

Freud described dreams as "the royal road to the unconscious". It can be revealing as activists to ask what our dreams might be showing us. How might the feelings, associations and motifs that they evoke shed light on actual events that are happening, or perhaps even, about to happen? Here is an example.

Alastair and his wife, Vérène Nicolas, had been working with a group of rural development officials over several years. They came from a part of the world that had experienced brutal American-backed military repression. Often, they still had to wrestle with corrupt political and corporate power. On this occasion, the group were on a week-long training in spiritual activism. As the levels of psychospiritual depth increased, they reached a point of starting to talk about the dangers of their work back home. The fear of being arrested and the knowledge of what happened in police and military prisons. The bag pulled out of the river containing the body of a neighbour's grandfather. That kind of thing.

Alastair went to bed that night feeling troubled for their safety. In the early hours of the next morning he had a vivid dream. He was sitting in the back of a bus in a British city, a centre of government. Two sharp-suited men nearby rose from their seats. They moved in on him with an air of suffocating evil. These were American intelligence agents. They tried to wrest his computer away, wanting to remove a memory chip that contained his work and contacts. The struggle proceeded in an eerie silence. Just as he could feel his strength failing, he saw a further two men rising from their seats at the front of the bus. Unbeknown to him, Alex George and Rusty - village friends from childhood days back on the Isle of Lewis - were also travelling on the bus. Burly men of crofter stock, they moved slowly up the aisle to give protection. The intelligence agents saw them coming. They realized that Alastair had a strong support base from within his own community. At that, they evaporated.

On awakening, it felt like it had been a "big" dream - a significant one. Alastair lay for half an hour reflecting on its possible meanings; the way in which the psyche, both individually and perhaps collectively, might be trying to organize his experience and shed insight. That evening, one of the course participants asked to speak privately through a trusted interpreter. He said how important the training programme was becoming in his community. He had already trained a team of ten others like him, but this was starting to draw unwelcome attention from powerful interests. Also, his attendance on this course abroad was being monitored by his country's security agency.

Alastair read this as a cue to tell the man the dream. It fitted like a key into a lock. It underscored the need to carry out the work of transformation from a base of solid grounding within one's wider community. The man observed that this can't be achieved overnight. It takes time to build up understanding, support, trust, sufficient goal convergence and a shared hunger and courage for fundamental change. Violence functions on the short temporal wavelength. Nonviolence operates more slowly on the long wave. While that's happening, in solidarity is safety. Old school friends can be there with one for more than just reunions. As graffiti on a wall in Nicaragua had it; "Solidarity is the tenderness of the people."

Living with a prophet

Spiritual activism can therefore bring up heavy and deeply-energized issues. Our lives extend beyond our own and into those of others. This brings joy but can also place strains both on ourselves and on those closest to us. To live with a partner who tosses and turns in crazy dreams all night and who is polygamously married to vital causes is not an easy shout. (*Hello Vérène! Hello Kath!*). Prophetic calling, even when a very much lower case "p" and part-time, can be a right pain for everybody else!

The Sufi holy fool, Mullah Nasrudin, was asked by his friend who was about to marry whether he himself had ever considered marriage. Nasrudin replied that he had. He'd once tried to find the perfect woman. In Damascus he found a woman who was beautiful and gracious but lacked a spiritual side. In Isfahan he met someone who was beautiful, gracious and spiritual, but somehow they did not communicate well. Finally, in Cairo he found the perfect woman: beautiful, gracious, spiritual – and easy to relate to.

"Well," asked the Mullah's friend. "Did you marry her?"

"No," said Nasrudin. "Unfortunately, she was looking for the perfect man."

The spiritual journey is in itself a marriage – a gradual uniting with the divine. The *Song of Solomon* from the Jewish tradition says it in lusciously erotic language, as do the poems of Mahadeviyakka who considered Shiva, the Zeus of Hinduism, to be her lover. Christianity speaks of becoming "participants in the divine nature". In Tantric Buddhism, spiritual union finds human expression where Sky Dancer, Yeshe Tsogyel, joins in cosmic ecstasy with Padmasabhava, who brought Buddhism from India to Tibet.

Spiritual marriage can be directly with God and/or in human conjunction. In the latter case, a marriage is not so much about two people, as three. Understood in this way, the divine is at the centre of a human marriage. It is that of God in one that marries that of God in the other, and so we transcend our limitations. "We marry none; it is the Lord's work," said George Fox of the Quakers.

Relationships today are very diverse and most of us have had our share of trials and disappointments. We raise the matter only because activists are people who, from time to time, burn with passion. Our deepest love for others and our activism may share a common source. The cleaner burns the flame, the more we see the heart of the fire. Both our love lives and our activism entail a shift from unconscious to conscious relationships. As John Welwood says; "Something vast inside us connects with something vast in another."[223] No wonder poor Nasrudin found it heavy going!

Erotic activism

"I think that Heaven is the fulfilment of the erotic," says the Reverend Ian Fraser of the Church of Scotland. As he approaches his first century of life, this Presbyterian clergyman is the most elderly member of the Iona Community. He explains:[224]

> In our earthly life we can experience... the colour of God's money thrown on the table in the gamble for life's transformation in justice, truth and peace. Lovers who search one another out to the point where they pour their beings into one another anticipate a larger heavenly fulfilment.

Has the old boy lost his marbles? More likely, found them! The German liberation theologian Dorothee Söelle says; "One cannot think of mystical experience and certainly not speak of it without eroticism. All religions testify to intersections of Eros and religion that arise from a sacred power."[225]

Audre Lorde, the Caribbean-American "lesbian, mother, warrior, poet" would have concurred. She wrote in an essay; "Uses of the Erotic: the Erotic as Power":[226]

> There are many kinds of power, used and unused, acknowledged or otherwise. The erotic is a resource within each of us that lies in a deeply female and spiritual plane, firmly rooted in the power of our unexpressed or unrecognized feeling. In order to perpetuate

itself, every oppression must corrupt or distort those various sources of power within the culture of the oppressed that can provide energy for change. For women, this has meant a suppression of the erotic as a considered source of power and information within our lives.

For Lorde, the truly erotic is "the personification of love in all its aspects... the passions of love, in its deepest meanings". The true experience of Eros is the enjoyment of *sensation* – and not just sexual sensation – with the heart's capacity for *feeling* fully engaged. She contrasts this with pornographic relationship where sensation is dead to the heart's feeling.

Through such a lens, the whole of consumerism – consumption in excess of dignified sufficiency – could be defined as being pornographic. That's what's wrong with naked capitalism where there is no heartfelt connection. It's pornographic. It implies, as Sigmund Freud and Wilhelm Reich first glimpsed, that many of the world's problems are erotic dysfunctions. *Om mani padme hum* is the antidote with its reconnection to the heart. As the Buddhist activist Joanna Macy puts it, this means coming to see the material world not so much as a battlefield of good and evil, as a trap from which we must escape with a transcendent spirituality, but as our lover. "World as lover, world as self."[227] This is an immanent spirituality that grounds the transcendent in the here-and-now. It is "incarnate", coursing through carnality. Anything less would be obscene.

The quickening

We have been talking about the ways of magic, and reached what C.S. Lewis in the *Chronicles of Narnia* called; "the deeper magic from before the dawn of time". Here, says Lewis, "death itself would start working backwards". Such is salvation; the "salving" or healing of our deepest wounds. Those wounds are the consequences of that cringe-inducing little word "sin" as defined in the liberation theology of Gustavo Gutiérrez; "the deepest root of all servitude; for sin is the breaking of friendship with God and with other human beings."[228]

In mystical cosmology, this "deeper magic" is *apocatastasis*; the revelation of all that is, was and will be in all its abundance. As in the title of

Donovan's 1968 compilation album, "Like it is, Was, and Evermore shall be." Or as in the words of the original old hymn, "which wert, and art, and evermore shalt be."

Here is reality, including human-beingness, outside of the constraints of space and time. This is the sacred time of eternity as distinct from the interminable mathematical time of infinity. Eastern orthodoxy portrays it as becoming "one as all things... a return from many to one."[229] Here, "the past is entirely preserved and the present open" because "everything points to and is totally present to the eye of the Eternal."[230] That is how death starts "working backwards", the mystical understanding of "resurrection".

These ideas are found not just in the early Christian mystics, but in the Vedic sages of India and the poetry of the early Celtic bards. The latter describe the "green world" of the ever-young, *Tír na nÓg*, the timeless realm of faerie.[231] Such "deeper magic" sustains the activist's hope and feeds the roots of life when all else, all of lesser depth, has run dry. Yes, we remain immersed in the suffering of the world, our own included; but like a storm raging in the bottom of the valley, the higher we climb the mountain the more we see it in proportion. Then our lives *quicken*.

"Quick" is one of those strange old Saxon words, rarely used today. The "quick" are the living who contrast with the dead. A mother "quickens with child" when she feels the first movement in her womb. "The quick" is the tender, sensitive part of the body, akin to the marrow, thus we might get "chilled to the quick". When Thomas Hardy writes that; "Tess's breath *quickened*," he implies more than just a huffing and puffing. Thus, too, the original wording of an Iona Community prayer; "Quicken us in mind and in spirit."

One of the most mystical lyrics to have emerged from English rock music is Led Zeppelin's *Stairway to Heaven*.[232] Robert Plant had reputedly been reading works of Celtic magic and hinted that the lyrics were channelled from beyond.[233] In the song the materialistic world - where "all that glitters is gold" and the path to Heaven can be bought - is contrasted with the spiritual world; a quickening of nature "when I look to the west,/ And my spirit is crying for leaving".

Here, expressed in everyday culture, is *apocatastasis*, that cosmic restoration where "the piper will lead us to reason./ And a new day will dawn for those who stand long,/ And the forests will echo with laughter."

Here, in the bustle in the hedgerow, is the "May queen", the "Dear lady".

Her stairway to Heaven is what the Franciscan priest, Richard Rohr, calls the "true liminal" - the threshold between the worlds.[234] This is the line the shaman must cross to bring back healing for the people. This is the path that, as the lyrics have it, "lies on the whispering wind."

Here, facing "our shadows taller than our soul," we meet the Lady, the feminine divine, "Who shines white light and wants to show/ How everything still turns to gold.../ When all are one and one is all."

"Ooh, it makes me wonder."

On the field of Truth, on the battlefield of life, what came to pass, Sanjaya?

In Scottish folklore, the Highland soldier dying on the battlefield quickens in his last breath. His blinded eyes open to a beatific vision. The weary guns at last fall quiet, and he whispers to his comrades: "The Pipes! The Pipes!"

"Then the piper will lead us to reason."

That's what came to pass, Sanjaya.

"Ooh, it really makes me wonder."

CASE STUDY

Gehan Macleod: Urban Poverty and Rural Vision

Gehan Macleod by Muhammad Idrees Ahmad
GalGael Trust, 2015

In 1989, the British government announced what it called the "largest road building program for the UK since the Romans" to advance prime minister Margaret Thatcher's vision of "the great car economy". Many were outraged, especially in the face of mounting concerns about climate change. Some took to tree houses at protest camps, placing life, limb and reputations in the way of politicians and developers who came to rip the woodlands apart.

Some defined themselves by nonhierarchical anarchist values. Others, by dietary choices such as vegetarianism, or an eco-pagan spirituality. Here was a communitarianism, even a tribalism, that rejected advanced capitalism in favour of togetherness. Their names said it all. The Dongas Tribe of Twyford Down. The Flowerpot Tribe of Jesmond Dene. The Autonomous Area of Wanstonia, on a motorway just outside London.

Gehan Macleod was born Gehan Ibrahim in Essex in the 1970s. Her mother is an Anglo-Scot; her father, an Egyptian Muslim. She left university without graduating, preferring to cut her teeth at the University of Life. She met her future husband, Colin Murdo Macleod, in direct action at Twyford Down in Hampshire. She was also involved in protests against Britain's weapons of mass destruction - Trident nuclear submarines - at the Faslane Peace Camp in Scotland.

In the early 1990s, Colin started the Pollok Free State protest camp at the M77 motorway construction site in Glasgow. Their family - eventually Tawny, Iona and Oran - began in a tree house, which must have been the most awe-inspiring home that any child could imagine.

After several years of holding ground, the battle was lost. The M77 was driven through. However, the wider war was won convincingly.

Public support for new roads had collapsed and, in 1996, the government slashed £4 billion off its construction budget. Colin's response was; "We've shown what we were against. Now let's show them what we're for."

The Pollok Free State had been a folk school, a people's free university, a place of social levelling where people came to learn rustic skills and use tools; to share their food and stories, their music and humanity.

The GalGael Trust was formally founded in 1997. In Scots and Irish Gaelic the *Gal* are the strangers and the *Gael,* the heartland people.

"We're all GalGael now" was the motto. Many of us are strangers in today's world, but with indigenous roots and needing to rebuild communities of place upon the ground on which we tread.

In 2005, Colin suddenly passed away at the age of thirty-nine. Gehan was left to press on and, with immense courage and effectiveness, grow the GalGael Trust. Today, many hundreds of people from Glasgow's hard-pressed ship-building district of Govan have been through training programmes such as *Journey On*. These teach basic work skills using hand tools, just like the ethic passed from hand to hand around the Free State's campfire.

GalGael is also renowned for building traditional wooden boats. These carry folks on trips down the river Clyde. In this way, the city and its rural hinterland find reconnection. The boats and voyages are metaphors for life's journey - the departure, the initiation, and the return - opening out new vision. Gehan has to wrestle endlessly to balance people issues and project funding, but what matters most, she tells us, is *spiritual bravery*:

Spiritual bravery is the willingness to go beyond what is traditionally perceived as "right" or "wrong" so as to discern the correct action at each moment. Colin had shed-loads of that kind of bravery. It ruffled a lot of feathers. But grains of truth were shaken free in the process. It means to live each moment by balancing head, heart and hand not by the day-to-day dogma that keeps you "in the right", but by being willing to take the risk with each step that you may be wrong. Being wrong can be a wonderful thing. It's learning. It's growth. It is the kind of vulnerability that opens up the space of solidarity. It's connection.

AFTERWORD

This is a terrible time to be advocating spiritual activism! If you've read this far, or even if you've just sneaked ahead, you might be wondering what sort of a medieval planet we've been living on.

As we worked on this book, the bodies of French cartoonists were being laid into the ground. Shortly afterwards, the so-called "Islamic" State burned a Jordanian pilot alive in a cage. Next, twenty-one Coptic Christians were beheaded on a lonely Mediterranean beach. So it is that the litany of violence rolls on, an eye for an eye, tooth for tooth, sanctioned in God's holy name.

Flip to the other side of that particular balance sheet, and historically the West colonized the Middle East more deeply than almost any other part of the world. In 2001, George W Bush launched the recent wave of warfare, calling it; "This crusade, this war on terrorism". The mission in Afghanistan was codenamed *Operation Infinite Justice,* until protestors pointed out that such an attribute usurps the role of God. In 2003, the invasion of Iraq was carried out by *Shock and Awe* - a terror doctrine dreamed up by the US Defence University. Later, it was reported that Tony Blair had felt his part in the proceedings to be a religious obligation.

As Iraq turned sour and body bags came home, Donald Rumsfeld's daily intelligence briefings to Bush ceased to feature cartoons on their covers. They carried Bible quotes instead. No great surprise, therefore, when in 2010 ABC News broke the story that Trijicon rifle sights - widely used by both the US and British forces - had Bible references coded into their embossed model numbers. Finally, in a national commemoration of the Afghan War at St Paul's cathedral in March 2015, the Archbishop of Canterbury blessed a cross brought in by soldiers. It had been made out of brass casings from used artillery shells; weapons fired to maim and kill.

Shocked and awed, what can we say before such poisoning of the spiritual well? We can attack religion as a whole and join the "new" atheists in treating life as a vast engineering project. Or, we can confront the fact that public religion has been hijacked, stoned and crucified by the god of war. Then we must put up resistance as "the secret of possessing joy". Such is why, in the aftermath of the Charlie Hebdo massacre, we applaud the Muslim Council of Britain for having posted on its website; "Nothing justifies the taking of life... Nothing is more immoral, offensive and insulting against our beloved Prophet than such a callous act of murder."[235]

This book has been about the need to understand the way corrupted power will always seek to colonize the soul. Our deepest activism must therefore be to decolonize; to set the soul free. We must refuse to collude in writing off its grace and power by othering the spiritual, by letting it be rendered impotent. We have seen how Gandhi lived the full spectrum of such spiritual activism. To those who wonder where to start, remember how he started: as a young man, he willingly stuffed envelopes for Congress members. Later, on the road to independence, he addressed them.

Adrienne Rich was a poet of both Jewish and Southern Protestant heritage. She said that we must cast our lot "with those/ who age after age, perversely/ with no extraordinary power/ reconstitute the world."[236] Such is the Beloved Community. Such is Heaven on Earth, where we belong.

Only then, shall we walk fearless even through the harrowed fields of Hell. Only then, the joyous anthem; "stardust... golden... and we've got to get ourselves/ Back to the garden."

Walk on, dear friends, stand in your love and power, go out to bless and be blessed. This is, indeed, a terrible time to be advocating "spiritual" activism. That's why the time is right.

A website with events and materials supporting this book is at:
www.alastairmcintosh.com/spiritualactivism/

GLOSSARY

Atman - in Hinduism, the individual level of soul which, at its ultimate depth, is one with **Brahman**.

Bhagavad Gita - a central portion in the sacred epic, the *Mahabharata*, sometimes called the gospel of Hinduism.

Buddha Nature - Roughly akin to Jung's deep Self, the Christ within, and Hinduism's "thou art that" where **Atman** is **Brahman**. Buddha Nature is the universal in us all.

Brahman - in Hinduism, the universal Spirit, similar to God in monotheistic religions.

Christian Bible - term for the New Testament that allows for recognition that for Jews the "Old Testament" is the complete Bible. See **Hebrew Bible**.

Conscientisation - in popular education and liberation theology, the process of people coming to an awareness of the structural injustices of their society and world; a synthesis of conscience and consciousness. It is the first stage of individuals and communities being able to work for change.

Dharma - Indian term (sometimes spelt Dhamma) common to Buddhism, Hinduism, Jainism and Sikhism. Loosely translates as the Way, the (natural) Law, or the Truth. Implies a divine core of reality which, if we discern and are true to it, leads to social and ecological harmony.

Epistemology - the study of the nature and structure of knowledge, asking deep questions about how we know things.

Essentialism - in philosophy, the idea that a whole thing (eg a person) can have its own inner being, vitality, soul or essence, which gives cohesion and is more than the sum of its parts. This idea is rejected by **materialism**.

Frankfurt School - a loose affiliation of social theorists associated with the Institute for Social Research at the Goethe University in Frankfurt. Many sought to reinvigorate Marxism, which was being narrowly interpreted to support European communist parties. Relevant names for us include Max Horkheimer (philosopher, sociologist and social psychologist), Theodore Adorno (philosopher, sociologist and musicologist), Eric Fromm (psychoanalyst), and Herbert Marcuse (philosopher).

Hebrew Bible - term for what Christians call the "Old Testament", acknowledging that for Jews there is nothing "old" about it. See **Christian Bible**.

I Ching - an ancient Taoist and Confucian divination text, in which short mystical texts are consulted, corresponding to the fall of either coins or yarrow stalks.

Materialism - in philosophy, materialism is the belief that only matter (and energy) exist - there is no soul, spirit or divine milieu.

Metaphysics - literally "beyond" or "behind" the physical - the study of intangibles and abstractions. Often and in our usage, a philosopher's way of talking about the spiritual.

Modernism - the history of Western thought is often divided into three eras. From the pre-Socratic philosophers of ancient Greece up to René Descartes (1596-1650) is considered pre-modern. Modernism covers the era from Descartes until the 20th century, and is associated with science, materialism, the 18th-century Enlightenment, the rise of reason and the conquest of nature. It mostly assumes an ability to take an objective view that leads to truth - an assumption that **postmodernism** challenges.

Mysticism - a strand running through all religious traditions, which is less concerned with religious tradition and doctrine, and more with direct spiritual experience. Mystics insist that the source of life cannot be known by the intellect alone, only through direct relationship and with the heart. The mystics report similar ideas and experiences across cultures, emphasizing the unity of all things, the centrality of love, and the importance of encounter with transcendent realities. In its intellectual expression, also called the "Perennial Philosophy".

Ontology - in philosophy, the study of the nature and structure of being and existence.

Postmodernism - see **modernism**. Post-modernists question the modernist assumption that there can be a neutral perspective from which to arrive at objective conclusions. Instead, they say, everything we know is subjective. What we think is solid - like the category of gender, or soul, can be "deconstructed" to show that it was a social construction. Because post-modernists, like modernists, tend to think reason is the only way of knowing anything, this leads many to the conclusion that ultimate reality is not knowable, and may not even be real.

Premodernism - see **modernism**. Pre-modernism considered **metaphysics** - the spiritual realm - to be central to understanding the world. The Earth was thought of as a living entity and not a dead machine. Everyone had a soul. Ethics were essential to the organization of public and private life. This was often mixed up with a lot of superstition, as well as not treating some categories of people as fully human. That acknowledged, the term can also cover ancient wisdom, indigenous worldviews and emergent neo-paganism and re-indigenization.

Satyagraha - Gandhi's word, meaning truth force, soul force, reality force or God force. For him it was the best way to explain the power of nonviolent direct action to bring about change. When speaking truth to power, or demonstrating it, such truth has its own power, so long as it is not obscured by the denial of other truths, such as the innate human dignity of the enemy.

Secular – 1. of government – adhering to the principle of keeping religion and state separate at the level of administration. 2. commonly used to mean "non-religious" in a wider sense, as in "secular thinker" or "secular discipline".

Shadow – in **transpersonal psychology**, the unprocessed emotional baggage we all carry, unawares. Shadow-work involves becoming more aware of our potential for being side-tracked by ego and neuroses, and trying to deal with potential issues as they arise.

Shadowstrike – term developed by Alastair in teaching spiritual activism for how the shadow can trip people up, lashing out in unexpected and inappropriate ways.

Spiritual abuse – just as people can be abused sexually or psychologically, our spiritual nature can be abused. Religions and cults can force spiritual practices on people or use them to their own ends at the cost of the individual's sense of integrity and authentic spirituality.

Tao – in Taoism (also spelt Daoism), Tao roughly translates as the Way, the Truth, or the Principle. It is the primal reality behind the outward manifestation of the hundred thousand things of the created world, the interplay of the complementary forces of Yin and Yang.

Tao Te Ching – (also spelled *Dao De Jing* or *Daodejing*) sacred text of Taoism, credited to Lao Tzu (also spelled Laozi). Sometimes simply called the *Laozi*.

Transpersonal psychology – psychology that allows for a spiritual grounding of reality, for transformation beyond ego limitations, and a worldview open to the interconnection of all things.

Vipassana – a Buddhist school of meditation focused on developing insight into the nature of reality.

Zen – a mystical branch of Buddhism, heavily influenced by Taoism, which uses paradox and koans in its teachings to try to point to the spiritual core of reality.

RECOMMENDED READING

These have been some treasures on our journey.

Brueggemann, Walter, *Hopeful Imagination: Prophetic Voices in Exile*, Fortress, Philadelphia, 1986. *Brilliant commentary on the social and ecological activism of the Hebrew prophets, Jeremiah, Ezekiel and Isaiah, bringing them bang up to date.*

Cardeña, Etzel, Steven Jay Lynn & Stanley Krippner (eds), *Varieties of Anomalous Experience*, American Psychological Association, Washington, 2002. *Scholarly literature reviews including near-death, paranormal and mystical experiences.*

Day, Dorothy, *Loaves and Fishes: The Inspiring Story of the Catholic Worker Movement*, Orbis, Maryknoll, 1997. *Biography of a modern saint.*

Deikman, Arthur, *Meditations on a Blue Vase: the Foundations of Transpersonal Psychology*, Fearless Books, USA, 2014. *A lifetime's research on mystical perception, cult psychology and authentic spiritual leadership.*

Eisenstein, Charles, *The More Beautiful World Our Hearts Know Is Possible*, North Atlantic Books, Berkeley, 2013. *A radical vision of a way of knowing, being and doing that can offer hope in dark times.*

Freire, Paulo, *Pedagogy of the Oppressed*, Penguin, Harmondsworth, 1972. *Classic study of dehumanisation, rehumanisation through popular* (people's) *education.*

Friedman, Harris L. & Glen Hartelius (eds), *The Wiley-Blackwell Handbook of Transpersonal Psychology*, Wiley-Blackwell, London, 2013. *Scholarly overview of the emerging field of spiritual psychology. A landmark new textbook.*

Gilligan, James, *Violence: Reflections on a National Epidemic*, Vintage, New York, 1997. *The roots of psychopathic behaviour, and paths towards rehumanization - by a prison psychiatrist, married to the feminist thinker, Carol Gilligan.*

Leech, Kenneth, *Doing Theology in Altab Ali Park: A Project in Whitechapel, East London, 1990-2004*, Darton, Longman & Todd, 2006. *From the community-based theologian who founded Centrepoint for advocacy on homelessness.*

Gottlieb, Roger S. (ed), *This Sacred Earth: Religion, Nature, Environment*, Routledge, London, 1996. *A magisterial compendium on nature and the sacred; reprinting classic texts including indigenous, interfaith and activist contributors.*

Green, Peter, Peter Woodrow & Fran Peavey, *Insight and Action: How to Discover and Support a Life of Integrity and Commitment to Change*, New Society, Philadelphia, 1994. *First-rate handbook on clearness, discernment and support groups.*

Grof, Stanislav & Christina Grof (eds), *Spiritual Emergency: When Personal Transformation Becomes a Crisis*, Tarcher/Putnam, Los Angeles, 1989. *Top of the list for navigating the pitfalls and openings of spiritual growth.*

Hesse, Hermann, *Siddhartha*, Picador, London, 1973. *Beautiful fable of life's journey, gentle and joyful reading.*

Hirschfield, Jane (ed), *Women in Praise of the Sacred*, HarperCollins, NY, 1994. *43 centuries of spiritual poetry by women with excellent contextualising comments.*

Hope, Anne & Sally Timmel, *Training for Transformation: a Handbook for Community Workers* (4 volumes), Mambo Press, Zimbabwe, 1984 onwards. *Graphically applied liberation theology and Freirian pedagogy for grassroots development.*

Horwitz, Claudia, *The Spiritual Activist: Practices to Transform your Life, your Work and your World*, Penguin, NY, 2002. *Strong on rituals, stories and spiritual practices - "addiction is a denial of the present moment".*

Jacobi, Jolande, *The Psychology of C.G. Jung*, Routledge, London, 1942. *The classic account of the pioneering transpersonal psychologist's thought.*

James, William, *The Varieties of Religious Experience*, Fontana, Glasgow, 1960. *The century-old but seminal study of religious and mystical psychology.*

Jones, James, *Jesus and the Earth*, SPCK, London, 2003. *A beautiful little primer in ecotheology by the now-retired Anglican Bishop of Liverpool, who devotes much of his ministry to fresh understandings of the Creation.*

Kornfield, Jack, *A Path with Heart*, Bantam, New York, 1993. *Rich sharings from one of the world's great Western Buddhist teachers.*

Lerner, Michael, *The Left Hand of God: Healing America's Political and Spiritual Crisis*, HarperOne, USA, 2007. *A spiritual "politics of meaning" from the editor of "Tikkun" and founder of the Network of Spiritual Progressives.*

Macy, Joanna and Molly Young Brown, *Coming Back to Life: Practices to Reconnect Our Lives*, New Society, Gabriola Island, 1998. *A classic of practical exercises for those wrestling with their feelings about the state of the Earth.*

McIntosh, Alastair, *Soil and Soul: People versus Corporate Power*, Aurum Press, London, 2001. *Spiritual activism explored through land reform on the Isle of Eigg and the Isle of Harris superquarry campaign.*

Miller, Alice, *For Your Own Good: the roots of violence in child-rearing*, Virago, London, 1987. *Study of the childhoods of tyrants, questioning the childhoods of us all.*

Palmer, Parker J, *A Hidden Wholeness: The Journey Toward an Undivided Life*, Jossey-Bass, San Francisco, 2004. *A veteran Quaker teaching trust, clearness and discernment.*

Posey, Darrell Addison (ed), *Cultural and Spiritual Values of Biodiversity*, ITDG and United Nations Environment Programme, Nairobi, 1999. *Anthology and context from indigenous activists around the world speaking for the Earth.*

Nicholson, Shirley (ed), *Shamanism: An Expanded View of Reality*, Quest, Wheaton, Ill., 1997. *Not the most academic study, but a rich edited collection of shamanic experiences.*

Rohr, Richard, *Adam's Return: The five promises of male initiation*, Crossroads, NY, 2004. *Women's initiation follows different paths, yet much will speak to all.*

Roszak, Theodore, Mary Gomes & Allen Kanner (eds.), *Ecopsychology: Restoring the Earth; Healing the Mind*, Sierra Club, San Francisco, 2002. *Edited collection that helped establish ecological psychology.*

Rowland, Christopher (ed), *The Cambridge Companion to Liberation Theology*, Cambridge University Press, 2007. *Christianity in the process of liberation from churchianity – by analogy, also relevant to other faiths.*

Rowson, Jonathan, *Spiritualise: revitalising spirituality to address 21st century challenges*, RSA, London, 2014. *Helpful report on what spirituality means in Britain today.*

Sabini, Meredith (ed), *The Earth Has a Soul: C.G. Jung's Writings on Nature, Technology and Modern Life*, North Atlantic Books, US, 2002. *The most profound anthology of Jung's spiritual thought.*

Seed, John, Joanna Macy, Pat Flemming & Arne Næss, *Thinking Like a Mountain: Towards a Council of All Beings*, New Society, Gabriola Island, 1988. *John Seed is the grandfather of Australian deep ecology – a practical and reflective guide to doing and being.*

Shaw, Martin, *A Branch from the Lightning Tree: Ecstatic Myth and the Grace of Wildness*, White Cloud Press, Oregon, 2011. *Myth and story on the search for meaning in our times.*

Shields, Katrina, *In the Tiger's Mouth: An Empowerment Guide for Social Action*, Millennium Books, Newtown NSW, 1991. *Brilliant on the "heart politics" of kindling vision and avoiding burnout – a dear book from a veteran Australian activist.*

Starhawk, *The Empowerment Manual: a Guide for Collaborative Groups*, New Society, USA, 2011. *Fearlessly tackles such prickly issues as leadership for leaderless groups, conflict and working with difficult people.*

Tart, Charles T. (ed), *Altered States of Consciousness*, Anchor, NY, 1969. *Dated but timeless: a foundation stone of transpersonal psychology.*

Walker, Alice, *Revolutionary Petunias*, The Women's Press, London, 1988. *Poetry to inspire and salve a weary soul. From the author of The Color Purple.*

Walsh, Roger & Frances Vaughan (eds), *Paths Beyond Ego: The Transpersonal Vision*, Tarcher/Putnam, New York, 1993. *A pioneering anthology of pioneers.*

Watts, Alan, *Nature Man & Woman*, Abacus, London, 1976. *First published in 1955, remains at the cutting edge of insight into ecology, sexuality and mysticism.*

Wink, Walter, *Engaging the Powers: Discernment and Resistance in a World of Domination*, Fortress Press, Philadelphia, 1992. *For activists, probably the most important work on the Christian theology of power since the gospels.*

Wink, Walter (ed), *Peace is the Way: Writings on Nonviolence from the Fellowship of Reconciliation*, Orbis Books, Maryknoll, 2000. *Outstanding anthology of writings by a wide range of practitioners of nonviolence.*

Writers of the gospels – *How to check out the teachings of Jesus? Start with Luke's or Mark's gospel in any modern translation, or the King James version for poetry.*

Yogananda, Paramhansa, *Autobiography of a Yogi*, Rider, London, 1969. *A memorable account of a Hindu mystic, a pioneer of bringing yoga to the West.*

ENDNOTES

All hyperlinks valid at time of going to press. Lengthy ones have been shortened.

1   Martin Luther King, "The Beloved Community", The King Center, http://goo.gl/Ouk92W.

2   Charles Landry, David Morley, Russell Southwood & Patrick Wright, *What a Way to Run a Railroad: An Analysis of Radical Failure*, Comedia, London, 1985, pp. 28-31.

3   Jo Freeman, "The Tyranny of Structurelessness", Anarchist Workers' Association, http://goo.gl/IlO799.

4   Katrina Shields, *In the Tiger's Mouth: An Empowerment Guide for Social Action*, Millennium Books, Newton NSW, 1991, p. xiii.

5   Alice Walker, "The Nature of This Flower is to Bloom", *Revolutionary Petunias*, The Women's Press, London, 1988, p. 70.

6   MK Gandhi, *An Autobiography or The Story of My Experiments with Truth*, Penguin, London, 1982, pp. 212-14.

7   Paul Heelas, *The New Age Movement: The Celebration of the Self and the Sacralization of Modernity*, Blackwell, Oxford, 1996.

8   Gustavo Gutiérrez, *A Theology of Liberation: History, Politics, Salvation*, SCM, London, 1988, p. xxxvii.

9   Borrowed from the geologist James Hutton, *Theory of the Earth*, Book 1, Chapter 1, 1795, http://goo.gl/N7oVh1.

10 Juan Mascaró (trans), *The Bhagavad Gita*, Penguin Classics, Harmondsworth, 1962, 9:4-5, p. 80. The same point can also be drawn from Christian and Taoist scriptures.

11 Lao Tzu, *Tao Te Ching*, (trans DC Lau), Penguin Classics, Harmondsworth, 1963, XVI, p. 72.

12 See C.G. Jung, *Synchronicity: an Acausal Connecting Principle*, Routledge & Kegan Paul, London, 1972.

13 Mircea Eliade, *Shamanism: Archaic Techniques of Ecstasy*, Arkana, London, 1989, chapter 2.

14 Don Oldenburg, "Julia Butterfly Hill: From Treetop to Grass Roots", *Washington Post*, 22 September 2004, http://goo.gl/p982Wv.

15 Julia Butterfly Hill, *The Legacy of Luna*, Harpercollins, NY, 2000, pp. 114-15.

16 Justin Berton, "Catching Up With Julia Butterfly Hill", *San Francisco Chronicle*, 16 April 2009, http://goo.gl/iZTR83.

17 Pers. com. with Alastair McIntosh, Aberdeen University Parapsychological Society, 1975.

18 RM Bucke, *Cosmic Consciousness*, University Books, New York, 1961 (1901), p. 6.

19 Letters, *New Scientist*, Issue 2838, 12 November 2011, p. 38.

20 Charles T Tart, "States of Consciousness and State-Specific Sciences", *Science*, 176, June 1972, pp. 1203-10.

21 William James, *The Varieties of Religious Experience*, Fontana, Glasgow, 1960, p. 374. The chapter on "Mysticism" remains an outstanding account to this day.

22 Throughout the 20th century a rich research literature developed, an excellent literature review of which can be found in Etzel Cardeña, Steven Jay Lynn & Stanley Krippner (eds), *Varieties of Anomalous Experience*, American Psychological Association, Washington, 2002.

23 Abraham Maslow, *Toward a Psychology of Being*, Van Nostrand, Princeton, 1962 and *The Farther Reaches of Human Nature*, Penguin, Harmondsworth, 1975.

24 Walter N. Pahnke & William A. Richards, "Implications of LSD and Experimental Mysticism", in Charles T. Tart (ed), *Altered States of Consciousness*, Anchor, NY, 1969.

25 William James, *The Varieties*, p. 407.

26 Juan Mascaró (trans), *The Upanishads*, Penguin, London, 1965, p. 83.

27 Ian McGilchrist, *The Master and His Emissary*, Yale University Press, London, 2012, pp. 235 & 237.

28 Robert Greenway, "The Wilderness Effect and Ecopsychology", in Theodore Roszak, Mary Gomes & Allen Kanner (eds.), *Ecopsychology: Restoring the Earth; Healing the Mind*, Sierra Club, San Francisco, 1995, pp. 122-135.

29 Rex Ambler (ed), *Truth of the Heart: An Anthology of George Fox*, Quaker Books, London, 2001, p. 101.

30 Judith Plaskow & Carol P. Christ, "Two Feminist Views of Goddess and God," *Tikkun,* Vol 29:3, Summer 2014, 29-32.

31 Tart, "States of Consciousness and State-Specific Sciences". Also, Charles T. Tart (ed), *Altered States of Consciousness*, Anchor, NY, 1969.

32 Ram Dass, "Promises and Pitfalls of the Spiritual Path", in Stanislav Grof & Christina Grof (eds), *Spiritual Emergency*, Tarcher/Putnam, NY, 1989, pp. 171-190. See also Galatians 2:20, where the deepest sense of *I* is Christ within. In the Orthodox churches this doctrine is well developed and variously called *theosis, deification,* or *divinization* - see Stephen Finlan & Vladimir Kharlamov (eds), *Theosis: Deification in Christian Theology*, Vols 1 & 2, James Clarke & Co, London, 2006 & 2008.

33 David Hay, 1982, in Michael Argyle, *The Psychological Perspective of Religious Experience*, Occasional Paper 8, Religious Experience Research Centre, Oxford, 1997.

34 Andrew Greeley, 1975, in Michael Argyle *The Psychological Persepective of Religious Experience*; see also Beit-Hallahmi & Argyll in the same.

35 Walter Pahnke & William Richards, "Implications of LSD".

36 Todd Murphy and Michael Persinger, papers on *Spirituality and the Brian*, www.innerworlds.50megs.com. Also Wulff's chapter in Cardeña et al., *Varieties of Anomalous Experience*.

37 Arthur Deikman's papers are now collected as *Meditations on a Blue Vase: and the Foundations of Transpersonal Psychology*, Fearless Books, USA, 2014.

38 Michael Eysenck, *Psychology: a Student's Handbook*, Psychology Press, Hove, 2000, p. 33.

39 Glenn Hartelius, Geffen Rothe & Paul J. Roy, "A Brand from the Burning: Defining Transpersonal Psychology", in Harris J. Friedman & Glenn Hartelius, *The Wiley-Blackwell Handbook of Transpersonal Psychology*, Wiley-Blackwell, Malden, MA & Oxford, 2013, pp. 3-22.

40 Hau de no sau nee, "Basic Call to Consciousness", 1977, http://goo.gl/YU6aKs .

41 Eriel Deranger, *Idle No More*, http://www.idlenomore.ca/.

42 Sigmund Freud, "A Religious Experience", (1927), *Complete Psychological Works*, Vol. XXI, Vintage, 2001, pp. 171.

43 Sigmund Freud, "The Future of an Illusion", (1928), *Complete Psychological Works*, Vol. XXI, Vintage, 2001, pp. 22, 31, 43, 44.

44 Sigmund Freud, "The Future", pp. 15 & 44.

45 Carl Jung, *Memories, Dreams, Reflections*, Fontana, Glasgow, 1967, pp. 102 & 121.

46 Carl Jung, *Memories, Dreams, Reflections*, p. 190.

47 There are over a dozen biographies of Jung. Two that were authorized by him, both written by women, are: Frieda Fordham's *An Introduction to Jung's Psychology* (1991) and Jolande Jacobi's *The Psychology of Jung* (1968). Jung's autobiography, *Memories, Dreams, Reflections* (1967), is a most readable account of his life and times. We also recommend Anthony Storr's *Jung: Selected Writings* (1983) and most stunning of all in its depth, approachability and relevance to activist concerns, Meredith Sabini's anthology, *The Earth Has a Soul* (2002), now being translated into French by the Salvia Foundation.

48 Carl Jung "The Concept of the Collective Unconscious" (1936), in *The Archetypes and the Collective Unconscious*, Routledge, London, 1992, pp. 42-53.

49 Carl Rogers, *On Becoming a Person,* Constable, London, 1961.

50 See Manfred Max-Neef's "Development and Human Needs" at http://goo.gl/10B6Ku.

51 An independent version of this known as the Development Wheel was created in the Solomon Islands in the 1980s to ascertain village quality of life and to agree local development priorities. See http://goo.gl/ZrltXy.

52 Sam Keen, "The Golden Mean of Roberto Assagioli", *Psychology Today,* 1974, pp. 97-107, http://goo.gl/ytl7LW. Also, Roberto Assagioli, *Psychosynthesis,* Turnstone, London, 1965.

53 Rosemary Randall, John Southgate and Frances Tomlinson, *Co-operative and Community Group Dynamics: Or, Your Meetings Needn't Be So Appalling,* Barefoot Books, London, 1980, pp. 8, 10

54 James Gilligan, *Violence: Reflections on a National Epidemic,* Vintage, New York, 1997.

55 Max Rosenbaum (ed.),*Compliant Behaviour: Beyond Obedience to Authority,* Human Sciences Press, NY, 1983.

56 The updated edition of Pennington is; Donald Pennington, Kate Gillen & Pam Hill, *Social Psychology,* Arnold, London, 1999.

57 Stanley Milgram, *Obedience to Authority,* Tavistock, London, 1974.

58 Craig Haney, Curtis Banks, & Philip Zimbardo, "Interpersonal Dynamics in a Simulated Prison", *International Journal of Criminology and Penology,* 1, 1973, pp. 69-97.

59 Joanna Bourke, *An Intimate History of Killing: Face-to Face Killing in Twentieth-Century Warfare,* Granta, London, 2000.

60 David Hackworth website, www.hackworth.com/biography.html.

61 Basavanna in AK Ramanujan, *Speaking of Siva,* Penguin Classics, London, 1973, p. 19.

62 Paulo Freire, *Pedagogy of the Oppressed,* Penguin, Harmondsworth, 1972, pp. 24-25.

63 Mathew 20:16; Matthew 18:12-14; Luke 21:1-4.

64 This is retold from distant memory.

65 The story is told in full in Alastair McIntosh, *Soil and Soul: People versus Corporate Power,* Aurum, London, 2001. For a full log of Alastair's work on Lafarge's Sustainability Stakeholder Panel including the debate about "greenwash", see http://goo.gl/R9vghO.

66 Alastair McIntosh, *Soil and Soul: People versus Corporate Power,* pp. 121-124.

67 2 Kings 2.

68 Isaiah 6:5; Exodus 4:10; Jeremiah 15 & 20.

69 Ali Rahnema (ed), *Pioneers of Islamic Revival,* Zed Books, London, 1994.

70   Pers. com. with Alastair, 1990s. Christine passed away as this book was being finalized, God rest her.

71   Numbers 11:29, KJV.

72   Gary Trompf (ed), *Prophets of Melanesia*, Institute of Papua New Guinea Studies, Port Moresby, 1977, pp. 1 & 4.

73   Max Weber, *The Sociology of Religion*, Methuen, London, 1965, pp. 47-48.

74   Mircea Eliade, *Shamanism: Archaic techniques of ecstasy*, Arcadia, London, 1989, pp. xix & 8.

75   Shirley Nicholson (ed.), *Shamanism: An Expanded View of Reality*, Quest, Wheaton, Illinois, 1987, p. vii.

76   Matthew 4:2.

77   Luke 8:49-56.

78   Jean Houston's *Introduction* to Nicolson, *Shamanism*, p. xiii.

79   In the Outer Hebrides where Alastair was raised, belief in telepathy and pre-cognition remains common, especially around such emotionally-charged events as deaths and marriages (see Alastair McIntosh, *Island Spirituality*, Islands Book Trust, Kershader, 2013). It also finds recognition within local Presbyterian circles where, as "the secret of the Lord", it has some recognition as a charismatic gift (John Kennedy, *The Days of the Fathers in Ross-Shire*, Christian Focus, Inverness, 1979). For scholarly literature review of such phenomena see Etzel Cardeña, *Varieties of Varieties of Anomalous Experience: Examining the Scientific Evidence*.

80   Colossians 1:16. See also the opening of John's gospel.

81   Juan Mascaró (trans), *The Upanishads*, Penguin, London, 1965, p. 113 (3.13.7) & pp. 117-19 (7.6).

82   Genesis 1:27.

83   Moving Breath, "We all Come from the Goddess" - lyrics at http://goo.gl/K5sNQY.

84   2 Peter 1:4, reflecting the idea of mystics in many traditions, Eastern and Western.

85   "Our Lady of the Isles", RC Diocese of Argyll and the Isles, http://goo.gl/Fsr07E.

86   Starhawk, *Dreaming the Dark: Magic, Sex and Politics*, Beacon Press, Boston, 1982, p. 13.

87   Eliza Filby, *God and Mrs Thatcher: The Battle for Britain's Soul*, Biteback, London, 2015.

88   Morton W. Bloomfield & Charles W. Dunn, *The Role of the Poet in Early Societies*, D. S. Brewer, Cambridge, 1989, p. 39.

89 Anne Hope & Sally Timmel, *Training for Transformation: a Handbook for Community Workers* (4 volumes), Mambo Press, Zimbabwe, 1984 onwards.

90 For TfT's international programme run from The Grail in South Africa, see http://goo.gl/jsgzNj. For the programme run by Partners out of Ireland, see www.trainingfortransformation.ie/.

91 Anne Hope & Sally Timmel (eds), *Training for Transformation in Practice*, Practical Action, Rugby, 2014, p. 7.

92 Based on interpretations of Isaiah 11:1-3.

93 David V. Barrett, *The New Believers: Sects, Cults and Alternative Religions*, Cassell, London, 2001, p. 46.

94 Marc Galanter, *Cults: Faith, Healing & Coercion*, Oxford University Press, 1999, pp. 176-9; Barrett, *The New Believers*, pp. 91-92.

95 In Barrett, *The New Believers*, p. 20.

96 Arthur Deikman, *Meditations...* pp. 263, 287 & 294.

97 From Alastair McIntosh, "The Cult of Biotechnology", *Resurgence*, 188, 1998, pp. 8-11.

98 Émile Durkheim (ed WSF Pickering), "The Elementary Forms of Religious Life", *Durkheim on Religion*, Scholar's Press, Atlanta, 1994, p. 106.

99 Leon Festinger, Henry Riecken & Stanley Schachter, *When Prophecy Fails*, Harper, New York, 1964, p. 220.

100 Based on but developed by us from Festinger's *When Prophecy Fails*.

101 Donald Pennington, *Social Psychology*, pp. 84-91.

102 Dorothee Söelle, *Beyond Mere Obedience: Reflections on a Christian Ethic for the Future*, Augsburg Publishing, Minneapolis, 1970.

103 Marc Galanter, *Cults*.

104 Deikman, *Meditations on a Blue Vase*, p. 283.

105 *The Searl Solution: the Official Website for Professor John Searl*, www.searlsolution.com.

106 Wikipedia, *Articles for deletion / John Searl*, http://goo.gl/VUd2z5.

107 Guy McPherson, *Contemplating Suicide? Please Read This*, http://goo.gl/6wmn1b.

108 Guy McPherson, *Nature Bats Last: Climate-Change Summary and Update* (updated as of 27 February 2015), http://goo.gl/8YZ7pn.

109 SJ Gould, *The Richness of Life: The Essential Stephen Jay Gould*, W. W. Norton & Co, NY, 2007, p. 594.

110 Clifford Longley, *Chosen People: the big idea that shaped England and America*, Hodder & Stoughton, London, 2002, p. ix.

111 Giuliani in Clifford Longley, *Chosen People*, p. 20.

112 Richard H Roberts, *Religion, Theology and the Human Sciences*, Cambridge, Cambridge University Press, 2002, p. 85.

113 "Microsoft's Nadella sorry for women's pay comments," *BBC News*, http://goo.gl/WrdltU.

114 Katherine Rushton, "Apple and Facebook offer to freeze eggs for female staff", *Daily Telegraph*, 14 October 2014, http://goo.gl/2Ij7hp.

115 Max Weber, *Economy and Society*, Vol. 1 & 2, California University Press, Berkeley, 1979, p. 241.

116 Max Weber, *Economy and Society*, 1979, p. 244.

117 Max Weber, *Economy and Society*, pp. 1122-23

118 Charles Lindholm, *Charisma*, Blackwell, 1993, p. 6.

119 Luke 8:40-56.

120 Charles Lindholm, *Charisma*, pp. 103-4.

121 Charles Lindholm, *Charisma*, p. 107; Alice Miller, *For Your Own Good: the roots of violence in child-rearing*, Virago, London, 1987.

122 In Lindholm, *Charisma*, pp. 137-55; see also Max Rosenbaum, *Compliant Behaviour*.

123 The Who, "Sally Simpson," *Tommy*, 1969 LP and 1975 film - http://goo.gl/VBh4Yp.

124 Lindholm, *Charisma*, pp. 4, 175, 186 & 105.

125 Marc Galanter, *Cults*, pp. 21-5.

126 Arthur Deikman, *Meditations on a Blue Vase*, p. 268.

127 Thomas Merton, *Wisdom of the Desert*, New Directions, 1970, p. 18; also 1 John 4:8.

128 RD Laing, "Transcendental Experience in Relation to Religion and Psychosis", in Stanislav Grof & Christina Grof (eds), *Spiritual Emergency: When Personal Transformation Becomes a Crisis*, Tarcher/Putnam, Los Angeles, 1989, pp. 49-62.

129 UNICEF, "Female Genital Mutilation/Cutting: What might the future hold?" New York, 2010, http://goo.gl/CqQBmD.

130 FORWARD & Muslim Council of Britain, "Female Genital Mutilation", London, 2014, http://goo.gl/E40Je4.

131 Tobe Levin, "Feminist (and 'Womanist') as Public Intellectuals? Elfriede Jelinek and Alice Walker", in Ethan Goffman & Daniel Morris (eds), *New York Public Intellectuals and Beyond*, Purdue University Press, 2009, pp. 243-274. This chapter explores the criticism Walker received from some postcolonial intellectuals for getting involved in FGM. Mama Efua had death threats.

132 This account is from Alastair's memory, possibly elaborated from other memories as Efua became a family friend when setting up FORWARD. The

interview was on *The South Bank Show*, episode 16:2, ITV, broadcast 11 October 1992.

133 *Meryl Streep Reads Alice Walker's Tribute to Efua Dorkenoo*, YouTube, 4 February 2015, http://goo.gl/7BHOlB. The words are also on the blog of her son, Kobby Graham, "For Mom" at http://goo.gl/OK6DvC.

134 Lucian Leustean (ed), *Eastern Christianity and the Cold War, 1945-91*, Routledge, London, 2009.

135 The seminal work is Gustavo Gutiérrez, *A Theology of Liberation: History, Politics, Salvation*, SCM Press, London, 1988 (revised edn). An approachable collection is Christopher Rowland (ed), *The Cambridge Companion to Liberation Theology*, Cambridge University Press, 2007 (2nd edn). Key texts include Isaiah 61:1-2 as reiterated by Jesus in Luke 4:18-19 in proclaiming his mission statement, Mary's *Magnificat* in Luke 1:46-55, and Matthew 25:42-45, culminating with; "Verily I say unto you, Inasmuch as ye did it not to one of the least of these, ye did it not to me" (KJV). In Catholic social teaching, the principles of integral human development trace their roots back to Pope Leo XIII's encyclical, *Rerum Novarum* (Of Revolutionary Change), 1891, and Pope Paul VI's encyclical, *Populorum Progressio* (The Development of Peoples), 1967. Surprisingly, but pleasingly, its most explicit development is in Pope Benedict XVI's *Caritas in Veritate* (Charity in Truth), 2009. In his 2015 encyclical (forthcoming at the time of writing), Pope Francis is expected to develop human ecology as "integral ecology" bound in with integral human development.

136 "Grand theory" is Harris L. Friedman's characterization of Wilber's *A Theory of Everything* as providing only "comforting illusions of sense-making to the largest questions of meaning and purpose" - see *The Wiley-Blackwell Handbook*, pp. 301-4. Our reservations about Wilber's "integral theory" are that its neo-scholastic systematic rationalism offers little to the poor and misunderstands the heart-based nature of spirituality in general, and the spiritualities of many indigenous peoples in particular.

137 Alastair McIntosh, *Healing Nationhood*, Curlew Productions, Kelso, 2000.

138 See http://goo.gl/2aXhdq. Pussy Riot's full source documents were at http://www.freepussyriot.org/documents. However, this site became unavailable as this book went to press around April 2015.

139 Walter Wink, *Engaging the Powers: Discernment and Resistance in a World of Domination*, Fortress Press, Philadelphia, 1992.

140 Walter Wink, *The Powers That Be: Theology for a New Millennium*, Random House, New York, 1998, p. 42.

141 Walter Wink, *The Powers That Be*, p. 81.

142 Genesis 32:22-31.

143 Matthew 10:14.

144 Joanna Macy, *Despair and Personal Power in the Nuclear Age*, New Society

Publishers, Philadelphia, 1983, p. 31.

145 Pussy Riot: Statement in Response to Patriarch's Speech on 24/03/12, from Free Pussy Riot website, currently defunct, see endnote 138.

146 "Punk prayer lyrics", Free Pussy Riot, from Free Pussy Riot website, currently defunct, see endnote 138.

147 "Letter to Supporters July 24, 2012, Free Pussy Riot, from Free Pussy Riot website, currently defunct, see endnote 138.

148 "Tim's Story," Peaceful Uprising, http://goo.gl/X1Ikpj.

149 Sarah van Gelder, "The Boomers 'Failed' Us: Climate Activist Tim DeChristopher on Anger, Love, and Sacrifice", *Yes! Magazine*, 30 May 2014, http://goo.gl/PfXigi.

150 Camara's book from 1971 is long out of print, but a PDF can be downloaded from http://goo.gl/ZBmVy4.

151 Martin Luther King, "The Beloved Community," The King Center, http://goo.gl/Ouk92W.

152 Dozens of examples are tabulated, for example, in Erica Chenoweth & Maria J Stephan, *Why Civil Resistance Works: The Strategic Logic of Nonviolent Conflict*, Columbia University Press, 2011. Surprisingly, this book makes no reference to *satyagraha* - as if the juicy essence of such issues troubles academic reserve?

153 Bo Lidegaard, *Countrymen: The Untold Story of How Denmark's Jews Escaped the Nazis*, Atlantic Books, London, 2014.

154 Michael Bar-Zohar, *Beyond Hitler's Grasp: The Heroic Rescue of Bulgaria's Jews*, Adams Media, 2001.

155 Arthur Deikman, *Meditations on a Blue Vase*, p. 276.

156 See Alastair McIntosh, *Soil and Soul*; also, Chriss Bull, Alastair McIntosh and Colin Clarke, "Land, Identity, School: Exploring Women's Identity with Land in Scotland Through the Experience of Boarding School", *Oral History: Journal of the Oral History Society*, Autumn 2008, Vol. 36:2, pp. 75-88, http://goo.gl/1aHiby. A key figure on political psychohistory is Nick Duffell, *Wounded Leaders*, Lone Arrow, London, 2014.

157 Gene Sharp, *The Politics of Nonviolent Action*, Vols. 1-3, Expanding Horizon Books, Boston, 1973.

158 Some of these case studies are explored in a paper based on lectures at the UK Defence Academy - Alastair McIntosh, "A Nonviolent Challenge to Conflict", in David Whetham (ed), *Ethics, Law and Military Operations*, Palgrave Macmillan, Houndmills, 2011, pp. 44-64, http://goo.gl/WP1wR4.

159 A wonderful anthology is Walter Wink (ed), *Peace is the Way: Writings on Nonviolence from the Fellowship of Reconciliation*, Orbis Books, Maryknoll, 2000.

160 "Show no pity: life for life, eye for eye, tooth for tooth, hand for hand, foot for foot" - Deuteronomy 19:21 NRSV.

161 Isaiah 2:2, 4 NRSV; Micah 4:1, 3.

162 See especially Marcus J. Borg and John Dominic Crossan, *The Last Week: What the Gospels Really Teach About Jesus's Final Days in Jerusalem*, SPCK, London, 2008.

163 Mark 11:15-17; John 2:13-22 NRSV.

164 See, for example - Angie Zelter and contributors, *Trident on Trial: the case for people's disarmament*, Luath Press, Edinburgh, 2001; and for Trident Ploughshares, www.tridentploughshares.org.

165 Matthew 5:38-48; Matthew 11:12 NRSV; Mark 3:17; Luke 9:51-56.

166 Luke 22:35-38; Matthew 26:52 GWT, KJV and Luke 22:51 ISV; cf. Mark 14:47 and John 18:10; Luke 22:51.

167 John 18:36 TEV; John 18:37.

168 J. Denny Weaver, *The Nonviolent Atonement*, William B Eerdmans Publishing Co, Grand Rapids, 2001.

169 Raimon Panikkar, "Nine Sutras on Peace", *Interculture*, XXIV:1, 1991, pp. 49-56, http://goo.gl/PmhT4W.

170 Abdullah Yusuf Ali (trans), *The Holy Qur'an: Text, Translation and Commentary*, Islamic Education Centre, Jeddah, 1946, p.75.

171 Philip J. Stewart, *Unfolding Islam*, Garnet Publications, UK, p.76.

172 For example, Mohammed Abu-Nimer, *Nonviolence and Peace Building in Islam: Theory and Practice*, University of Florida Press, Gainesville, 2003.); and the online resource, Glenn D. Paige, Chaiwat Satha-Anand (Qader Muheideen) and Sara Gilliatt (eds), *Islam and Nonviolence*, Center for Global Nonviolence, Honolulu, 1986, http://nonkilling.org/pdf/b3.pdf.

173 Abdullah Yusuf Ali, *The Holy Qur'an*, p. 251.

174 Mohammad Raqib, "The Muslim Pashtun Movement of the North-West Frontier of India - 1930-1934" in Gene Sharp, *Waging Nonviolent Struggle*, Extending Horizon, USA, 2005, pp. 113-34.

175 Eknath Easwaran, *Nonviolent Soldier of Islam: Badshah Khan, a Man to Match His Mountains*, Nilgiri Press, Tomales, 1999, pp. 84 & 63 respectively.

176 Mohammad Raqib, "The Muslim Pashtun Movement", pp. 117-18.

177 Mohammad Raqib, "The Muslim Pashtun Movement", p. 117.

178 Eknath Easwaran, *Nonviolent Soldier of Islam*, p.195.

179 Eknath Easwaran, *Nonviolent Soldier of Islam*, p.7.

180 Gandhi cited in Michael Nagler, *The Nonviolence Handbook: A Guide for Practical Action*, Berrett-Koehler, USA, 2014, p. 10.

Endnotes 215

181 W. Montgomery Watt, "Women in the Earliest Islam", *Studia Missionalia*, Vol. 40, 1991, pp. 162-73, http://goo.gl/PssZpM.

182 For example, the Muslim Council of Britain has on its website, *The Covenant of Prophet Muhammad (PBUH) with Christians*, from Saint Catherine's Monastery in Egypt - www.mcb.org.uk/prophet-muhammad-covenant-christians/. Based on the precedent that Muhammad let his mosque in Medina to be used for prayer by visiting Christians, Muslims and Christians each held prayers together in Saint Giles Cathedral, Edinburgh, as part of their expression of sorrow following the First Gulf War in 1991 - http://goo.gl/wyL85G.

183 Jack Kornfield, *A Path With Heart*, Bantam, NY, 1993, p. 198.

184 Richard Rohr, *Falling Upward*, Jossey Bass, San Fransisco, 2011, p. xiii

185 Juan Mascaró (trans), *The Bhagavad Gita*, Penguin, Harmondsworth, 1962, section 2:47-50.

186 Matthew 6:3.

187 Matthew 6:12, Jubilee Bible 2000.

188 Psalm 118:24.

189 Beverly Wildung Harrison, "The Power of Anger in the Work of Love: Christian Ethics for Women and Other Strangers", in Ann Loades (ed), *Feminist Theology*, SPCK, London, 1990, pp. 194-213.

190 Juan Mascaró (trans), *Bhagavad Gita* chapter 1; Mark 3:31-35; Matthew 10:34-36.

191 Gerald Davison, John Neale and Ann Kring, (2004) *Abnormal Psychology*, John Wiley & Sons Inc, Hoboken, 2004, p. 29.

192 John 14:5; Exodus 3:14.

193 Brian Edward Brown, *The Buddha Nature: A Study of the Tathagatagarbha and Alayavijnana*, Motilal Banarsidass Publishers, Delhi, 1991.

194 Jeremiah 2:13.

195 TS Eliot, *Four Quartets*, Faber, London, 1959, p. 57.

196 Thomas Merton, *The Wisdom*, pp. 52-53.

197 Matthew 5:8.

198 Michael J. Sheeran SJ, *Beyond Majority Rule: Voteless decisions in the Religious Society of Friends*, Philadelphia Yearly Meeting, 1983. Sheeran was sent by the Jesuits to help recover their lost traditions of discernment by studying the Quakers in the aftermath of Vatican II. His book has been adopted as a Quaker classic.

199 Religious Society of Friends, *Quaker Faith and Practice*, Britain Yearly Meeting, 1995, 3.02.

200 Quaker Life Team, *Clearness*, Britain Yearly Meeting, http://goo.gl/lELROi.

201 Parker J Palmer, *A Hidden Wholeness: The Journey Toward an Undivided Life*, Jossey-Bass, San Francisco, 2004, p. 134.

202 Parker Palmer, *A Hidden Wholeness*, pp. 58-9.

203 Tova Green and Peter Woodrow, *Insight and Action*, p. 12.

204 Katrina Shields, *In the Tiger's Mouth: An Empowerment Guide for Social Action*, Millennium Books, Newtown NSW, 1991, p. 120.

205 Joseph Campbell, *The Hero With A Thousand Faces*, Fontana, London, 1993, p. 12.

206 Matthew 10:39.

207 Richard Rohr SF, *Adam's Return: The five promises of male initiation*, Cross-roads, NY, 2004, pp. 12-13.

208 Hermann Hesse, "The Poet", *Strange News from Another Star and Other Stories*, Penguin, London, 1976, pp. 30-7. http://goo.gl/Lha4Ul.

209 Desmond Tutu, *No future Without Forgiveness*, Rider, London, 1999, p. 5.

210 Desmond Tutu, *No future Without Forgiveness*, p9.

211 Starhawk, *Dreaming the Dark*, Beacon Press, USA, 1982, p. 13.

212 Aniela Jaffé, *From the Life and Work of C.G. Jung*, Daimon Verlag, Einsiedeln, 1989, pp. 75-7.

213 Mikhail Bulgakov, *The Master and Margarita*, Vintage, London, 2004, p. 311.

214 Joshua ES Phillips, *None of Us Were Like This Before: American Soldiers and Torture*, Verso, NY, 2012. Martha K Huggins, Mika Haritos-Fatouros & Philip G Zimbardo, *Violence Workers: Police Torturers and Murderers Reconstruct Brazilian Atrocities*, University of California Press, Berkeley, 2002. Also, James Gilligan, *Violence*, and Joanna Bourke, *An Intimate History of Killing*.

215 Martin Luther King, "My Pilgrimage to Nonviolence", in Walter Wink (ed), *Peace is the Way: Writings on Nonviolence from the Fellowship of Reconciliation*, Orbis Books, Maryknoll, 2000, pp. 64-71.

216 M. Scott Peck, *People of the Lie: the Hope of Healing Human Evil*, Arrow, London, 1990, p. 91.

217 Jeremiah 5:1, NLT.

218 Karen Armstrong, *Twelve Steps to a Compassionate Life*, The Bodley Head, London, 2011, pp. 93 & 169.

219 Anthony de Mello, *Sadhana: A Way To God*, Bantam Doubleday Dell, USA, 1978, pp. 3-34.

220 Cited in Ben Pink Dandelion, *Open for Transformation: Being Quaker*, The 2014 Swarthmore Lecture, Quaker Books, London, 2014, pp. 19-20.

221 Walter Wink, *Engaging the Powers*, pp. 297-8.

222 Richard Wilhelm & CG Jung (commentary), *The Secret of the Golden Flower: A Chinese Book of Life*, Routledge & Kegan Paul, London, 1962, p. 142.

223 John Welwood, *Journey of the Heart: The Path of Conscious Love*, Harper Perennial, NY, 1991, p. 39.

224 Pers. com. with Alastair McIntosh, c. 2000, and he's still going strong as we went to press.

225 Dorothee Söelle, *The Silent Cry: Mysticism and Resistance*, Fortress Press, Minneapolis, 2001, p. 113.

226 Audre Lorde, "Uses of the Erotic: the Erotic as Power," *Sister Outsider: Essays and Speeches*, The Crossing Press, Freedom, 1984, pp. 53-9. See http://goo.gl/by4Xbi.

227 Joanna Macy, *World As Lover, World As Self*, Paralax Press, Berkeley, 1991, p. 8.

228 Gustavo Gutiérrez, *A Theology of Liberation*, p. xxxviii.

229 Vladimir Kharlamov (ed), *Theosis: Deification in Christian Theology*, Vol 2, James Clarke & Co, London, 2008, p. 93. The Greek mystical notion of *apocatastasis* is closely connected to *theosis*, divinization or deification - the idea, also central to Eastern faiths, that our human destiny is to participate in the divine nature. *Apocatastasis* (pronounced apoc-at-ast-asis) means the revelation of that which is most deeply there, underneath outward appearances. In Christianity and especially as developed by the Eastern Church, it implies the revelation of all things in their primal or essential state of being, from outside of space and time. In Acts 3:21 of the Bible, *apocatastasis* is variously translated as "the times of restitution of all things", "the final restoration of all things" and "the time of universal restoration". In Protestant evangelicalism it is often taken to imply the "second coming" of Christ.

230 Paul Evdokimov, *Orthodoxy*, New City Press, NY, 2011.

231 John Carey, *A Single Ray of the Sun: Religious Speculation in Early Ireland*, Celtic Studies Publications, Aberystwyth, 2011.

232 *Led Zepelin IV*, 1971. *Stairway* lyrics at http://goo.gl/pyz4aN.

233 Sian Llewellyn, "Stairway to Heaven," *Total Guitar*, December 1998, pp. 61-62.

234 Richard Rohr, *Adam's Return*, pp. 140-42.

235 "News," *Muslim Council of Britain*, http://goo.gl/YxlBnz.

236 Adrienne Rich, "Natural Resources" in *The Dream of a Common Language*, W.W. Norton & Co, 1978, p. 67.

INDEX

ALSO BY GREEN BOOKS:

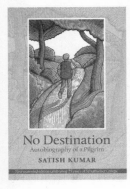

No Destination:
Autobiography of a Pilgrim
Satish Kumar

No Destination tells the extraordinary story of activist and pilgrim Satish Kumar, from his 8,000 mile peace walk to protest nuclear armament during the cold war to his most recent work promoting spiritual teachings and sustainable living. With additional chapters to bring it up to date, this beautifully finished hardback edition celebrates 25 years of Schumacher College, where Kumar continues to be involved in holistic courses for sustainable living.

Rekindling Community: Connecting people, environment and spirituality
Alastair McIntosh

This Schumacher Briefing explores three integrated pillars of community with one another, with the natural environment and with the spiritual ground of all being. McIntosh draws not just on his own extensive experience, but also on the work of a dozen associates at the Centre for Human Ecology mostly his former students.

About Green Books

green books

Environmental publishers for 25 years. For our full range of titles and to order direct from our website, see: **www.greenbooks.co.uk**

Send us a book proposal on eco-building, science, gardening, etc.
– **www.greenbooks.co.uk/for-authors**

For bulk orders (50+ copies) we offer discount terms. Contact **sales@greenbooks.co.uk** for details.

Join our mailing list for new titles, special offers, reviews and author events: **www.greenbooks.co.uk/subscribe**

 @ Green_Books   /GreenBooks